THE PARIS AIR SHOW

Don Berliner

MBI Publishing Company

First published in 2000 by MBI Publishing Company,
729 Prospect Avenue, PO Box 1, Osceola, WI 54020-0001USA

© Don Berliner, 2000

MBI Publishing Company books are also available at discounts in bulk quantity for industrial or sales-promotional use. For details write to Special Sales Manager at Motorbooks International Wholesalers & Distributors, 729 Prospect Avenue, PO Box 1, Osceola WI, 54020 USA.

Library of Congress Cataloging-in-Publication Data Available

ISBN 0-7603-0728-8

On the front cover (clock-wise from top left): *Strange looking and exceptionally loud, the Dornier Do31 VTOL aircraft performed its novel maneuvers, but reportedly could lift little more than the weight of its crew. DaimlerChrysler Aerospace*

A member of the support crew sits in the cockpit as a Swedish Air Force SAAB J-37 Viggen is prepared for display. Don Berliner

One of France's and Europe's great hopes for the future: the wide-bodied Airbus A340 airliner. Almost as large as the popular Boeing 747, it is considered more of a pilot's airplane, having a user-friendly cockpit. Bernard Thouanel

A ticket stub from the 1977 show illustrates the aviation-themed graphics that year.

On the frontispiece: *A Fouga Lutin C.M.82R scale prototype of the coming Fouga Magister jet trainer is pictured here at the 1951 show. The Magister would be a big success, as both a trainer and the choice of the French formation acrobatic team. Flight International*

On the title page: *An aerial view of the Paris Air Show in 1989 captures a host of aircraft. At left center, a row of Soviet airliners and the shuttle-carrying An-225 dominated the Russian aircraft display. Flight International*

On the back cover: *The Paris Air Show has played host to nearly the entire history of aviation. No matter where your aviation tastes or loyalties lie, there was always an incredible aircraft there for you. This montage of photos provides a peek at the show across the years.*

Edited by Mike Haenggi
Designed by Tom Heffron

Printed in China

CONTENTS

INTRODUCTION

Although it didn't seem that way to most people, 1908 was the sixth year of heavier-than-air flight. In America, the brothers Wright were continuing their methodical attack on the forces of nature, and they were winning. Although few people believed they had flown even once, by the beginning of 1908, Wilbur Wright had flown their 1905 Flyer more than 24 miles in 38 minutes. But this was done quietly outside Dayton, Ohio, and the world had yet to toast them as world-class inventors.

In Europe, a host of men who had their sights set on making history were struggling to stay in the air long enough for their compatriots to see them. The official best as 1907 ended was Henri Farman's barely controlled flight of 1 1/4 minutes, during which he covered almost two-thirds of a mile. The Europeans, being unconvinced that the Wrights had ever flown, and certain that true flight could only be achieved by the culturally and educationally superior residents of the Old World, cheered Farman as the best yet.

Nineteen eight was to be a year of great shocks. On August 8, Wilbur Wright flew at Le Mans, France, and with great ease broke all the existing records with a flight of almost 2 minutes. While his time was not that much greater than Farman's, his total control of his airplane was instantly recognized by the Europeans as proof that they had lost the race to be first.

In September, one of Orville's flights at Fort Myer, Virginia, in demonstrations aimed at selling the U.S. Army its first airplane, lasted 1 hour and 15 minutes. A few days later, Wilbur flew at the French Army's Camp d'Avours, east of Le Mans, for 1 1/2 hours. His sharp turns and effortless figure eights demonstrated control far beyond anything the Europeans had managed or even thought possible.

Since both brothers were now flying in public, the world at long last could see them for what they were: the masterful inventors of the airplane. Millennia of envying the flight of eagles and robins and even parakeets had come to an end. Suddenly, man's imagination was let loose and anything was possible.

Still, only a few thousand people had actually seen an airplane. And so when the annual Paris Auto Show included a display of flying machines, the crowds poured through the doors of the Grand Palais, just off the Champs Élysées, as soon as the show was formally opened by the president of France on December 24.

Officially, it was the First Aeronautical Salon, held as part of the Exhibition of Industrial Vehicles and Motor Boats. But to those who gaped and gasped upon their first close-up look at airplanes, it was a dream world. Even though cars and trucks were still a novelty, they lacked the mystique of machines that could actually lift themselves into the air and go more or less where they wished. Automobiles were fascinating, but noisy and dirty. Airplanes, on the other hand, were pure magic.

In the center of honor of the display was Clement Ader's *Avion III*, a steam-powered, bat-winged craft the French trumpeted as the first airplane to fly. According to legend, it had flown almost 1,000 feet at Satory on Oct. 14, 1897. It would be several years before the official French government report on the flight was released, confirming that the *Avion* had never left the ground.

Around this were displayed no fewer than 15 aircraft: 5 biplanes, 9 monoplanes, and the Brequet helicopter. They bore the names of Wright, Voisin, Bleriot, Breguet, Antoinette, Esnault-Pelterie, Santos-Dumont, and others that would soon rise to fame. Above them were suspended several balloons and the huge *Ville de Bordeaux* dirigible.

In addition, there were displays of engines, propellers, accessories, and models of airplanes that just might become reality in the wildly unpredictable future of this New World.

The exhibition in Paris in late 1908 wasn't the first of its kind. That honor goes to the 1868 Aeronautical Exhibition in London's Crystal Palace. And while the first one certainly deserves a place in history, the second was far more important, as it led directly to a series of displays of unprecedented duration.

At first it was called the "1909 Exposition Internationale de la Locomotion Aerienne." Properly translated as "International Exposition of Aerial Locomotion," it was immediately called simply the "Paris Aero Show" by English-speaking enthusiasts and journalists.

Today it is officially called the "Salon International de l'Aeronautique et de l'Espace," and it is known throughout the rest of the world as the Paris Air Show.

8

BEFORE THE FIRST GREAT WAR

*T*he airplane was invented in 1903, but this was not widely recognized until 1908, thanks to poor communications, the Wrights' lack of interest in publicity, and the attitude of their European rivals. The French, in particular, felt that this great achievement certainly must be made by them, not by a pair of unsophisticated bicycle mechanics from Dayton, Ohio, wherever that might be.

Once the world realized just how great was the Wrights' mastery of flight, aviation took off! After Wilbur and Orville showed that it could be done, dozens jumped on the flying bandwagon.

Close-up of a small part of the Grand Palais display showing the emphasis placed on balloons. In the lower right, on a Stand of Honor, is an Antoinette. In the lower left is another. Behind it is the Farman, while the highly decorated balloon is a scale model of the original Montgolfier of 1783. Bleriot's Channel-crosser is in front of the balloon, while the R.E.P. is at the far right. USiAS

In 1909 it was just a corner of the annual Automobile Show, but it led to much bigger things. At the left front is Clement Ader's Avion III, *which the French long insisted was the first airplane to fly. At the front left is a pair of wings used as decoration, while in front of that is an R.E.P. monoplane. Behind the long pole topped by a set of wings is a Delagrange biplane, and in the distance are balloons and cars.* Flight International

The French, assumed to be leading the way toward flight, were forced to face the simple reality that someone else had invented the airplane. It was not pleasant to face such reality, but that being said, they proceeded to make the best of it.

On July 25, 1909, the painfully shy Louis Bleriot took off in his Type XI monoplane from Les Baraques, near Calais on the eastern side of the English Channel. Thirty-six and a half minutes of wobbly, uncertain flying over nothing but water ended with a hard landing near Dover Castle, above England's famed White Cliffs. His 21-mile excursion was one of the most significant trips in history, making obsolete the centuries-old security of Great Britain's natural moat. It was the first international flight. Many years later, high-speed trains would streak through a tunnel under the English Channel on almost the same route, and in less time.

Four weeks after Bleriot's flight, at Reims in France's lush champagne country, an eight-day public extravaganza introduced the world to record setting, to air shows, and to closed-course air racing. By the end of the Great Week of the Champagne, every important flying record had been broken, most of them several times.

Bleriot became the new holder of the World Speed Record at 47.8 miles per hour; Henri Farman had a tenuous grip on the World Nonstop Distance Record with a flight of 112 miles, and Hubert Latham had climbed higher than anyone

before in history with a flight to 509 feet above the earth. America's Glenn Curtiss had won the James Gordon Bennett Trophy with two laps around the 6-mile course in the first major pylon race.

Also in 1909, Robert Peary became the first man to reach the North Pole. Bakelite had just gone into production as the world's first example of plastic. Eugene Lefebvre had become the first pilot to die in the crash of an airplane, when his Wright Model A dove into the ground at Juviasy.

All of these brave men are long gone, as are their records. But the third of France's epic contributions to aviation in 1909—the Paris Air Show—remains a major part of the aviation (now aerospace) world after 90 years.

The first event in this amazing series of events was held from September 25 through October 17—just over three weeks—in the very heart of Paris. It was strictly a static display, any flying being far in the future. But right from the start, it offered the very best the world had in the way of complete airplanes, engines, propellers, and all manner of associated equipment and dreams.

It was held under the auspices of the Syndicate of the Aviation Industries and its president, M. Albert de Dion. The general commissioner of the show was M. Andre Granet.

The interior of the Grand Palais was decorated as only the French could have done in the early part of the twentieth century: ornate, elaborate, and perhaps slightly overdone. Potted palms, garlands of flowers, acres of banners and bunting and flags. And everywhere, white-painted wrought ironwork. Sleek, modern airplanes would have looked utterly out of place. But the airplanes of 1909 were intricate collections of struts and wires, with hardly any parts hidden inside streamlined covering, and they fit perfectly.

In the place of honor was Louis Bleriot's channel-crossing monoplane, elevated and surrounded by beds of flowers. On stands of honor around it were examples of some of the best-known types: a Voisin, a Wright, an Antoinette, and an R.E.P. from Rene Esnault-Pelterie.

Hanging from the ceiling were all shapes and sizes of gas-filled balloons, including one of the same design as the one flown by the brothers Mongolfier in 1783 for history's first free flight.

They had launched it from a park just 2 miles west of the site of the first Paris Air Show.

It was widely believed, at the time, that the Wright brothers' first airplane was on display, and there certainly was a Wright airplane, which may well have been so labeled, hidden away on the second floor. But the 1903 Flyer remained parked, broken, and bent in the back of the Wright Cycle Co. shop in Dayton, Ohio, where it had lain since returning from its single day of glory at Kitty Hawk six years before.

The show was formally opened by French President Armand Fallieries, whose elation upon entering the building was cooled by the whispered news that the famed French dirigible *La Republique* had just crashed and killed all on board. So little was known about flight in those days that such accidents were disturbingly frequent.

According to published reports at the time, more than 100,000 persons passed through the gates in just the first four days. By the time the show had ended, more people had seen airplanes and their attachments and related gadgetry up close in the Grand Palais than in all other public events held up to that time.

It was clear that aviation appealed not just to designers, builders, pilots, and other visionaries. It had captured the hearts and imaginations of the

The interior of the Grand Palais, sumptuously decorated as was the custom in those days. Clockwise from lower right: Farman biplane, French-built Astra-Wright (on the center Stand of Honor), Louis Bleriot's Channel-crosser, Antoinette monoplane, a Voisin, another Bleriot, and an R.E.P. The ceiling was hung with full-scale and model gas-filled balloons.
Flight International

public, for most of the visitors were average people. It would be many years before aviation would welcome them as paying passengers. But the thought of actually flying had been indelibly written in the memories of all who had looked into the crude designs of those first years and had seen something more than just bamboo and cotton cloth.

1910 PARIS AIR SHOW

The success of the first show could hardly be questioned. It had brought out great numbers of curiosity seekers, along with government officials and others who would play major roles in aviation's future. In addition, it had provided a forum for the more technically inclined types to study what had been achieved to date, and to speculate about the potential of a hundred new ideas. They may not have been able to predict where aviation was headed, nor to what uses it might eventually be put. But there was no question in their minds that flying machines would become a major part of the future.

Aviation, especially in Europe, was seeing one of history's greatest assaults on performance records. In the year since the first Paris Air Show, the World Air Speed Record had risen 40 percent to Alfred Leblanc's 68 miles per hour.

The distance record grew even more, with Maurice Tabuteau's flight of 289 miles in 6 hours easily eclipsing the 1909 record of just 112 miles. Men were just beginning to see the performance potential in flying machines.

The second Paris Air Show was held for two weeks, from October 15 through November 2. It almost failed to open on schedule, due to a nationwide railway strike that held up deliveries of a lot of airplanes and display materials. Stories of airplanes being smashed by mobs of angry strikers turned out to be no more than rumors, but they were enough to convince the French premier that it would be too risky for him to take part in the formal opening.

At least 24 types of airplanes were on display, along with one helicopter. One of the airplanes hinted at a major development that would not be realized for almost 30 years.

This was Henri Coanda's jet-propelled monoplane. It used a reciprocating engine to drive its compressor, much as a more successful Italian airplane would do in 1940. Had the Coanda jet flown, there is no way to estimate its impact on the future of flight. Coanda later claimed that he got the airplane into the air briefly in December 1910, just before it crashed in flames and was destroyed. Historians challenge this and insist that no attempt was ever made. Still, it was in full public view, and clearly looked like a jet-propelled airplane.

Another major trend in evidence, and one that unfortunately was an omen of things to come, was the development of military versions of otherwise standard designs. In fact, most of the two-seaters in the exhibits were called "military," with the assumption that the passenger could take on a secondary job as an observer, gunner, or bombardier, since the complexities of those specialized functions had not yet been demonstrated. A Voisin pusher-biplane carried a large machine gun, to be aimed and fired by the pilot, all of whose skills would already be seriously taxed just trying to keep the airplane headed in the right direction.

Not quite as obvious to the casual passerby was the trend toward more useful flight controls for the pilot. Many of the early airplanes had controls that were anything but natural, and this played a

The airplanes are almost hidden by the ornate decorations. In the foreground is an Antoinette monoplane. At right is a Wright Model B biplane. At left is a Maurice Farman biplane. And just past its far wingtip is another Farman. In the fancy center "cage" is the Antoinette factory display. Flight International

role in the terrible accident rate. Several of those in the show (including a Voisin and the Turcat-Mery & Rougier) had a steering wheel for combination roll and pitch control, and a rudder bar for directional control. The Bleriot-like Sommer even had a trim wheel for its horizontal stabilizer. Standardization of controls, and the accompanying increase in safety, was starting to show.

There were clear signs of a trend toward increased power, which probably will never end. The Clerget tandem-monoplane (actually a biplane with one wing in front and the other in back) had a 200-horsepower Clerget V-8 engine. And a Deperdussin, from a firm whose primary goal was speed, used a thin-bladed propeller with six blades. Such ideas would eventually have solid science behind them, but 1910 was far too early for such innovations to offer any great benefit.

While the obvious object of most visitors' interest was the design of airplanes, their construction showed advances just as great. Steel tubing was increasingly used for basic structures, and steel was being used more frequently for fittings. And amazingly, airplane constructors were using less aluminum. Fewer external bracing wires were to be seen, as improved engineering began to have an impact. There were minor additional signs of streamlining, along with improved finishes and fewer examples of hurried completion. In all, there was a welcome trend toward increased professionalism.

Almost all the airplanes on display were new since 1909. A few, from Antoinette and Maurice Farman, were basically the same but showed signs of sensible modifications. The license-built Astra-Wright biplane had wheels in place of skids, an utterly logical move that the Wright brothers were not yet ready to make.

The engine display was larger and more interesting, with examples of airplane engines from a variety of firms known best for their auto engines: Renault, Daimler, Fiat, Darracq, and Panhard. There were more examples of horizontally opposed engines, though the idea would not really catch on until the late 1930s.

With aviation still so young, recognition of "historic" airplanes was downplayed, though Henri Fabre's first-in-the-world seaplane was on display.

"Freak" airplanes were scarcer than in 1909, with only the Sloan biplane with its converging wingtips and the aforementioned Clerget tandem-monoplane as types that weren't conventional in their basic layout.

1911 - 1912

The third Paris Air Show was held from December 16, 1911, through January 2, 1912. It presented increasing evidence of the growing maturity of aviation. At midyear, Edward Nieuport raised the speed record to 83 miles per hour at Chalons, and during the show, Andre Gobe added 60 percent to the closed-course distance record with a 460-mile flight at Pau in just over 8 hours. Both records were set with Nieuport monoplanes. In the outside world, Charles Kettering had just invented the self-starter for cars, and Irving Berlin had just written "Alexander's Ragtime Band."

The show was formally opened by the president of France, M. Fallieres, accompanied by a host of high government officials. The decor of the Grand Palais exceeded anything before seen.

From some angles, the airplanes were completely overwhelmed by potted plants and ferns and even trees, making it look as much like a garden show as an air show. But such was the atmosphere at Paris in 1912. In the foreground is only the second in a long line of metal Breguet airplanes to show themselves at Paris. Flight International

It isn't clear why the organizers felt the Grand Palais should look like something out of the ancient world, with columns topped by winged people, but those intent on studying airplanes could ignore all that. From the bottom right: an unidentified pusher with Wright influence, a Zodiac biplane, and a Borel monoplane. Flight International

According to *Flight* magazine, "On entering . . . one is immediately struck with the magnitude of the uniform decorative scheme. Under the central dome of the building is hung a huge light cloth bearing the monogram of the exhibition, and radiating on all sides are brightly colored hangings, each stand having its double name banners. The scene at night with the lights full on is really magnificent."

There were 44 airplanes from 30 manufacturers on display, along with 70 types of engines from 32 makers. The trend toward the Paris Air Show becoming an international event began slowly, with airplanes from Great Britain and Germany on display, though the French continued to supply more than 90 percent of everything in sight. The most obvious change from the previous year was the rapid progress in streamlining. Many of the monoplanes had fully enclosed fuselages, and a majority of the biplanes were at least partly enclosed.

The most impressive job of streamlining could be seen at the Paulhan & Tatin stand, where its *Aero Torpedo* was there for all to see. Not only was the fuselage fully covered, but it had a circular cross-section, and a pointed nose, as the propeller was in the extreme tail. A top speed of 85 miles per hour was claimed, on only 50 horsepower. The term "hype" had not yet been coined, but the concept was in full view.

Along with improved streamlining came increased power, the combination still seen as the obvious route to ever-greater speed. Five engines were said to be rated at 200 horsepower. There was a fairly even distribution of radial and vertically arranged cylinders, while most of the radials were of the rotary type in which the cylinders and crankcase revolve as a unit, and the propeller is attached to them rather than to a revolving crankshaft.

The most novel engine was the six-cylinder Helium rotary, in which one group of three cylinders revolved clockwise and another revolved counterclockwise. The same system was used on a two-row, 10-cylinder Helium. This eliminated the severe torque of the conventional rotary, while adding mechanical complexity.

Aviation may have begun with a biplane, but by the 1911–1912 Paris Air Show, two-wingers

There was less greenery and more flying machines than in the past years. From the front: Caudron amphibian, Drzeweicki double monoplane, Zodiac triplane, Savary biplane, and others too dim to make out. Note the lack of lighter-than-air craft hanging from the rafters. Flight International

appeared to be on the way out. Fully two-thirds of the airplanes were monoplanes. And most of the biplanes were tractors (engines in front) rather than pushers (propellers facing rearward).

This movement in the direction of what we now consider modern and perfectly logical, was countered by the continued reliance on wing warping for lateral control instead of ailerons. One of the few with ailerons was a Henri Farman biplane with biplane "ailerons" attached to the outermost interplane struts . . . and oriented 90 degrees to the trailing edge of the wing. Proof of the long-term popularity of this idea can be found with a quick survey of your nearest airport!

Before 1911 had ended, two major events occurred that would have inestimable impact on the future. An airplane was first used in war by the Italians on October 11, when a Bleriot monoplane made a reconnaissance flight over the North African coast. And Marie Curie was awarded the Nobel Prize for Chemistry for her work with the radioactive element radium. As yet, few people could locate Hiroshima on a map.

1912 PARIS AIR SHOW

The fourth show was held from October 26 through November 10. During the 10 months since the previous show, the Air Speed Record had been raised to 108 miles per hour by Jules Vedrines, flying a Deperdussin monoplane near Chicago, Illinois. And the distance record had been extended to 628 miles per hour in 13:22 by Maurice Farman in one of his own airplanes at Etampes, France.

Roald Amundsen had become the first person to reach the South Pole. Victor Hess had discovered cosmic rays, the *Titanic* had hit an iceberg and sunk on its maiden voyage, and the first Woolworth's 5 & 10 cent store had been opened.

The show was not merely a technical exhibition. It was a way for France to show its own people how it was spending some of their tax money, and the rest of the world how it was using the latest technology for defense. The French turned out in great numbers and were suitably impressed. Displays from other countries were not so plentiful as to detract from the feeling that the Paris Air Show remained an essentially French event.

The most obvious change from the previous year's show was the growth in interest in "hydravious," or water-airplanes. The first of these wasn't flown until 1910, by Henri Fabre, but they quickly caught on. There were 11 in the Grand Palais in late 1912, including several that qualified as flying boats, having a combined fuselage and hull. The others had one or two floats, and generally were land planes that had been quickly modified for water operations.

Among the better thought-out hydro-monoplanes was the Borel, which had fittings on its floats for oars, to be used to row the machine up to its landing slip. In addition, it had a hand-operated device, which the passenger could use to start the engine, in yet another small step toward practicality.

In numbers alone, the 1912 show was almost double the size of the previous years: 77 aircraft of all types, to 44 for 1911. In the past, the ceiling of the great hall would have been full of balloons and dirigibles, but this year there were but two balloons. The airplane was winning out.

An even more surprising trend was the rush toward monoplanes, no doubt to a great extent because of the success and subsequent popularity

Drzeweicki double monoplane, with what looks like a front canard surface, and plates on the wingtips that are something like modern winglets. A rear-mounted engine drives a pusher propeller, making it possibly an ancient ancestor of Burt Rutan's Vari Eze? At the time of the show, the Drzeweicki had yet to leave the ground. Library of Congress

The Zodiac biplane was displayed for the second year, with the only obvious change being a semienclosed cockpit for the comfort of the pilot and passenger. The designer knew enough about the new science of aerodynamics to use high-aspect ratio wings to give him superior performance. Library of Congress

of Bleriot's designs. In 1912 there were 46 monoplanes and only 20 biplanes.

Another development evident at the Bleriot stand was the monocoque fuselage (without internal bracing) made from laminated paper, cork, and fabric. This could be considered the first "composite" structure, though one seriously doubts that radar-invisibility was Bleriot's main goal. Still, it was of great interest, and showed how such a technique could produce clean lines.

Caudron, which had yet to gain fame with exceptionally streamlined racers, displayed one of the first amphibians. The main wheels were integral with the central floats, and placed aft of the step where they allegedly would not interfere with water operations.

Henri and Maurice Farman were by now among the most prolific of manufacturers, and their airplanes at the show were particularly well finished. Some observers got the impression that at least one of the Farman airplanes had been especially prepared for the show, and that production machines might not be quite as well finished.

As evidence of the crude-but-advancing state of knowledge of streamlining, the Ponche and Primard

airplane now had aluminum covering on both surfaces of its wings. In 1911 only the lower surface was covered, leaving the top open so that the spars and associated bracing could create yet more drag.

There was continued interest in the "torpille" layout, so named because the propeller was in the tail, as in a torpille or torpedo. It was not because the fuselage was shaped like a torpedo, though this was often the case. D'Artois offered one of these, in which the rotary engine was located in the center of the fuselage and drove the propeller via a long shaft. This is such a great way to streamline an airplane that designers continue to try, but rarely with much success.

But the award for the greatest advances in streamlining had to go to Deperdussin, whose single-seater won the James Gordon Bennett Race in 1912. With a 140-horsepower Gnome rotary engine, it led off with a large spinner around the propeller hub and a tight, rounded engine cowling. The struts were of streamlined cross-section, the wings were unusually thin, and the pilot's headrest was small. The result: an official 105 miles per hour around a 4-mile closed course.

Louis Breguet, who would become one of the greats of French aircraft design, produced for this show his most unusual flying machine, *La Marseillaise*. A flying boat, it had auxiliary floats attached to the sides of the main float; these later would be called "sponsons."

But the engine was the shocker. The 110-horsepower Canton-Unné was a radial, which included a set of gears, which turned the driveshaft 90 degrees. It was mounted flat in the fuselage and drove the four-bladed propeller via an additional shaft. This placed the prop in the extreme front of the amphibian.

If that wasn't enough, the machine was a canard, with its elevator just behind the propeller, and a full tail just behind the high-mounted wing. If the engine location was supposed to improve streamlining, the myriad of struts and wires must have worked quite effectively in the opposite direction.

With European flight still just a few years old, it was to be expected that there would be few signs of stability or much agreement on the shape of an airplane.

1913 Paris Air Show

The sixth annual show was held in the Grand Palais from December 5 through 25, a full three weeks. No doubt this was an effort to reduce the crowding experienced in previous shows.

Since the 1912 show, Maurice Prevost had raised the World Speed Record to 127 miles per hour, and M. Seguin had flown 635 miles nonstop. The zipper and the fox trot were well on their way to worldwide popularity, and unnoticed by most, the Geiger counter had been invented.

Rumbles of approaching war were getting louder, and yet the number of clearly military airplanes was down. Manufacturers were more interested in filling orders for their own governments than in trying to sell their wares to other countries.

The correspondent from *Flight* magazine described the scene in a manner unfamiliar to modern air show fans:

"In the center of the Grand (Nave) is a great fountain of flowers standing some 30 feet high, and round it are ranged six stands, which are separated from each other by terraces of flowers, radiating from the plinth of the great floral fountain. Along the center of the Grand (Nave), three on each side of the central fountain, are arranged a half-dozen giant Egyptian drinking cups, each overflowing with beautiful flowers, and running between each vase are stepped terraces of flowers."

But there were clear signs that designers and manufacturers were thinking in a more military way. The two-seat Bristol biplane had a bomb-dropping device consisting of a drum, around the outside of which were 12 very small bombs, which could be dropped singly, or in groups. Tests of this device had already been made in "actual warfare" in the Balkans, where tests of advanced military equipment continue.

One of the odder-looking airplanes on display was the Moreau *Aerostable*, which had recently won a stability competition. What makes it prophetic is the covering of transparent material intended to make it very difficult to see at a distance. Perhaps it was the world's first "stealth" airplane, even if that word had not yet been used in this sense.

At the opposite end of the spectrum from military uses for airplanes were the improvements in comfort and convenience seen in several designs. The tandem style of seating in two-seaters was being replaced by side-by-side seating, known as a "Sociable," the term apparently borrowed from the early cars. Crude metal bucket seats had, in some cases, given way to fully upholstered seats. Some cockpits boasted such conveniences as map holders and cupboards for storing small items that otherwise would bounce around and possibly jam the controls.

For primary structures, there was a trend away from wood and toward steel. Its greater weight had to be dealt with, as light aluminum alloys were not yet in existence. Several of the airplanes used steel for the frames of their wings, fuselages, and tails, and paid the price. Also adding to the weight, at least of the military airplanes, was armor plating for the protection of the pilot and whatever crew was along.

Among the intriguing new bits of apparatus on display was the large light mounted between the front struts of the main float of a Breguet hydroplane. Just what the purpose was remains vague, as night flying, especially by watercraft, was rare in 1913.

The display of the Avions Caudron factory. At left is the hydro-biplane with combined wheels and floats for the main landing gear and the smaller unit at the tail. At right is the monoplane displaying some of the best of contemporary streamlining, including a semicowled engine. Library of Congress

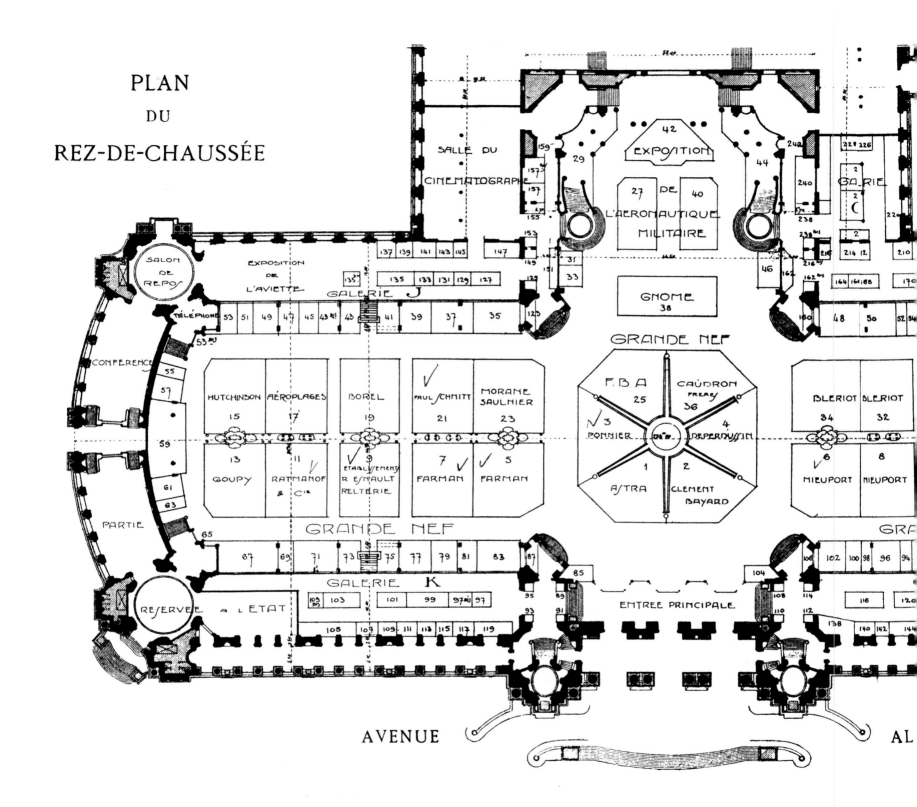

PLAN

DU

REZ-DE-CHAUSSÉE

SALLE DU
CINÉMATOGRAPHE

EXPOSITION

42

27 DE 40

L'AÉRONAUTIQUE

MILITAIRE

29 44

240

238

SALON
DE
REPOS

EXPOSITION
DE
L'AVIETTE

GALERIE J

135 133 131 129 127

137 139 141 143 145 147

53 51 49 47 45 43 43 41 39 37 35

TÉLÉPHONE

CONFÉRENCE

55

57

59

61

63

PARTIE

65

GNOME
38

214 12

48 50 52 54

GRANDE NEF

F.B.A
25

CAUDRON
FRÈRE
36

3 4

BONNIER PEUGEOT

1 2

ASTRA CLÉMENT
BAYARD

BLÉRIOT BLÉRIOT

34 32

6 8

NIEUPORT NIEUPORT

HUTCHINSON AÉROPLAGES BOREL PAUL SCHMITT MORANE
SAULNIER

15 17 19 21 23

13 11 9 7 5

GOUPY RATMANOF
& Cie
ÉTABLISSEMENT
R. ESNAULT
PELTERIE
FARMAN FARMAN

GRANDE NEF

67 69 71 73 75 77 79 81 83 87

85

106 102 100 98 96 94

104

GALERIE K

103 101 99 97 97

RÉSERVÉE A L'ÉTAT

105 107 109 111 113 115 117 119

95 89

93 91

108 114

110 112

116 120

ENTRÉE PRINCIPALE

138 140 142 144

AVENUE

AL

20

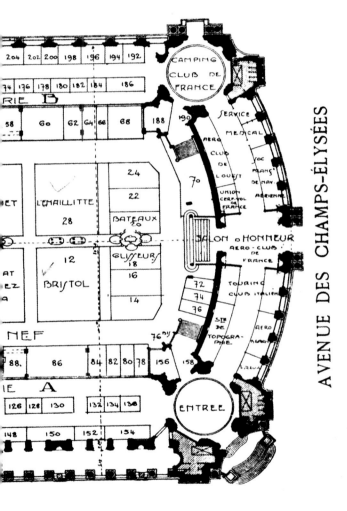

CINQUIÈME EXPOSITION INTERNATIONALE
DE
LOCOMOTION AÉRIENNE
GRAND PALAIS
1913

DRE III

Of more practical use was the wireless telegraph mounted in the fuselage of an unfinished Breguet. The observer's station included a writing desk, which was quite an elaborate concept for the time.

One of the airplanes on the Morane-Saulnier stand was a then-uncommon parasol type, with its top wing mounted above the fuselage, on struts, and giving the pilot exceptional visibility. The one at Paris in 1913 was a military two-seater, which had a camera behind the observer's seat, pointed straight down so it could take photographs of enemy defenses and formations.

The display of Deperdussin was one of the more impressive, with three airplanes, including the latest James Gordon Bennett Race winner. Far ahead of all rivals when it came to streamlining, the company's bright future faded rapidly after this show when its head, Armand Deperdussin, was jailed for having established his firm with embezzled money.

Yet another idea that was new in 1913 but has attracted the interest of engineers ever since was a variable-incidence wing on a Paul Schmitt biplane. It could be changed in flight so that as the airplane's speed varied, the attitude of its fuselage could remain the same. While such wings are still talked about, Mr. Schmitt soon faded away.

The sixth Paris Air Show was scheduled for December 1914. Unfortunately, there were those who had other ideas. In June 1914, Austrian Archduke Ferdinand was assassinated, which got a lot of people terribly upset. By September, the major powers of Europe were slaughtering young men by the tens of thousands in the Battle of the Marne.

Airframes and engines and equipment that were first revealed at Paris Air Shows had gone into mass production. Names like Nieuport, Sopwith, and Fokker that had been known to relatively few outside aviation, were now commonplace. Aerial combat and bombing were added to the original, nonlethal, military functions of observation and scouting.

World War I raged on for four years, ending finally in November 1918. The Paris Air Shows would not resume until a year later, in late 1919.

Plan of the Ground Floor of the Fifth International Exposition of Aerial Locomotion, Grand Palais. The Grand Nave (Nef) in the center highlighted the main exhibitors' airplanes: Caudron, Deperdussin, Clement Bayard, Ponnier, and F.B.A. Radiating from it in three directions were the displays of dozens of manufacturers and vendors of devices aeronautic. Official Guidebook of the Salon

21

2

CONTRIBUTION AND DEVELOPMENT

*T*he "War to End All Wars" ended in November 1918. It had seen slaughter on a scale never before known. Hundreds of thousands of soldiers died in single battles. In its aftermath, hatred of the defeated Germans led the victors to impose punishment so severe that it would lead to an even worse war.

The airplane, however, had come of age. No longer was it a novelty. It was now a useful device, if only for making war even more terrible, as it began to bring the fighting to the home front. England, in particular, saw its age-old immunity wiped out by lumbering zeppelins that dropped their bombs on homes from many thousands of feet above.

The SPAD-Herbemont 45, a big step forward in the design of large airliners. Setting it apart from all the others was its streamlining: the smooth curves of the laminated wood fuselage, the completely cowled engines, the single I-strut between the wings. It was designed to carry 17 passengers and a crew of three at over 100 miles per hour on four 300-horsepower Hispano engines. U.S. National Archives

The 1920 Paris Air Show saw the first use of aircraft designations by manufacturers. No longer were aircraft just described as biplanes or monoplanes, now they had letters and numerals in their names to designate each model.

All of the major fighting powers except the United States fielded thousands of scout planes, pursuits, and bombers over the Western front, and a new category of military hero, the combat pilot, was born. Those who survived the takeoffs and landings from ill-prepared fields, let alone the dogfights and intense antiaircraft fire from the ground, were glorified and offered as an inspiration for the next generation.

Technical advances, spurred on by each country's need to survive and win, came at a rapid rate: better engines, propellers, fuels, and structures. Each month produced more experience in operating airplanes than the entire prewar period, leading to far greater reliability, especially among engines.

1920 PARIS AIR SHOW

The sixth in the series of Paris Air Shows was held from December 19, 1919, to January 4, 1920, in a more modestly decorated Grand Palais. Like its predecessors, it was a primarily French show, though five British manufacturers displayed, as did three from Italy, which had been a member of the wartime Allies. Germany was prevented from building or operating aircraft.

On the day before the show opened, Sir Arthur Whitten Brown was killed in a crash in France. It had been just six months since he and John Alcock, in a converted Vickers Vimy bomber, had completed the first nonstop airplane flight across the Atlantic Ocean.

One of the most significant changes from prewar days was not the sort to lead to many comments at the time. Previously, airplanes had been described, more than named: Bleriot monoplane, Breguet biplane, etc. Now, with the great increase in the number of types, most were given designations by their manufacturers: Caudron C-25, Farman F-60, and Nieuport 29C.1.

With this came the first identifications for individual aircraft. In 1919, by international agreement, civilian aircraft first received national registrations, each starting with the prefix of the country of origin: N for the United States, G for Great Britain, F for France, etc. Both these innovations continue to the present day and are now considered indispensable.

Probably the most striking new idea to gain a foothold in 1920 was one that grew to such proportions that it now is the main connection between average people and aviation: the airliner. These ranged from the four-seat Airco (later DeHavilland) 16 with a single engine to the huge (89-foot wingspan), four-engined Bleriot Mammoth that carried 28 passengers within its lump-shaped fuselage. Some of their immediate predecessors had initiated more-or-less regular service between London and Paris for travelers willing to face the very real risks of bad weather and engine failure.

The impact of air racing on airplane design was as marked as that of car racing on the progress of automobiles. Streamlining was increasingly evident, especially on the smaller airplanes, with several resembling the fast Deperdussin racers of 1913. One particularly advanced machine was the Clement racer, with a cantilever (internally braced) wing and retractable landing gear. While one noted journalist referred to it as a "freak," such speed-increasing techniques would soon become standard.

Another "new" idea that today seems absolutely obvious was placing passenger seats entirely within the fuselage of most airliners. Here, comfort was as great a motivator as speed and fuel efficiency.

The prewar trend toward monoplanes was clearly being reversed, to a great extent because of wartime experience with single-wingers breaking under stress. Pilots simply preferred two wings, as they were easier to brace effectively. And they looked safer. The engineering knowledge and the materials needed to make a monoplane wing as strong were both on the horizon. A few triplanes were on display, even though their increased drag should by now have relegated them to museums.

Although the era of long, hard-surface runways was still off in the future, there was a noticeable drop in the number of water-based craft. There were but three flying boats: Marcel Besson's little triplane, the Loire et Olivier trimotor, and the Fiat-powered Savoia S.16. And a single float plane, the Breguet XIV T, which was almost identical to Breguet land planes.

Commercial uses began with the airmail, which by now was well established between major European cities. Next to follow was airline service. This grew more slowly because the airplanes in use insisted on crashing when they were flown into bad weather, and their pilots had difficulty navigating around high ground that was hidden by clouds.

But air travel was coming, and to entice nervous passengers, the interiors of airliners were made to look as much like expensive cars as possible. Patterning after shipping lines, they offered first, second, and third class cabins, with appropriate decorations. Flight crews saw their instruments improve and increasingly useful air-to-ground radios fitted.

There was considerable contrast among airplanes from well-known makers. The Farman and Voisin airplanes were little changed from prewar days, having uncovered structures in place of rear fuselages. The Bleriot Mammoth airliner, on the other hand, had a fully enclosed cabin in which passengers were carried on two decks. Perhaps sensing this was a bit too modern, they arranged to have the passengers enter the airplane via a ladder and up through a trap door in the fuselage bottom.

A hint of things to come was on the Boulton & Paul stand. The type P.10 was almost completely uncovered, displaying its steel construction for all to see. This was not an airplane designed for wood and then built of metal, but one designed to be metal right from the start. Rather than using stainless steel, which seems logical, the manufacturer preferred more common steel and then coated it to prevent rust. By using carefully engineered components, the weight was reportedly kept below that of a comparable wooden airplane, while the durability must have been considerably greater.

For many years, landing gears had been so complex that they added a lot of unnecessary drag to otherwise fairly clean airplanes. Now, serious attention was being paid to the struts and wires, which held wheels in place. Axles were submerged in streamlined spreader bars, and fewer parts, such as skids, were being left out in the breeze.

In many ways, the 1920 Paris Air Show showed little evidence of the terrible war that had ended just 12 months earlier. There were armed airplanes on display, but no arrays of bombs such as later became common. People were mourning their dead and needed no reminders.

1921 Paris Air Show

The seventh show, now called the "Salon de l'Aéronautique," was held from November 12 to 27. Continuing the trend away from ornate decorations, it was dominated by large airplanes called by such wonderful names as *Mammoth, Leviathon,* and *Juggernaut.* By using up such names on airplanes, which today seem barely average in size, no extravagant

The Rene Tampier roadable folding-wing biplane. It had an extra set of wheels amidship and separately powered for moving it down the street. This seemed to work reasonably well, but the extra weight of the wheels and motor cut into the airplane's payload, and so little more was seen of it. Flight International

names were left for today's enormous airliners. This may explain the popularity of the colorless designations with which such magnificent craft as the Boeing 747 are known.

In the world at large, KDKA in Pittsburgh, Pennsylvania, became the world's first commercial radio station. Herman Oberth founded the then-academic subject of astronautics. Barely a month before the Air Show opened, Sadi Lecointe became the first man to fly faster than 200 miles per hour, with a 205-mile per hour dash in a Nieuport-Delage sesquiplane (wing-and-a-half) at Villensauvage, France.

Many of the large airliners on display were powered by three engines, though the advantages remained debatable. At least one test had shown that the third (center) engine produced as much drag as thrust. But the idea that two engines would continue to develop power even if the third failed seemed to have a calming effect on passengers, if not on engineers.

One of the most prominent of the big airliners was a twin-engined biplane developed from the World War I Vickers Vimy. It had a bulbous fuselage to carry up to 12 passengers in amazing comfort. The individual seats resembled expensive curved-back chairs, and were covered with embossed leather. The walls were decorated with paintings. Obviously aimed at attracting the wealthy set, it was expected to be used on the 200-mile London-to-Paris route.

The Marcel Besson firm, which had displayed small flying boats before, this time showed off a prototype single-engined triplane with a most unusual wing arrangement. The lowest wing had the greatest span, with the middle wing having less, and the top wing being the shortest of all. The engine was encased in a very clean, compact nacelle, and the interplane struts had elaborate fairings at their ends. Evidently something was not quite right with the H.6, for it was never seen again.

The Breguet stand displayed the usual conventional large airplanes, plus the unfinished fuselage of one to be powered by a very unusual engine. The Leviathon had in its nose a 450-horsepower Breguet-Bugatti engine composed of four groups of cylinders, with a clutch arrangement to select which and how many of the banks to use at any one time. Power was transmitted to a pair of two-bladed propellers, which were on the same shaft and turned in the same direction. This "Quadrimotem" no doubt owed a lot to the genius of race car builder Bugatti, who had built aircraft engines during World War I, but it never got anywhere.

Pierre Levasseur, one of the veterans of the Paris Air Shows, offered a "school" (training) airplane intended to be inexpensive to build and to maintain. It had a greatly simplified structure, which resembled in some respects the balsa-and-tissue model planes of the 1940s.

Another futuristic idea on the Levasseur stand was a variable-pitch propeller, which reportedly had successfully completed a 10-hour test run at a French government laboratory. It would eventually enable airplanes to operate off much shorter runways or to take off with much higher wing-loadings. But it would be many years before such propellers were standard equipment.

Yet another novel technique was on display: the roadable airplane. Or at least an attempt at building one. Rene Tampier drove his airplane, its wings folded, along a street bordering the Grand

On the left is a Breguet 14 T bis of five-passenger capacity (F-ADBR), while at right is the advanced design all-metal fuselage structure of a Breguet Leviathon. It used duralumin tube longerons and pressed duralumin bar frames. Power is a Breguet-Bugatti quadrimotor, driving a quite modern-looking four-bladed propeller. U.S. National Archives

Palais, and even backed it up under its own power. To do this, he used an auxiliary engine to power a pair of wheels, and steered them with the rudder control. Sadly, he experienced what many others would in the future: in order to make his car/airplane do many things, he sacrificed so much performance that it could do nothing very well.

The Italian manufacturer, Ansaldo, built thousands of airplanes during the war and was trying to get into the commercial market. One way was with new ideas, including one that should have caught on. Its type A.300T was a clean cabin biplane with a pair of small windows that faced forward, allowing passengers to look past the engine to see where they were going. Maybe someone should try this one today.

All in all, the 1921 Paris Air Show offered a lot in the way of improved streamlining and comfort, without producing any huge technical advances. But Europe was still trying to recover from war.

1922 PARIS AIR SHOW

The eighth "Exposition Internationale de l'Aeronautique" was held in the Grand Palais from December 15, 1922, to January 2, 1923. Since the previous Paris Air Show, the *Readers Digest* had been launched, Irving Berlin had written "April Showers," and John Harwood had invented the self-winding wristwatch.

This Paris show produced some major advancements, as Europe continued to rebuild itself. Unlike most earlier shows, this one lacked

A Fokker glider, one of the few motorless aircraft seen so far at Paris. The wing is reminiscent of the World War I Fokker D.VIII, as is the tail. The wheels and struts at the rear merely serve to support the tail when the glider is parked on the ground. U.S. National Archives

A general view of the airplanes and the signs identifying manufacturers in 1922. In the foreground, the four-engined Schneider bomber with swept outer wing panels. Beyond it, a Latecore L.A.T.6 all-aluminum four-engined bomber. In the distance, a Potez XVIII 12-passenger airliner with three 275-horsepower Lorraine engines.
Flight International

any ornate decorations, being almost functional in appearance. Identical design banners with plain lettering announced the manufacturers displaying below.

Many of the new French airplanes, which continued to dominate the displays, were built of Duralumin, an aluminum alloy later known simply as "Dural." It combined strength and durability with low weight, enabling designers to create more efficient airplanes. And it would lead to more aluminum alloys for the next few decades of aviation.

Several of the new airplanes were low-wing, cantilever monoplanes with far less aerodynamic drag, hence greater efficiency and potential, than the usual strut- and wire-braced collections of wing panels. As usual, there were those airplanes that combined the new and the old in mixtures that could hardly produce anything better. Some had fairly clean airframes cluttered with all sorts of parts sticking out in the wind.

Dreams of high-speed, long-distance flying began to take form, as the French displayed a Rateau supercharger, which was said to have completed a 10-hour test successfully at a government laboratory. The advantages of greatly reduced drag at 20,000 feet and higher would soon translate into much higher cruising speeds.

Breguet this time displayed two quite different Leviathons, both powered by the complex Breguet-Bugatti four-in-one engine. One was the same single-engined design as last year, while the other was an otherwise fairly conventional twin.

The brothers Farman, who had produced little in the way of recent innovations, displayed a low-wing, cantilever monoplane with a 2-foot thick wing into which enough strength could be built to make it workable.

The other, similar design was the all-metal S.I.M.B. Bernard, which could have been an ancestor of the mid-1930s Boeing P-26 Pea-Shooter, so similar was its layout. Bernard would soon follow it with a World Speed Record airplane, the V.2.

The oddest looking machine in the Grand Palais had to be the Nieuport Astra Type 37.C1, modified from the 37.C, which was entered in the 1922 Coupe Deutsch Race but refused to fly. On the positive side, it had a fuselage with a near-perfect tear-drop shape. On the negative side, the fuselage was cluttered with so many protrusions that its performance had to be compromised.

Easily the most prophetic of all the displays was Raul Pescara's helicopter. Like all rotary wing craft of the era, it was terribly complicated, with two contra-rotating rotors, each composed of four biplane rotor blades. This time, however, the thinking behind it was solid, and in 1924, Pescara flew it to the world's first official record for a helicopter. He recorded a flight of almost a half-mile, in 4-plus minutes, at an altitude of 6 feet. The record would stand for 10 years.

More and more airplanes—large and small—were equipped to fold their wings for ease of storage and transport. One of the airplanes displayed by Morane was an unbraced high-wing cabin monoplane, a style that would soon become popular. The Hispano engine was mounted for ease of maintenance; with the removal of just four bolts and the instrument panel, it could be detached in a claimed 10 minutes.

1924 Paris Air Show

The ninth show, called the "Salon d'Aviation," was held from December 5 to 21. The two-year gap since the previous show would become permanent, giving manufacturers more time to develop new airplanes, engines, and equipment.

There was some movement back toward the elaborate decorations of the earlier shows, with the plain banners of 1922 style giving way to translucent yellow banners with fancier blue lettering. But the flowers and streamers of yore were long gone.

Since the last show, Hugo Eckner had flown across the Atlantic nonstop in the Zeppelin ZR3. In Japan, 120,000 people had died in earthquakes. Juan de la Cierva had invented the autogyro. And Jacob Schick had produced the first commercially viable electric razor. While the show was in progress, Florentin Bonet raised the World Air Speed Record to 278 miles per hour in the Bernard V.2.

The event was opened by the French under the secretary for air, M. Laurent-Eynac. The next day, French President Doumergue and Prime Minister Herriot attended, giving it the official stamp of approval.

Once again it was a primarily French event, with only two other countries represented: Great Britain with one manufacturer (Armstrong-Siddeley) and the Netherlands with three (Fokker, Koolhoven, and Pander).

There was a noticeable trend toward sesquiplanes and away from conventional biplanes. Lower wings on sesquiplanes ranged from little more than an airfoil-shaped axle to wings more than half as long as the upper. The idea was to combine the lower drag of a monoplane with the lightweight strength of interplane struts. It wasn't clear just how much science supported the theory.

Metal construction continued to increase in popularity. The French used more Duralumin, to some extent because they had to import thin, high-grade steel at considerable expense. Metal was also starting to show up in propellers, where laminated wood props were showing weaknesses at high rpm.

Prior to World War II, France developed a reputation for producing really strange looking multiengined airplanes. One that helped establish the pattern was the Farman Jabiru sesquiplane airliner. It had a high wing, with the pilot's head

and windshield poking through the upper surface of the wing. The nose was impossibly blunt, though rounded to reduce drag somewhat.

The nacelles for the pair of 400-horsepower Lorraine engines sat atop the lower wing, and looked like slightly rounded rectangular blocks. Contrasting with this lack of streamlined shape was the excellent attention paid to fairings. Something must have been right with the Jabiru, as one of them won the 1923 Grand Prix for commercial airplanes.

The fact that aviation had become a 21-year-old "adult" was recognized by the Dutch firm, Fokker. Its display featured Tony Fokker's original 1911 Spin, alongside the latest D.XIII pursuit, making an impressive silent contrast. This clean sesquiplane was powered by a British Napier "Lion" engine inside a tight cowl. It was said to have a top speed at sea level of 175 miles per hour.

The Barnard speed record machine offered a new solution to the growing problem of cooling an engine that is run at very high speed. The barrel-shaped Lamblin radiator had its surface covered with cooling fins, and was, in this case, hung from the wings. While it produced drag, it was so vital

The aircraft at the 1922 show incorporate many of the lessons learned from World War 1. Fully enclosed fuselages, moving ailerons (rather than wing warping), and conventional empennage appear everywhere.
Flight International

*Upstaged by the elaborate decorations
and partially hidden by the shrubbery, the
Aero Tovarna company from
Czechoslovakia displayed two of its latest
biplanes, including the Aero Ab.11 at
front center. Another Czech firm, Avia,
had its airplanes just behind Aero's.*
Service Presse USIAS

that there was little choice. For such a special-pur-
pose airplane, additional cooling radiators were
built along the undersurface of the wings.

One of many attempts to develop all-metal,
adjustable-pitch propellers produced a novel
solution: blades made from large-diameter steel
tubes. Carefully planned cutting away of portions
of a tube resulted in a blade having the desired
shape and curvature.

This head-long rush toward metal construction sometimes clashed with the needs of conservative customers. To cope with this, the SPAD 61
single-seat fighter was offered with metal wings.
But it also could be supplied with wood wings in
order to suit. It was equipped with an unusually
heavy armament: two machine guns on the top
wing, and two in the fuselage, firing through the
propeller arc.

With long-distance flights gaining popularity, Breguet chose to display, as an example of its Type XIX, the actual machine flown by Lieutenant Dropsy from Paris to China. By offering proof of its capability, the manufacturer attracted far more attention to its other airplanes on display. The all-metal XIX was offered for only $5,000, less engine.

Among the far-sighted developments revealed at Paris in 1924 was the beginning of the light plane movement, with several small, personal airplanes on display. On the Dewoitine stand was the D.7, powered by a 55-horsepower, six-cylinder, water-cooled Vaslin engine. A simple shoulder-wing design, it had a thick cantilever wing which gave it a top speed of 94 miles per hour, assuming its engine produced the advertised power.

Another light plane, and a much better looking one, was the Dutch Pander. It had a wingspan of 26 feet 3 inches, length of 16 feet 3 inches, and wing area of 116 square feet. It weighed just 385 pounds empty, and 615 pounds fully loaded. With a 30-horsepower, Y-type Anzani three-cylinder engine, it was supposed to have a very useful speed range of 25 to 80 miles per hour.

1926 PARIS AIR SHOW

The 10th show was held at the Grand Palais from December 3 through 19. In the two years that had passed since the previous Paris Air Show, the World Air Distance Record had risen from 2,470 miles to 3,353 miles with a flight made a few weeks before the show. Costes and Rignot had flown a Breguet XIX from Le Bourget Aeroport, north of Paris (and the future home of the Paris Air Show), to Persia.

Since late 1924, Malcolm Campbell had boosted the water speed record to over 150 miles per hour. Gene Tunney had beaten Jack Dempsey for the world heavyweight title. And Professor Robert Goddard had successfully launched the world's first liquid-fueled rocket, near Roswell, New Mexico.

While this show was predominantly French, the trend toward an international event continued. There were airplanes and associated equipment from Great Britain, Czechoslovakia, Italy, and the Netherlands. As yet, the United States had not been involved.

The trend toward metal construction and away from wood continued, though it would never become complete. Many European sport planes use wood in their structures to this day. But the long-term advantages of steel and aluminum alloys were too much to ignore.

Engines continued to grow more powerful, with several in the 700-to-800-horsepower range, at least in their advertising brochures. Air-cooled radials gained popularity, along with water-cooled inline V and W (or broad-arrow) arrangements. Half the airplanes on display were powered by some version of the Jupiter engine, a popular nine-cylinder, air-cooled radial.

The 1926 show offered fewer potentially significant new ideas, but built upon the last show. There were more airliners and more trainers, and hardly anything that would be recognized as a bomber. The value of proven performance, rather than manufacturers' questionable claims, was recognized by the increasing number of record-setting and competition-winning airplanes included in commercial displays.

The sesquiplane, with its small lower wing, began to fade out, to be replaced, at least for a few

General view from the south. In front, just to the right of center, is the Koolhoven F.K.35 in its monoplane configuration; addition of a top wing could turn it into a biplane. The white airplane at left center is the Farman 170T with a 500-horsepower Farman engine inside a clean cowling.
Flight International

years, by the parasol monoplane in which the wing was mounted above the fuselage on struts.

At the Bleriot stand, the SPAD 61 was trumpeted as the new holder of the World Altitude Record of 40,822 feet. But this was never recognized by the International Aeronautics Federation. Still, it had the effect of attracting a lot of interest among the tens of thousands who toured the Grand Palais. Of more significance was the Bleriot 165, a twin-engined, 16-passenger airliner scheduled for the increasingly popular (if not exactly profitable) Paris-London route.

Louis Breguet, one of France's most successful airplane manufacturers, displayed the Type 19 G.R. (for Grand Raid, or long distance) which had been used for several important distance flights. The hefty biplane was powered by a well-proven 500-horsepower Hispano-Suiza V-12. With minor changes, it could be a standard army observation or bombing type.

In the Farman display, this very old French builder was showing its Type F.170 transport, which was in use on the Paris-Amsterdam and the Paris-Cologne-Berlin routes. An example held the world duration record with a 45-hour flight in 1925, suggesting its 500-horsepower Farman V-12 engine was quite reliable.

The most popular airliner in Europe, Fokker's F.VII.3m trimotor, was a Dutch airplane equipped with British 185-horsepower Armstrong-Siddeley Lynx or American 240-horsepower Wright Whirlwind engines. As airline flights were gradually getting longer, its eight passengers were furnished with the luxury of a lavatory at the rear of the cabin.

Another Dutch product, the Koolhoven F.K.35, also offered a choice, but of wings rather than engines. It could be converted from a biplane reconnaissance into a monoplane fighter. It used a Bristol Mk.VI Jupiter engine, which gave a claimed top speed of 160 miles per hour. Other novel ideas included droppable fuel tanks suspended in the wings and a mechanically operated one-gun turret. The two latter ideas would reappear in more sophisticated form.

The shape of airliners to come was suggested by the Levasseur 7.T Limousine: a fuselage with passengers inside and a cockpit in front and above

At the right front is the Breguet 280T, an all-metal sesquiplane airliner with a 500-horsepower geared Renault engine. At left center is the Loire et Olivier LeO H.18, a two-seat, all-wood flying boat with a 120-horsepower pusher engine. In the center is the uncovered fuselage and stub wings of the LeO 20 Bn 3 night bomber. Flight International

them. The cockpit was still open, as pilots "knew" they needed to feel the wind in order to fly properly.

Another aircraft with a modern-looking fuselage, slowed by strut-braced biplane wings, was the Loire et Olivier LeO H.190 flying boat. The cabin carried six passengers, while the cockpit was behind it and included a wireless (radio) room. With a single 420-horsepower Gnome-Rhone Jupiter engine, it was advertised with a cruising speed near 100 miles per hour.

On show for the first time was Nieuport-Delage Type 42 C.1 fighter, destined to become a major airplane for the French Armee de l'Air. It was one of the very first such planes to be called a "light fighter," an idea that is still of great interest to air forces, even though it has rarely worked out as intended.

The Czech Avimeta AVM88 two-seat fighter was a parasol monoplane having fully faired (but

corrugated) landing gear struts, which made the lower part of the airplane look much more modern than the rest. It used the French Alferium aluminum alloy to reduce weight. Otherwise, the Czech airplanes offered few new ideas, resembling other countries' designs of several years earlier.

1928 PARIS AIR SHOW

The 11th Salon de l'Aviation was held in the Grand Palais from June 29 through July 15. Only 1 1/2 years had elapsed since the last show, but the shift to summer dates would not become permanent for more than 20 years.

The most important event since the last show was undoubtedly the solo, nonstop trans-Atlantic flight by Charles Lindbergh in May 1927. While its distance was exceeded within a few weeks, it was the emotional impact that has yet to be equaled. The world became air-minded overnight. When a lone pilot took off from New York and flew until he landed in Paris, the world shrank.

By the time the 1928 Paris show began, the World Nonstop Distance record had been extended to 4,467 miles with Ferrin and DelPrete's flight from Rome to near Natal, Brazil. The Speed Record was now over 300 miles per hour, as a result of a series of dashes by another Italian, Mario deBernardi, clocking 318.6 miles per hour in a Macchi M-52R seaplane. This extended the seaplane's domination of the absolute speed record that would not end until 1939.

Otherwise, color television had been demonstrated for the first time, and penicillin had been invented by Arthur Flemming. It was not yet clear which would prove the more beneficial.

Highlight of the Air Show was the first participation by Germany since before World War I. The show was smaller (only 40 airplanes on display), but there were more countries involved: France, Czechoslovakia, Great Britain, Germany, and the Netherlands. Among the German manufacturers were several whose products would become extremely well known, including Arado, Focke Wulf, Heinkel, and Junkers.

Decoration of the Palais was still limited to banners with manufacturers' names hanging from the ceiling, plus whatever modest additions each exhibitor wished to add. The show was becoming more functional in appearance, and more of a serious marketplace. Countries displaying their wares were France, Germany, the Netherlands, Czechoslovakia, Italy, and Great Britain. French domination was gradually ebbing, with France this year accounting for barely two-thirds of the aircraft.

There were no major new ideas in design or construction, as metal continued to replace wood, and streamlining extended to every part of an airplane, save its biplane wings.

Among the new military types was the prototype of the Bristol Bulldog, though it was called, simply, the Bristol single-seater. The all-metal machine was said to be capable of 170 miles per hour at 20,000 feet on the power of its 450-horsepower Bristol Jupiter nine-cylinder radial engine.

The Levasseur P.L.7T²B²b amphibious torpedo biplane was noted as much (or little) for having the most complicated alpha-numeric designation in

aviation history as for any achievements. Its landing gear could be dropped prior to alighting on water, and its wing-root fuel tanks could be used to assist in flotation, once emptied of fuel.

Potez introduced its Type 35, a high-wing, twin-engined night bomber that hinted at future bombers such as the Flying Fortress. It had five movable machine guns that were claimed to cover almost any angle from which an enemy might attack.

Fokker, of the Netherlands, showed a new single-engined, high-wing "strategic" reconnaissance airplane, the C.VIII. While it had a radius of action of barely 200 miles, one must keep in mind that it was built in a very small country, and even a 200-mile flight could take it over the territory of several other countries.

Yet another interesting military type was the little Mureaux M.B.35, a twin-float seaplane meant for antisubmarine scouting. With two seats side-by-side in the open cockpit, it was said to have appeal to sporting types, making it one of the more unusual dual-purpose flying machines ever developed.

Among the airliners on display was the largest yet: Farman's F.180, with facilities for as many as 22 passengers for short legs (up to 300 miles) in its modern-looking fuselage. The fully enclosed cockpit was in the extreme nose, with passengers behind, much as they are today. For long flights of 900 miles and taking up to 9 hours, the cabin could be outfitted with 12 berths for sleeping in comfort.

Another streamlined large airplane was the prototype of the C.A.M.S. 53 long-range mail carrier. A flying boat with a pair of 500-horsepower Hispano-Suiza engines in a single nacelle under the top wing, it had an advertised range of 600 miles at a little over 100 miles per hour.

Aimed purely at the growing private flying market were at least a half-dozen monoplane designs, mostly with engines in the 50–60-horsepower range. The largest was the Loire et Olivier LeO H.18, a side-by-side flying boat with a pylon-mounted 120-horsepower Salmson engine with a pusher propeller.

With the 1928 show, the first postwar decade ended. Aviation was experiencing healthy growth, thanks to booming business and the lack of any major war on the horizon. The future looked rosy.

CHAPTER 3

DEPRESSION INTO CONFLICT

The first Salon de l'Aviation of the 1930s was held from November 28 to December 14, 1930, in the Grand Palais, as ever. Thirteen months before, the world was rocked by the Wall Street crash, which was leading to the worst financial depression in modern American history. While its impact had yet to be felt as strongly in Europe, fear was beginning to spread, and it was obvious that all of aviation would soon be affected.

Herbert Hoover was now president of the United States. E.O. Lawrence had invented the cyclotron and Albert Einstein had published his "Unified Field Theory," though few had any hint of the significance of either. Jimmy Doolittle made the first flight relying solely on instruments.

In sharp contrast to all the airplanes parked sedately on the floor, this Morane-Saulnier 430 looked as if it were making a turn a little too low. A trainer in the AT-6 Texan class, it used a 390-horsepower Salmson or 400-horsepower Gnome Rhone engine good for a claimed 220 miles per hour. Flight International

General photo of the interior of the Grand Palais. In the foreground is the Caudron all-metal trimotored monoplane. At the left, under its wing, is the Caudron C.195 light all-wood sport plane powered by a 95-horsepower Renault. The wing at the very bottom, lettered with "PH-" is the Fokker F.1X trimotored airliner.
Flight International

The World Speed Record had been raised to 358 miles per hour by a British Supermarine racing seaplane, while that for land planes remained at 278 miles per hour.

Poland was added to the list of nations that had displayed at Paris, and the United States would have joined, too, had it not been for a door. The largest door to the Palais was too small, and the French refused to allow part of a wall to be removed so that a big Ford Trimotor could be rolled in. Excessive French nationalism was suspected, but not proven.

That, and the presence of an increasing number of jammed-together large airplanes, should have made the governing body of the show realize that a much larger, specially designed facility was needed, and that it should be on or very near an airfield to eliminate trucking airplanes through the streets of Paris.

One of the first German aircraft on display since World War I is this Dornier S flying boat. Larger than the well-known Wal, and much smaller than the giant X, it is powered by four Hispano-Suiza engines in push-pull nacelles. Twelve passengers can be carried in the forward cabin and 10 in the rear.
DaimlerChrysler Aerospace

A French Dewoitine D.27 single-seat fighter with a 500-horsepower Hispano-Suiza V-12 engine. It is in production and in squadron service, but only in Switzerland. It has a top speed of 190 miles per hour and a ceiling of 30,000 feet. Its armament is a pair of small machine guns.
U.S. National Archives

An obvious but temporary solution to the seemingly permanent problem of overcrowding was the increased use of models and photographs of new and proposed designs. Typical of this was the 174-foot Supermarine flying boat with six Rolls-Royce 900-horsepower V-12 engines, no doubt thought of as a rival to Germany's massive Dornier X flying boat with its 12 engines of 600 horsepower each, flying since 1929 but never especially successful. Models and photos of the Supermarine boat attracted attention, but it was never built.

A far more successful prototype was Britain's all-metal biplane Bristol Bulldog, which was on display at Paris, and which survived to go on display in 1999 in the Royal Air Force Museum in London. It became a classic service fighter in the early 1930s.

The airline industry, while still extremely crude by modern standards, had progressed far enough to demand both regular airliners and small ones for "feeder" routes. Safety, reliability, and comfort were at an early stage, but steadily improving.

A very different trimotor: The Rene Couzinet 20 light plane with three 40-horsepower Salmson engines in very clean nacelles (but with cylinders exposed). With a pilot and four passengers, it has an advertised cruising speed of 90 miles per hour and range of over 500 miles.
U.S. National Archives

Among the "feeder" airliners on display were the Nieuport-Astra 641 Icare, which offered seats for four passengers and a copilot alongside the pilot, both of them having full controls. The all-wood machine had a 300-horsepower Lorraine engine.

Another was the Bleriot III of about the same size and performance, but with retractable landing gear. While the advantages of pulling the wheels up into wings or fuselage had been common knowledge for at least a decade, it was only now coming slowly into use in military airplanes.

The continued ability to draw a crowd using record-setting airplanes was demonstrated by the Societe des Avions Bernard. To pull in the people, it displayed a Type 191 long-range monoplane that had recently made a nonstop East-to-West crossing of the Atlantic. Alongside it was the sleek forerunner of a powerful seaplane that never quite made it in time for the final Schneider Trophy Race.

The Bleriot stand's display contrasted the simple, functional monoplane in which Louis Bleriot first crossed the English Channel in 1909, with the ultramodern Bleriot 125 airliner. This had two bulbous passenger-carrying fuselages that resembled streamlined railroad cars, and a center pod with a 500-horsepower engine in either end, with an enclosed cockpit in between.

After several shows in which there was hardly an airplane of unusual design, let alone of radical or "freakish" form, creativity began to reemerge. The Breguet 270 A.2 had a fuselage that ended in a point a few feet behind the wings, continuing to the tail in the form of a slender boom. One reason for the odd shape was that it gave the rear gunner a wider field of fire. Certainly ugly, but potentially useful.

More and more small sporting monoplanes appeared with unbraced cantilever wings. To get sufficient bracing inside the wing, it had to be thicker than usual, which partly counteracted the reduced drag from the lack of exterior wires. As the knowledge of engineering advanced, wings would gradually return to their normal thickness without sacrificing strength. Other small airplanes were more traditional, like the DeHavilland Gipsy Moth two-seat, open-cockpit biplane that was being built on license in France by Morane-Saulnier.

The German exhibit lacked any sort of military aircraft, since the building of such was prohibited by international agreements. But some of those on display obviously could be converted to military uses with a minimum of effort, and truly military types were being built in secret. The only new design to be shown was the Dornier S flying boat.

Poland's exhibit included the P.VI gull-wing fighter that would lead to the P.11c, one of which would shoot down the first invading airplane of World War II. The only other Polish airplane was a parasol monoplane with a license-built Wright Whirlwind engine.

1932 PARIS AIR SHOW

The 13th Salon de l'Aviation was held in the Grand Palais from November 18 through December 14. While the décor remained mainly hanging banners with manufacturers' names, there were additions in the way of modern, interior-lit, sunburst-like fixtures suspended from the ceiling of the main hall. But it was still a far cry from the early days, when the decorations outshone the displays.

In the two years since the last show, Charles Lindbergh's baby son had been kidnapped and murdered; Franklin D. Roosevelt was elected president, bringing with him the economic New

Deal, and the Nazis assumed power in Germany. The Absolute Air Speed Record rose above 400 miles per hour with the 407-mile-per-hour dash by a Supermarine seaplane. The land plane record trailed far behind, with Jimmy Doolittle's 294 miles per hour in the GeeBee Super Sportster being the fastest with wheels.

While there were no revolutionary developments on display, there were continuations of trends that had begun a few years earlier. Retractable landing gears were seen more than in the past, though this obvious step didn't seem to be catching on as quickly as it should. The use of metal to supersede wood continued to spread as more was learned about how to employ various aluminum alloys to their best advantage.

Monoplanes were definitely on the ascendant, with the great majority of airplanes having

The overhead lighting suggests a very plush cocktail lounge, but it seems to be effective. At center bottom is a Mauboussin M121 Zodiac. At the far left is a Dewoitine 412 seaplane meant for the Schneider Trophy Race but not ready in time. F-AKEK is a Wibault-Penhoet 282 T 12 trimotor in service as an airliner. Service Presse USIAS

The parasol monoplanes are from Morane-Saulnier, all with their characteristic swept wings. The larger monoplane at the right is the Latecore Lat.290, twin-float seaplane. Partially hidden behind it is the Bleriot 111 single-engined airliner with an open cockpit aft of the cabin and retractable landing gear. Flight International

but a single wing. The aerodynamic advantages had long been known, but the engineering to support the changeover had come more slowly.

While there had never been any shortage of nationalism in Europe, relatively few of the displayed airplanes were admittedly military. Others, however, could be converted easily with the addition of machine gun mounts, bomb shackles, and the like.

The British portion of the display was their largest yet, with a Fairey Fox II single-engine day bomber and a Firefly II single-seat fighter, both biplanes powered by the 500-horsepower Rolls-Royce Kestrel V-12. Hawker had a single airplane, the Hart day bomber, which replaced the Fox; a Hart day bomber still flies in England.

Polish airplanes included two developments of the gull-winged fighter shown in 1930, each equipped with either a French or a British radial engine. In addition, there was a two-place R.W.D.6 that was flown to first place in the recent International Touring Competition that involved various tasks, fuel efficiency, etc.

The Italian display was that country's biggest yet, no doubt part of dictator Benito Mussolini's effort to convince the world that his fascist government was doing great things for his country. The only admittedly military airplane was the Fiat CR.30 biplane fighter. Powered by a Fiat A.30 R engine, it had a claimed top speed of 223 miles per hour and would figure in the Spanish Civil War.

Other Italian airplanes included the Savoia-Marchetti S.66 twin-hulled seaplane with three 700-horsepower Fiat engines mounted as pushers above the wing. The Caproni 97, a single-engined cabin monoplane transport, was the victim of a strange case of sabotage. And there were two machines from Breda: The Type 19 aerobatic trainer and the two-seat Type 25 trainer.

Everything else was French, with 46 airplanes from 23 manufacturers in the hall. Half were what is now called "general aviation" types, with the remainder military and commercial.

Military airplanes were from Mureaux (170 C.I fighter), Bernard (75 C.I fighter), Breguet (270 A2 pod-and-boom fighter), C.A.M.S. (55-6 reconnaissance bomber), Latecore (Type 29 twin-float military version of Type 28 airmail carrier), Levasseur (P.L. 151 torpedo sesquiplane). From Loire et Olivier, the LeO H.30 four-engined bomber, and from Morane-Saulnier, the 225 single-seat fighter equipped with a new NACA engine cowling.

Nieuport-Astra offered an all-metal, parasol-winged, long-distance reconnaissance airplane. There were two military airplanes from Potez: the Type 45 small patrol flying boat, which was to be catapult-launched from ships, and the Type 49, which could be a monoplane or biplane, and was planned as a recco-bomber and carrier of relief supplies.

Personal airplanes on display were mainly of the high-wing, side-by-side seating style, such as the Mureaux 160-T or Caudron 282, or low-wing monoplanes such as the Farman F.355. Even biplanes, such as the Bernard 200 TS, were on

The LeO 30 is a four-engined (two Hispano 12s in either wing-mounted nacelle) bomber with a futuristic multiwheeled landing gear. As displayed, it carried no engines, and the nacelles appeared to be unfinished. It has a wing area of 2,000 square feet, and gross weight of 33,000 pounds. Library of Congress

The Nieuport-Delage Type 590 Colonial powered by three 300-horsepower Lorraine engines. The lower rear fuselage tapers sharply inward, creating a pair of "tunnels" that would permit gunners to fire machine guns back or downward without having to get out into the slipstream. Library of Congress

This early Junkers Ju.52 trimotor was powered by a trio of Junkers Jumo diesels and sported very large twin floats. With radial engines and wheels, it became the Luftwaffe's main transport of World War II, despite its draggy, Ford Trimotor-like corrugated skins. Flight International

display. In addition, there were more specialized light planes, such as Morane-Saulnier's aerobatic Type 332 and Type 230 aerobatic/training parasol, several of which would remain in use in the 1990s.

Commercial airplanes ranged from the Mureaux 140-T, a six-passenger machine with three little 120-horsepower Salmson radial engines, to the Wibault-Penhoet trimotor (350-horsepower Gnome-Rhones) that is in airline service. Latecore displayed the wing for a proposed large commercial airplane.

The most interesting, or at least different, airplane on display was the Nieuport-Delage light plane. It was a tail-less monoplane with a 100-horsepower Lorraine radial engine turning a pusher propeller. On either wingtip was a large rudder, not all that different from the winglets becoming increasingly popular in the 1990s. Of perhaps the greatest significance was the tricycle landing gear with a steerable nose wheel. It was a good example of one of the purposes of the Paris Air Show, to display new ideas that some sharp engineer might turn into real progress.

A French Amiot 143 multipurpose fighter-bomber that wasn't as clean and modern looking as this view suggests. This one had a pair of Hispano V-12s, while the production version had 14-cylinder Gnome-Rhone radials. The low-drag cowls were counterbalanced by the fixed landing gear and extensive struts. Flight International

1934 PARIS AIR SHOW

The 14th Salon de l'Aviation (and 4th Exposition de Photogrammetrie!) was held from November 16 through December 4.

Since the last show, a rare set of quintuplets—the Dionnes—survived in Canada, John Dillinger (Public Enemy Number One) was shot by FBI agents, and Nazi Adolf Hitler was "elected" chancellor of Germany.

The World Absolute Air Speed Record had been raised to 441 miles per hour by a tandem V-12-powered Macchi MC.72 racing seaplane, complete with open cockpit. And the World Distance Record had been boosted to 5,657 miles by Rossi and Codos flying a Bleriot-Zapata 110 from New York to Syria.

Slowly, the Paris Show was growing, this time with 70 aircraft on display, including quite a few large ones, straining the capacity of the Grand Palais to its limits. Along with the still-dominating French exhibits came those from Great Britain, Italy, Germany, and, for the very first time, the pathologically secretive USSR. For the tens of thousands of visitors, this had to have been a major draw.

Radical designs were still to be seen. One that was to have a meteoric history was Henri Mignet's tiny Pou du Ciel, popularly known as the Flying Flea. It was a puddle-jumper with tandem wings and a control system utilizing a conventional rudder and a pivoting top-front wing. Following its first flying appearance, it inspired hundreds, if not thousands of Frenchmen, Englishmen, and others to become what later would be known as "homebuilders." But a series of fatal accidents pointed up a design flaw, and the Flea was outlawed in several countries; it rapidly faded from view.

Levasseur's P.L. 200 was a twin-float seaplane, with the two floats continuing back as tail booms. The central pod had a Hispano radial engine in the nose and a gunner's position behind the pilot. It was intended to be catapult-launched from ships.

The Soviet display spoke volumes about the country, as information was hard to extract. Even the precise designations of airplanes was concealed, and later became evident. A large biplane was identified only as that used on an Arctic rescue mission. It turned out to be a variation on the mass-produced Polikarpov Po-2 utility airplane known as a U-2.

A sleek low-wing with slotted flaps and ailerons was said to be an AIR-9, but current authorities say that type hadn't flown by that time, and so it probably was an AIR-7 built by Yakovlev as a sporting airplane. Why such secrecy? And why display in public, since sales to other countries were impossibly complicated? Was it to show that Soviet technology was up to that of the West?

Overall, there was significant progress in making airplanes cleaner and more efficient. Retractable landing gears and variable-pitch propellers were becoming common. Greater concern for streamlining was resulting in airplanes with excellent detail work.

The latest military airplanes were, in most cases, still held back to maintain secrecy and because there was no need to sell them. With war steadily getting closer, factories were busy turning out fighters and bombers to equip ever-more squadrons.

Germany displayed three military airplanes, none of them that important. One was a Fieseler STOL type, clearly a predecessor of the Fi.-156 Storch utility airplane. Another was a Focke Wulf FW.44 Stieglitz trainer. And the third was a float-equipped version of the Junkers Ju.52 trimotor

The partial fuselage at right is from a Bristol 143 and was displaying its construction methods: metal monocoque and wingroots of light alloy. At left is a Hawker Fury, typical of first-line RAF fighters. The displays, still under construction before the show opened, are bolstered by photographs, models, and uncovered sections of wings and a fuselage. Flight International

transport, which became Germany's World War II counterpart of the vastly superior American C-47.

Great Britain had two military airplanes at Paris. The Hawker Fury had been a standard RAF biplane fighter since 1931, but would be put out to pasture long before the war started. The Armstrong Whitworth Scimitar was a prototype that got no further.

Poland had two versions of its gull-winged P.Z.L. line: a P.11c and a later P. 24. It's hard to imagine, but Poland was considered a major air power in the early 1930s, and its technology supported this, even if its production did not.

From Czechoslovakia: the 250-mile per hour Letov S.231 and the equally fast Avia 534, both single-seat fighters. From Italy: two more single-seat biplane fighters, the Breda 27 and the Fiat CR.32, almost as fast.

But it was France, as usual, which displayed the most military airplanes. Fighters included the Morane-Saulnier 275, good for 225 miles per hour on a 600-horsepower radial engine, and the gull-winged two-seat Mureaux 180. More important was the all-metal, monoplane Dewoitine 511,

said to be capable of well over 250 miles per hour on 850 horsepower.

French bombers were far less aerodynamically clean, having gun turrets that appeared almost comical in their bulbous shapes. The Breguet 413 was a twin-engined sesquiplane with multiple gun turrets. The Amiot 142 had two engines and fixed landing gear, and was to be used for a variety of functions, including those of a fighter-bomber. The Marcel Bloch 211 had two engines, but retractable landing gear, and allegedly could hit 215 miles per hour.

Progress in many areas was accelerating, as fear of war intensified.

1936 PARIS AIR SHOW

The 15th Salon de l'Aviation was held from November 13 through 29 in the Grand Palais. Since the last Salon, American sprinter Jesse Owens had dominated the Berlin Olympics and thoroughly embarrassed racist Nazi dictator Adolf Hitler. The Spanish Civil War had begun and was being used as a testing ground for new weapons by Germany, Italy, and the USSR. China and Japan were at war, while Germany and Italy had allied themselves in the Rome-Berlin Axis. Aviation greats Billy Mitchell and Louis Bleriot had died.

With a European war becoming increasingly inevitable, it was understandable that the main focus of the Salon was on military airplanes. Most of the significant ones were kept home for security reasons: Britain's Spitfire, Hurricane, and Wellington, Germany's Messerschmitt 109. And of course America's B-17 Flying Fortress.

But others were on display, not for sale but for prestige. The most prophetic of all the military airplanes at Paris was the USSR's Polikarpov I-17, called the ZKB 17 at the time. It was a mostly metal, low-wing monoplane with fully retractable landing gear and a tightly cowled 850-horsepower Hispano-Suiza V-12. It was the first truly modern fighter plane to fly, reportedly with a top speed over 285 miles per hour. It never went into production, but eventually, all the major World War II combatants had fighters of similar layout.

There were two radical-design airplanes on display, neither of which produced much more than interesting ideas. Surprisingly, both came

A general view in the Grand Palais showing the muted decorations. In the foreground is the first production example of thousands of Bristol Blenheims, Britain's first all-metal bomber. Beyond it is the Amiot 341, advertised as a high-speed mail plane, but its glassed-in nose suggests it could house a bombardier. At the far left is a Caudron Typhon, inspired by the DeHavilland Comet racer. Flight International

from the Netherlands. The more conventional of the two was Fokker's G.1 twin-engined fighter with a general design similar to the later and much more successful Lockheed P-38 Lightning: twin tail booms and a pilot's central pod.

The more interesting was the purely experimental Koolhoven F.K.55, which had an 860-horsepower liquid-cooled V-12 engine buried behind the pilot and driving a pair of contra-rotating propellers in the nose. While plans for series production were announced, nothing came of it. Both airplanes were armed with two cannons and several machine guns.

Great Britain's display was to have featured the Hawker Hurricane low-wing fighter with a Rolls-Royce Merlin engine, but the Air Ministry decided to cancel its appearance. This left the Bristol Blenheim medium bomber to represent the rapidly rearming Royal Air Force.

Neither Germany nor Italy exhibited at Paris in 1936.

American participation at Paris began slowly and very quietly, with the display of a pair of Curtiss-Wright engines: a nine-cylinder radial Wright Whirlwind and a larger Wright Cyclone of similar arrangement and solid international reputation.

Major trends of recent years have become standard practice: all-metal construction, retractable landing gear, and variable-pitch propellers. The increasingly rapid and public spread of information (and no doubt more than a little spying) was producing similar levels of technical knowledge in the major advanced nations. It was also encouraging the application of heavy security over advanced technology. There was no hint of the efforts going into the development of jet engines.

Among the light-to-medium bombers, the Bristol Blenheim stood out. All-metal, midwing, and particularly clean, it had an advertised top speed of 260 miles per hour with a 1,000-pound bomb load. France's Marcel Bloch 131 was larger and slower, but carried almost twice the load.

Fighters were highlighted by the French Morane-Saulnier 405 and Dewoitine 510. Both, powered by modern Hispano V-12 engines, were prototypes that would lead to production airplanes. Mureaux continued to work on lightweight fighters, with the latest being the

fixed-landing gear 190 with a 450-horsepower inverted V-12 engine, equipped with a cannon firing through the propeller hub and two small machine guns.

Trainers, useful for military as well as civilian use, ranged from the Stearman-like Romano 80 primary trainer, to the Caudron Rafale advanced trainer, which showed the influence of the sleek Coupe Deutsch racers.

Rotary wing aircraft refused to go away, though they had achieved little to date. Loire et Olivier, best known for its flying boats, displayed a streamlined, 350-horsepower autogyro, intended for Army duties.

On the commercial side, few airliners or personal airplanes were on view. The Farman F.224 was a large twin-engined, strut-braced machine that could carry 40 passengers plus a crew of four. But it offered little besides size.

One of the clearest signs that performance was gaining in importance was the large number of new engines on display. There were no fewer than seven rated at 1,000-horsepower or higher, with the Gnome-Rhone 18-cylinder, two-row radial being the most powerful at 1,400-horsepower. An increasing number were equipped with superchargers for high-altitude operation.

The first modern Soviet fighter to be seen in the west: the Polikarpov I-17 (TsKB-19), the second prototype of the first V-12-powered, low-wing, retractable landing gear, fighter in the world. When it first flew in 1934, it preceded the Messerschmitt 109, the Hawker Hurricane, and others. Power was a 760-horsepower Hispano-Suiza V-12. Flight International

On display, despite being out of date, the *Loire Nieuport 46 C1 was clearly obsolete. Its profusion of struts, fixed landing gear and open cockpit would have made it a better sport plane than fighter. It first flew the same month as the sleek Soviet I-17, yet served with the French Air Force for two years.*
Flight International

1938 PARIS AIR SHOW

The final prewar show, the 16th Salon de l'Aviation, was held from November 25 through December 11. It was smaller than the last, the absence of known new types of aircraft being particularly obvious.

British Prime Minister Neville Chamberlain had gotten Hitler's promise of "peace in our time," but hardly anyone was fooled. The Germans were moving on Austria and Czechoslovakia, and most major countries were taking rearmament very seriously, for war seemed just around the corner.

In the Grand Palais, just off the ultrafashionable Champs Élysées, the mainly French show went on despite the turmoil in the French government and aircraft manufacturing that would soon lead to disaster. The confusion was illustrated by the reorganization of the aircraft industry, in which traditional firms such as Hanriot, Farman, Dewoitine, Breguet, and Potez were grouped into regional organizations identified by impersonal initials.

The first American airplane finally appeared at Paris in the form of the Vought SB2U-3 Vindicator dive bomber, which had been ordered by the French Navy. But no American manufacturer had yet taken part in the Paris show.

Fighters predominated, with an amazing range of quality from the obviously outdated to a few truly modern machines destined for immortality.

The shape of things to come was revealed, to those sufficiently perceptive, in the British and French displays of single-engined fighters. While the engineers of the two nations may have been

The British exhibit featured airplanes that would soon be in combat. At right is an early Hawker Hurricane fighter, while at left is a Bristol Blenheim medium bomber. Across the back are displays by the main British engine builders: Armstrong-Siddeley, Bristol, Napier, and DeHavilland. Together, they would power tens of thousands of airplanes that would help save their nation. Flight International

equally talented, the atmospheres were so different. England was preparing for war against a known enemy. France was too busy fighting itself to spend much time developing airplanes that would stand up against Me-109s, Me-110s, and Ju-88s or even Ju-87 Stuka dive bombers.

The Royal Air Force's Hawker Hurricane and Supermarine Spitfire were the most advanced of their kind, and both were in mass production. France's Morane 406 and Bloch 151 and Potez 63 and Arsenal were still being developed, and not even their final versions had both the power and

streamlining needed for late 1930s air combat. All of these airplanes were on display, in a manner that suggested they were about equal.

Other nations offered a look at a new generation of twin-engined fighters, including the Polish P.Z.L. Wolf and the Dutch Fokker F.23. The idea was to combine the qualities of a fighter and a light bomber, but only the Lockheed P-38 and DeHavilland Mosquito were able to deal with opposing single-engined fighters.

There were fewer bombers on display, though two of them turned out to be important.

At the very bottom is the history of Fokker in models of its many designs. At left is the trim Belgian S.A.B.C.A. fighter/bomber, which had no chance to see combat. Just above it is a Czech Zlin XII tourer, and beyond that on a pole is a Caudron Cyclone, an attempt to create a fighter from the highly successful Caudron 460 racer. Flight International

51

The Polish national exhibit. In the middle is the P.Z.L. Elan bomber, and at lower right is the P.Z.L. Wolf fighter, with P.Z.L.-Foka inverted-V engines then considered secret, and armament of four machine guns and a 20mm cannon. At top left is a light trainer. In all, the Polish Air Force was considered one of the best in Europe. Flight International

Germany's Dornier Do.17 "flying pencil" was developed into the effective Do.217, and Britain's Bristol Blenheim led to the Beaufort and to the Beaufighter night fighter. France's hefty Bloch 162 with its four 1,100-horsepower engines, allegedly had excellent performance, but faded away quickly.

The only new commercial design was the French Potez 662, which looked like a four-engined DC-3. Carrying but 12 passengers and said to cruise at 250 miles per hour, it was smaller than a DC-3 and certainly would not

have been an economic success had it gone into production. Other companies displayed models of future airliners that were aimed at trans-Atlantic service, long a dream.

Light planes were displayed by several countries, despite the overwhelming emphasis on military craft. There were two Belgian Tipsy two-seaters, and Czechoslovakia displayed the two-seat Zlin XII and Benes & Mraz Be 555.

In a special grouping were several small, light machines called "ultralights," in one of

The Fokker D.XXIII from the Netherlands. It combined a soon-to-be-common tricycle landing gear with tandem engines that reduce drag and single-engine control problems. It was powered by Czech Walter straight-12 engines of 540 horsepower, good for 325 miles per hour at 30,000 feet, according to Fokker. Flight International

the first uses of that now-common term. They were heavier and more powerful than modern ultralights, and really were more like American light planes such as the Piper Cub, Aeronca Champ, etc.

More than any previous Paris Air Show, this one was marked more by absences than appearances. Great Britain, France, Germany, the USSR, and the United States were so busy building warplanes that they had little time to display. Besides, the show was a marketplace, and the entire productive capacity of these nations was devoted to filling government contracts. There was no need to sell.

The next show—what would have been the 17th—was scheduled for late 1940. But long before that time, war had engulfed Europe. Germany had overrun Poland, Norway, Denmark, Luxembourg, Holland, Belgium, and much of France. German troops had been in Paris since June 1940.

About the only source of optimism was the victory of the Royal Air Force over the Luftwaffe in the Battle of Britain. Airplanes that had been displayed side-by-side in downtown Paris had turned aggressive and slugged it out in the sky.

Nationalistic exaggerations of performance on signs in front of airplanes in the Grand Palais had been replaced by reality. And by small enemy

insignias painted on the sides of airplanes whose pilots had ignored questionable claims of speed and maneuverability.

As the time for the 1940 Paris Air Show came and went, great aerial flotillas were assembling for air battles far larger than had ever before been seen. They prepared to rain thousands of tons of bombs on homes and factories, not merely on enemy armies and navies. It was total war far more than any before, and the outcome was yet to be determined.

Nazi Germany opened the door to its secret armada to permit a look at its standard medium bomber, the Dornier Do.17 "Flying Pencil." Performance claims for what was called a "fighter" include a top speed of 310 miles per hour, maximum range of 1,550 miles, and maximum payload of 6,600 pounds. While it started out as an airliner, it served into 1942 and led to the Do.217. DaimlerChrysler Aerospace

CHAPTER 4

THE POSTWAR BOUNTY

*T*he 17th Salon International de l'Aeronautique was held from November 15 through December 1, 1946, in the Grand Palais in downtown Paris. It was different in so many important ways from the last one, eight years before.

In the intervening time, the world had gone through far too many changes. As a result of World War II, much of Europe and Asia was in ruins. As many as 50 million people had died unnecessarily. From Great Britain to China, millions remained close to starvation, and the deplorable conditions would not ease for many years.

The French Nord exhibit. In the center, the twin-engined 1500 Noreclair, a large carrier-based purpose-built recco-bomber with folding wings that resembles a Douglas A-20 Havoc. To the left are, in front, a three-seat 1203 Norecrin, and behind it a four- or five-seat 1101 Noralpha, both with the tricycle landing gear. Of the three, only the Noralpha was built in any quantity. Flight International

Postwar dreaming: The Dutch Fokker F.26, to feature two Rolls-Royce Nene turbojets and a pressurized cabin. It was ahead of its time, but the Fokker F.27 twin-turboprop and F.28 twin jet became important airline types a few years later. Flight International

The entire world was exhausted. But it was also eager to take advantage of whole new areas of knowledge that had come out of history's most terrible war. Amazing changes were created in medicine, power generation, and transportation, especially air transportation.

In the year and a half since the end of the war, America had created an Atomic Energy Commission to oversee the peaceful uses of this awesome new power source. The Allies had held the Nuremberg trials of German war criminals. And Winston Churchill had declared that "an Iron Curtain has descended," separating the Soviet bloc and the West.

When the war began, more than one air force was still operating fabric-covered, open-cockpit biplanes. When it ended, several had introduced turbojet-powered airplanes whose airframes had been designed entirely with mathematical formulas. Science and aviation had been joined for eternity.

As evidence of the enormous involvement of aviation in the war, two-thirds of all the airplanes built to the end of the twentieth century were built during, or were somehow related to, World War II. Approximately one million airplanes built in 1939–1945, out of a grand total of 1.5 million were built from 1903 through 2000.

The biggest change to aviation was the birth of the jet airplane, with potential so great that few were brave enough to make predictions. Already, a near-operational Gloster Meteor twin-jet had raised the World Speed Record from the 469 miles per hour in 1939 by a wildly experimental German "fighter" to 616 miles per hour. Jet planes were not only faster, they sounded completely different, thus making the great change obvious to those who knew little about airplane engines.

A few weeks before the Salon opened, a U.S. Navy P2V Neptune patrol bomber broke the World Distance Record with an 11,236-mile flight from Australia to Columbus, Ohio. The author played hooky to see it land.

Once again, the majority of airplanes and other displays in the Paris Air Show were from France. Missing from prewar shows were Germany (for obvious reasons) and the Soviet Union, as the latter was trying to rebuild a shattered economy without the tools or techniques needed. The United States, Italy, Czechoslovakia, and the Netherlands were there with small exhibits, and Sweden was taking part for the first time.

More than ever before, emphasis was on models of proposed aircraft, for the French industry had but a year to re-create itself after the long, bitter German occupation. Only Germany, Great Britain, and the U.S. had jet airplanes flying, and so the others had to do whatever they could to catch up. This meant building research airplanes with which to explore this new regime, and planning to produce military and some day maybe even commercial jets.

The most interesting idea from France was the Rene Ledue ramjet-powered research airplane that was to be launched from the top of a Languedoc airliner. Once built and proved, it could produce considerable data on the nature of high-speed and high-altitude flight.

The sole French research airplane known to have flown, and then only briefly, was the SO 6000, which was a flying test bed for captured German Juno 004 engines and various French and British turbojets. Others displayed as real airplanes, rather than as maquettes (mock-ups), included the impressive Arsenal VG 70-01 with swept wings and its air intake under the fuselage.

Small French airliners on show were the conventionally twin-engined SO 90, and the SO 7010 Pegase with two V-8 engines driving a single, three-bladed propeller. Larger airliners were represented by the SO 30R Bellatrix with twin rudders at the tips of a horizontal tail having considerable dihedral.

While the airplane in the center looks like an early executive jet, it is actually one of the first two-seat, side-by-side jet trainers, the SO 6000 Triton, powered by a Rolls-Royce Nene engine. At top left is an SO M2 scaled prototype for the planned SO 400 twin-engined bomber. Pierre Gaillard

Despite the major problems facing its aircraft industry, France showed surprising interest in very light, personal airplanes. Both the Nord 1101 Noralpha 4-seater and the Nord 1203 Norecrin 3-seater not only went into production, but remained in production for several years. There was even an amateur-built two-seat biplane—LeLevrier (the Greyhound)—from a man named Chapeau.

The British exhibit included the only production jets in the Grand Palais: a pair of Gloster Meteors, including the speed record holder. Other types were the Hawker Sea Fury, the last piston-engined fighter to be produced by a major power, and a carrier-based Fairey Firefly.

Czechoslovakia displayed a Meta Sokol low-wing three-seater, examples of which can still be seen in Europe; and the tiny two-seat Praga. From the Netherlands came the Fokker F.25 Promotoer, a twin-boom four-seater with retractable tricycle landing gear and a 190-horsepower Lycoming six-cylinder engine. It came to naught.

The main impact of the American display was from its engines, many of them well proven during the war. Foremost among these was the rugged

Seen here in flight during the Paris Air Show is the prototype SO 30, a 30-passenger transport powered by 2,000-horsepower Pratt & Whitney R-2800 engines. When powered by more powerful engines, it was expected to carry up to 37 passengers at 270 miles per hour. As yet, none had entered service. Pierre Gaillard

2,000-horsepower Pratt & Whitney R-2800 14-cylinder radial, which had great potential in larger airliners.

1949 PARIS AIR SHOW

The 18th Salon de l'Aeronautique was held from April 29 through May 15 at the Grand Palais. It had been a full two years since the last one, and the change to permanent spring dates was at least partly because of the September dates of Britain's similar biennial Farnborough Air Show.

Since the last Paris Show, NATO had been formed, the Soviets had blockaded West Berlin, and the Western Allies had broken the blockade. The People's Republic of China had been established, the USSR had tested an atomic bomb, and Chuck Yeager had flown faster than sound in the little Bell XS-1 rocket plane.

While the core of the show remained the same, there was for the very first time, a flying program at Orly Airport, south of the city. And for most of the two weeks, a major meeting, the First International Congress of the Aeronautical Industry, was held. Sessions dealt with such topics as advanced aircraft design, quantity production of aircraft, and light aircraft.

France, as usual, provided the bulk of the displays, along with Great Britain, Holland, Czechoslovakia, Italy, the United States, and newcomers Switzerland and Turkey. Sweden was absent, as was the Soviet Union.

The rapidly increasing variety of airplane types forced the exhibitors to make use of more models and photos, especially when it came to larger aircraft. Only one of any size airliner was on display, the twin-pusher-engined, high-wing, seven-passenger Nord N.2100. The long wings of a prototype Breguet 100-passenger, four-engined, double-decker were there to give an impression of its considerable size.

Other airliners seen only as models included the Douglas DC-3 and Super DC-3; Lockheed Constellation; Bristol Brabazon, Freighter, and Britannia, and Vickers Viscount. A day of flying at Orly Airport allowed the crowd to see many of these types in operation.

Military aircraft were almost as scarce as commercial types. Examples of the few fighters included France's first production type, the Marcel Dassault (formerly Bloch) Ouragan (Hurricane). Shown with straight wings, it would go into production with swept wings. And the Sud Oest 6020 Espadon with a ventral air intake for its French-built Rolls-Royce Nene engine.

Fiat of Italy and Fokker of the Netherlands had groups of military trainers on show, with most powered by British Rolls-Royce or American Pratt & Whitney engines. Under development was the two-seat jet Fokker S.14 trainer, whose details were shown in cutaway models.

France's ramjet powered Leduc 010 research airplane was claimed to have hit 440 miles per hour on a recent test, using only half its available power. In the same category was the SO M2, with its flush canopy and pair of turbojets tucked in close to the fuselage.

Most of the aircraft at Paris were what are now called "general aviation" types: trainers, sport, utility, sailplanes, and small helicopters. All but the last were easier to develop, cheaper and quicker to build, and took up less display space in the crowded Grand Palais.

The first two genuinely new American four-seat, all-metal light plane designs attracted a lot of attention: the Beech Bonanza and the North American (later Ryan) Navion. The former, with its novel V-tail, has remained in production in much the same form for a half-century.

From Czechoslovakia came several personal planes, ranging from one of the first to carry the Zlin name, to the Bonzo N.3 with its 160-horsepower Walter Minor engine, to the five-place Aero 45 light twin. They suggested that at least one of the countries in Soviet-controlled Eastern Europe remembered how to build machines well.

The first Swiss airplane to be shown at Paris was the Pilatus P.4, a utility airplane intended to lift sizable loads from short fields at high elevation. Pilatus airplanes would grow in usefulness and popularity.

Italy, which had played a relatively minor role in the air war, was charging into peacetime aviation with several civilian airplanes based on its excellent Fiat G.55 fighter. Two two-seat trainers were on display: the G.46 with a DeHavilland Gipsy Queen engine, and the Fiat G.59 with a

Something of a throw-back, the SO 95 Corse II is a piston-engined (two Renaults) airliner with a tail wheel, in an era in which the switch to nose wheels appeared nearly unanimous. An early production model was the winner in the 1948 Cannes Rally, suggesting better-than-average performance. Pierre Gaillard

This Marcel Dassault M.D.450 Ouragan (Hurricane) was said to be France's first "world class" jet fighter. Powered by a license–built Rolls–Royce Nene engine, it was expected to see its wing swept back in later versions. Shortly before the show opened, the first prototype set a climb mark by reaching 26,500 feet in 5 minutes. Pierre Gaillard

Rolls-Royce Merlin. In addition, the sleek civil four-seat Ambrosini Grifo was said to be capable of 150 miles per hour on only 115 horsepower.

Among the many French light planes was the novel Fouga Cyclone glider with a small Turbomeca jet engine. Other modern sailplanes were aimed at the flying enthusiast who could not afford the high cost of operating a powered airplane.

The beginnings of a strong amateur-built airplane movement, with vital government support, could be seen in the little Echard Roitelet. It had a gross weight of about 500 pounds and could use any of several engines between 20 and 40 horsepower.

The flying display on May 15 included many aircraft that had not been on static display in the Grand Palais. Among the American airplanes were the Lockheed P2V Neptune *Truculent Turtle*, which had set the World Distance Record of 11,236 miles in 1946. The U.S. Air Force showed off its huge Douglas C-124 Globemaster cargo plane and a formation of B-29 Superfortresses.

The British contributed a team of DeHavilland Vampire jet fighters, a formation of Gloster Meteor

jet fighters, the prototype Hawker P.1052, and an imposing sextet of Avro Lincoln heavy bombers.

But it was the French who dominated the flying display. Military airplanes included jet fighters (Dassault Ouragan and SO Espadon), trainers (S.I.P.A. 11 and Morane Saulnier 475), and freighters (N.C.211 Cormoran and S.E. 2010 Armagnac).

There were many light planes in the air, such as the French S.I.P.A. 901, Czech Zlin 22, and American Beechcraft Mentor. Light twins included the Czech Aero 45 and the French Morane 700.

1951 PARIS AIR SHOW

The 19th Salon International de l'Aeronautique was held from June 15 through July 1 and was split between the traditional Grand Palais in downtown Paris and Le Bourget Aeroport to the north of the city. The smaller aircraft, along with displays of engines, equipment, etc., were in the Grand Palais, while the larger airplanes, long hampered by space limitations, were parked at the airport for the last half of the show, and many were demonstrated on the final day.

In the two years since the previous show, the Korean Conflict had become a major war. Electric power had been produced by atomic energy for the first time, and the first practical color TVs had been built.

The Grand Palais struggled in vain to retain its glamour and stature, much like an aging movie star. The decorations, like heavy cosmetics, may have been impressive, but simply could not hide reality: The Paris Air Show was undergoing the biggest change in its history. It was moving out of the city to a new site that would offer nearly unlimited space, plus the stimulating atmosphere of an historic airfield.

The Grand Palais was as crowded as ever, but most of the airplanes on display were light planes and trainers, along with helicopters, a few French fighter planes, and a variety of piston and jet engines.

One of the most intriguing new designs was the Fouga Lutin, a two-place trainer with long wings, a V-tail, and a pair of small turbojets slung under the wings, much like droppable fuel tanks. It was clearly descended from earlier Fouga sailplanes, and was said to be a scale model of a future military trainer. Even so, it was advertised with a 310 miles per hour top speed.

New from Italy was the clean, all-metal, prop-driven Piaggio P.148 trainer, along with several other trainers seen at previous Paris Air Shows. The Ambrosini Super Seven was available as a single- or two-seater, with or without a .30 caliber machine gun, depending on its use for military or sporting purposes, which seems like the polite thing to do.

So far, it had been a traditional Paris Air Show. But starting on June 21, the focus of attention was on Le Bourget Aeroport, where the ramp of the major airport was crowded with large aircraft and small. To wind up the biennial event, July 1 saw a major flying display, few of which had been held since the end of the war.

Parked on the concrete slab were French jet fighters: the new Dassault Mystere and the slender Espadon, as well as an American Republic F-84E Thunderjet fighter and Fairchild C-82 Packet cargo plane, the single-engined Cessna 170 and 195, and a Douglas DC-3, which was boosted into the air with a small turbojet engine mounted under the fuselage.

But it was the finale air show that drew a crowd estimated at 250,000. The indoor display had become increasingly attuned to those with technical backgrounds, leaving the average person and even the enthusiast standing around with their hands in their pockets. The air show would be for everyone.

It started out on a novel note, with a pair of Emouchet gliders having several small pulse jets under their wings for power. Never very popular due to their extreme noise, they first became famous as the power for the German V-1 buzz bombs, and later as the Dyna-jet in model airplanes, until noise regulations appeared on the scene.

Other light airplanes followed: the Aubert 204 four-seater, the Dutch Fokker S.11 trainer, the French Morane Saulnier 733 trainer. A pair of light jet Fouga Cyclopes enjoyed themselves with aerobatics, as the crowd was slowly being warmed up for the big, fast airplanes still sitting on the taxiway.

Next came the airliners: French Breguet Province and Armagnac, both with four engines and the announcer's predictions of great futures, which never quite materialized.

Immediately after came a formation of 11 Boeing B-50s, which were B-29 Superfortresses with more power. Their combined roar was meant to make a statement about American air power. They were followed by a tight Vee formation of three mammoth Convair B-36s, each with six piston engines and four jet engines.

The Royal Air Force did itself proud with well-synchronized aerobatics of 13 DeHavilland Vampire jet fighters. This was followed by solo and dual presentations by many French and British military airplanes, some of which simulated their wartime missions.

It was the U.S. Air Force that really wowed the French crowd with its "Skyblazers," four brightly painted Republic F-84E Thunderjets that were the precursor to today's Thunderbirds. Their tight-formation loops and rolls and extremely low passes left the audience gasping and then cheering, which was of course just what the pilots wanted.

The combination of outstanding static displays of large airplanes and a great air show made the indoor exhibit at the Grand Palais seem old-fashioned and ineffective. Its days were numbered.

CHAPTER 5

FLY ON AT LE BOURGET

1953 PARIS AIR SHOW

The 20th Salon International de l'Aeronautique, held from June 26 through July 5, saw its biggest move completed. The Grand Palais, as the site of the biennial show, was a thing of the past, as everything was shifted to Le Bourget Aeroport, where it would remain. The classic, traditional, and, let's face it, *antique* atmosphere of the 50-year-old building gave way to the expanse, dynamism, and modernity of a new facility that offered room for expansion and the feel of a place as new as the aircraft to be displayed.

The permanent facility begins to grow. At lower right is the main display building, while at lower left are two rows of customer hospitality chalets. In between, the airplanes on static display are parked. In future years, all three elements will grow substantially. Pierre Gaillard

The world's first purpose-designed jet trainer, unlike others that were modified for use as trainers. This Fokker S.14 uses a Rolls-Royce Derwent turbojet engine to achieve 440 miles per hour at 25,000 feet, where it can fly for up to 3 hours. To the left are two Italian light piston-engined trainers for contrast.
Flight International

Since the last Paris Air Show, Dwight Eisenhower and Queen Elizabeth II had assumed their lofty perches. In the still-ominous USSR, Josef Stalin had died, but the Soviets had exploded the world's first hydrogen bomb. The world was still not a particularly safe place to live.

Only a single building (now part of the much larger Building 2) was built for the first show at Le Bourget, but with almost 100,000 square feet of display space for a record 10 exhibitors, it dwarfed anything previously used. Spread out in front of it was the static display area, filled with aircraft from France, Britain, the United States, Sweden, Spain, and Italy.

Major flying displays were held on both weekends, with that on the last day's show extending from midmorning until late afternoon. There was flying on a much reduced scale on every day, spaced so as not to interfere with scheduled airline traffic at one of Paris' two major airports.

Aircraft on display were still primarily French, though many of them were license-built versions of British airplanes: e.g., the Sud Est Mistral jet fighter was actually a DeHavilland Vampire. The French aircraft industry had not fully recovered from its wartime suffering.

Series production was just around the corner for France's Dassault Mystere IV delta-winged fighter, the V-tailed Fouga Magister light jet trainer, and the hefty Nord Noratlas cargo plane that resembled the American Fairchild C-82 Packet.

Other French military airplanes appeared as prototypes, some of which it was assumed would eventually go into production. Perhaps the most interesting of these was the Sud Est OO Baroudeur, a ground attack jet using a rocket-powered dolly for takeoff, and landing on a belly skid. Just how it was supposed to taxi after landing was unclear.

The Breguet Super Deux Ponts (double-decker) was developed from a current Air France airliner and was expected to use either the large Wright Turbo-Cyclone or Pratt & Whitney Wasp Major piston engines.

Among the helicopters, the French showed the S.E. 3120 Alouette, just going into production and destined to become a staple of the industry. The little SO 1220 Djinn used compressed air to turn its rotor, thus eliminating troublesome torque problems and a lot of the usual rotor noise.

The French parade of light planes was led by the sleek and fascinating two-seat, twin-boom SIPA Minijet that had a claimed cruising speed of 235 miles per hour on just 300 pounds of thrust, while weighing barely 800 pounds empty. Considerably more practical and economical were some of the pioneering postwar homebuilts, such as the wooden, single-seat Druine Turbulent and the two-seat Turbi. These and some of the early crank-winged wooden Jodels would give the French light plane industry a desperately needed shot-in-the-arm.

From the United States came a variety of military, airline, and personal planes, many of them flown in the finale air show. The U.S. Air Force contributed a Douglas B-26 Invader, Fairchild C-82, Republic F-84 Thunderjet, North American F-86 Sabre, and Grumman SA-16 Albatross. Airliners included a Douglas DC-6B and a pair of Lockheed Super-G Constellations, both piston-engined and in regular service.

There were helicopters from Bell and Hiller, light planes from Piper and Cessna, and a Happy

This neat little SIPA 20 Minijet looks like a lot of schoolboy's doodles and older boys' dreams. It was promoted as a formation trainer for aerobatics and for high-speed transport up to 275 miles per hour with a single 330-pound Turbomeca Palais jet engine. Flight International

Elephant, the last being a French-built Sikorsky S-55 helicopter called an *Eléphant Joyeux.* Even less known was the license-built Grumman Widgeon amphibian, powered by DeHavilland Gipsy inline engines.

From Great Britain came its latest jet fighters—the Hawker Hunter and Supermarine Swift. Barely two months later, examples of both types would break the World Speed Record. There was a Shackleton patrol bomber and a Canberra, one of which had just broken the five-year-old World Altitude Record. Proof of superior performance beat questionable advertising claims any day.

With more than two acres of outdoor space in which to display full-size aircraft, the indoor area need not be crowded with items that were clearly too big, as had been increasingly the case at the Grand Palais. Instead, the first permanent building

This Bristol Type 171 Sycamore was the first British-designed and British-built helicopter; the prototype flew in 1947. The Mk. 3 version carries five, including the flight crew. Power is a nine-cylinder, 500-horsepower Alvis Leonides radial piston engine. Performance includes a top speed of 125 miles per hour, economy cruise of 90 miles per hour, and service ceiling of 15,000 feet. Flight International

A group of very serious French military and civilian officials ignore the model of the S.E.5000 Baroudeur single-seat, swept-wing jet fighter. The unusual feature of this yet-to-fly machine is its lack of wheels, preferring to take off from a dolly and land on skids. With the power of one SNECMA Atar 101, it should be capable of high speed. Flight International

could be used to show off engines, models of future aircraft, and a wide variety of parts and equipment for not only aircraft but airports.

With the big move complete, the show assumed the form it would retain for many years. It was both a marketplace for the growing aviation industry, and one of the world's greatest air shows for the public.

In a very real sense, the Paris Air Show had long been two quite separate events rolled into one. For the aviation industry, it was a trade show, peopled by industry leaders and government officials who spent their time examining their rivals' wares and talking business. For the aviation enthusiast, it was one of the year's premier air shows, the place to see more of what was new, both on the ground and in the air. Happily, this clash in needs and views had not become an obstacle to progress.

1955 PARIS AIR SHOW

The 21st event, called the Salon International de l'Aeronautique, was held at Le Bourget Aeroport from June 10 through 19. At about the same time, the European Community was established by France, Italy, and Germany. Faced with centuries-old, deep-seated animosities, it would struggle and slowly grow and eventually become a major force in the world. And it would lead the way to unprecedented international cooperation in aircraft design and manufacture.

Roaring low over the crowd at Le Bourget in the first real Paris Air Show, a Nord 2501 Noratlas wows 'em! Power is a pair of license-built 2,000-horsepower Bristol Hercules sleeve-valve engines. While its design and dimensions are similar to the American Fairchild C-119, the latter's increased power permits a greater payload to be carried. Flight International

This head-on view of the experimental Hurel-Dubois H.D.31 transport emphasizes its outstanding characteristic, a very high aspect ratio wing. With just a pair of 800-horsepower Wright Cyclone engines, and at a take-off weight of 30,000 pounds, it can get to an altitude of 35 feet just 2,000 feet from the start of its take-off roll. Flight International

The process of Paris Air Show growth had begun already, with the main building experiencing the first of many expansions to meet the demand for additional indoor display space. The outdoor show area, too, was becoming crowded with more and larger aircraft, though its expansion into additional concrete areas was considerably simpler.

Displays located under cover are independent of weather, but not so for the outdoor displays, and the 1955 Paris Show had more than its share of chilling rain. Any experienced air show–goer knows of this risk, and quickly gets under cover, a move certain to please those with displays in the main building. A greater problem is the flying portion of the operation, which had to be redesigned or rescheduled.

A constant limit on the types of aircraft to be displayed had long been the need for security, whether military or commercial. The requirement to keep the most advanced ideas secret from rival air forces or manufacturers is understandable, if unfortunate. Lined up against this are the needs to show off one's technical prowess and advanced thinking. The need for secrecy does not always win out.

Take American fighter planes, for example. The U.S. Air Force's operational Republic F-84 Thunderjet and North American F-86 Sabre were on display, but not the supersonic F-100 Super Sabre, even though the prototype had flown two years before. And as for Lockheed's Mach 2 F-104 Starfighter, or the delta-winged Convair F-102, they were nowhere to be seen. On an even more secret list was Lockheed's soon-to-fly U-2 spyplane, not even a model or sketch of which was on display.

Most of the more modern military airplanes that were present either as full-scale airplanes or detailed models were French and well behind American technology. Not so for helicopters, an area in which the French were charging ahead with designs that would soon become standards.

The Sud Est Alouette I was a piston-engined type that had the drawbacks which all such rotary-winged craft did, as their old-fashioned engines offered too little power and too much weight to permit the lifting of large loads. The newer, tur-

This tiny Jodel D.9 Bebe homebuilt is parked by the fence at Le Bourget during the air show. It was the first type of amateur–built airplane to appear in France since the war, and would lead to a major world aviation movement. In France, construction of such sport planes was subsidized by the government to help re-create lost skills. Pierre Gaillard

bine-powered Alouette II, with double the horsepower and less weight, had just set a world record by climbing to 26,272 feet. Successors would remain in production for decades.

Among the new airliners, France's Caravelle stood out, with a clean fuselage and rear-mounted jet engines, a style that would become increasingly popular. Although flying in just prototype forms, it would be the first commercially successful jet airliner, as Britain's DeHavilland Comet had

About as simple as small airplanes can get, this Druine Turbulent is built entirely of wood and covered with fabric. Power is up to the builder, though many have used Volkswagen car engines of 1,100 to 1,500 cc. They made private flying possible again, after the Germans wrecked France's aircraft industry.

A spectacular combination: the amazing Leduc 021 ramjet-powered research airplane atop its carrier, a modified Languedoc piston-engined airliner. The Leduc went up in this condition, then fired up and cut loose. It tore past the fascinated crowd, in its first public demonstration, at more than 400 miles per hour, making surprisingly little noise. Flight International

The start of something big. The S.E. 3130 Alouette II gas turbine helicopter had just set a World Altitude Record at more than 26,000 feet. At first it was used primarily for medical evacuation duty, but quickly expanded its services to include most of those for which helicopters have become famous. The Alouette II and successors would be in use for decades. Pierre Gaillard

encountered serious structural problems, and the Soviet Tu-104 was underpowered, inefficient, and thus of no interest outside the Soviet bloc, where airlines needed to show a profit.

America's domination of the postwar light plane industry was starting to become apparent, as the products of Piper, Cessna, and Beech flooded the market. In France, government subsidy of amateur building was beginning to pay off, as little models were attracting the interest of manufacturers, and modified versions were going into limited production.

While many countries were experimenting with radical-design aircraft, only France was ready to show much. America's X-planes remained safely out of sight at Edwards AFB, while France was showing its stuff. The futuristic Leduc ramjet with its pilot in the air intake's centerbody, was launched from its carrier plane over Le Bourget and made several loud, fast passes. The SO 900 Trident, with jet engines on its wingtips and a rocket engine in the tail, took off on mixed power and roared past at just under Mach 1.

On show as merely models or mock-ups were even more exotic airplanes. Two coleopters (with shroud wings wrapped around their fuselages) included an unmanned interceptor with a projected rate-of-climb of 49,000 feet in 2 minutes, and the Bruche A ground-attack craft with a prone-position pilot. Few such designs would ever fly, but they indicated significant research effort.

One of the most intriguing new French designs was the Payen Pa 49 Katy, then the world's smallest delta-winged jet. M. Payen was known and admired for his highly advanced prewar designs: deltas with canard surfaces in front and contra-rotating propellers in the nose or tail. Most of them were aimed at racing or speed records, and few got much beyond design studies.

While complete aircraft got the lion's share of attention, those in the know paid just as much attention to engines, frequently the indicators of future serious design trends. In this, more than in airframe design, the United States, Great Britain, and France were nearly equal rivals.

Most of the new engines on display at Paris were in the under-10,000 pounds of thrust class.

Britain's ultimate heavy bomber, the Avro Vulcan, is the classic delta wing. With four powerful Bristol Olympus engines, it can carry a huge load for great distances. With everything battened down, it is capable of air show slow rolls. Pierre Gaillard

Slightly larger were the license-built version of the British Armstrong-Siddeley Sapphire and the Bristol Orpheus. Both were relatively compact turbojets that were to power a variety of fighters and bombers in the coming years.

1957 PARIS AIR SHOW

The 22nd show, called the "Salon International de l'Aeronautique," was held at Le Bourget Aeroport from May 24 through June 2. Since the last show, international rivalries had boosted the World Speed Record into the supersonic zone, with Britain's Fairey Delta 2 research airplane currently on top at more than 1,100 miles per hour.

For the first time, the show was clearly dominated by the United States, in particular the U.S. Air Force, which had a wide variety of its aircraft on display. But the major story was much more subtle, consisting not of spectacular new airplanes in the sky, nor even in the static display park, but of wooden models on pedestals.

Three major American companies' stands displayed large, well-made models of jet airliners they were preparing to build: Boeing's 707, Douglas' DC-8, and Convair's 880. Of novel but quite similar design with four engines hung below their wings on pylons, they forecast far more than almost anyone realized.

By the next Paris Air Show, 707s would be in airline service, DC-8s were close, and the prototype 880 had flown. Before long, the United States would be well on the way to a level of airline domination no country had known since the late 1930s, when America's Douglas DC-3 was in use by more than 80 percent of the world's airlines.

The transportation revolution propelled by these airplanes would color all future Paris Air Shows. They would cut transatlantic flight time from 14 hours to 7, and would almost eliminate weather as a source of concern and discomfort for passengers. With the increasing efficiency of high-altitude flight, they would enable airlines to

greatly reduce the impact of inflation on fares, thus bringing millions more travelers into the air.

The inconspicuous start of a second major trend was the appearance of the first Soviet airplane at Paris since the 1930s. The sleek Tupolev 104 twin-jet airliner may have wowed the crowd, but so lacked meaningful performance that it was little more than a propaganda effort. A long series of such technological stunts would follow in both aviation and space.

French airliner displays ranged from the flight-demonstrated Hurel-Dubois 34, whose efficient high-aspect ratio wing was forced to fight against a mass of wing struts, to models of the Sud

The first appearance of North American's F-86F Sabre included the first sonic booms heard by many at Paris. The standard U.S. Air Force fighter was well ahead of any other fighter, being able to exceed Mach 1 in a dive. It had already made a name for itself in Korea, with a kill ratio of over 10 to 1. Pierre Gaillard

If the aircraft isn't too big, it can fit into an indoor display, like this Bell 47J Ranger helicopter. The four-to-five seater was built by designer Bell, as well as, in this instance, licensee Agusta of Italy, which had delivered more than 200. With a 220-horsepower Lycoming engine, it could cruise at 100 miles per hour for 2 hours. Flight International

Caravelle, since the two flying versions were busy with tests and demonstrations for potential customers.

On the military research side, the French flew a VTOL (Vertical Take-Off and Landing) test bed called the Atar Volant, which was supposed to become a man-carrying coleopter, once a wrap-around wing was added. Instead, it was one of the first public demonstrations of technology that would lead to VTOL airplanes. Quietly, Britain's soon-to-be-very-noisy VTOL Harrier was about to move off the drawing board.

The beginnings of serious international cooperation could be seen among the helicopters. Bell's streamlined new 47J was shown alongside

the classic bubble-nosed 47G, both of them in licensed production by Agusta of Italy, which would go on to produce many Bell designs in the coming decades. Westland, in England, continued to expand its production of Sikorsky helicopters and components. Even Eastern Europe was showing signs of licensed production, with the Russian Mi-1 being built as the SM-1 in Poland.

The big tandem-rotor Vertol 44 (military H-21) was at Paris in three versions: civilian, U.S. Air Force, and French Air Force. Some of them demonstrated their utility by providing a shuttle service between Issy (a pioneer airfield to the south) and Le Bourget.

France retained its position of dominating the portion of the show devoted to fighter planes. It showed off single and twin versions of the Breguet Taon (horse-fly), Dassault's Super Mystere, Etendard, and Mirages, Sud's Durandel, Trident II, and Vatour.

Military jet trainers included the French naval version of the Fouga Magister, Britain's Folland Gnat (which would soon equip the RAF's Red Arrows formation team), and Spain's Hispano Saeta. This category would grow to the point where many of the trainers would attract barely enough foreign contracts to justify extended production runs.

American military aircraft on display were fighters (North American F-100D Super Sabre and its two-seat trainer version, the TF-100F), bombers (B-47 Stratojet, B-57 Canberra, and B-66 Destroyer), and cargo planes (C-123, C-124 Globemaster II, and C-130 Hercules). A Republic RF-84F Thunderjet was in French Air Force colors.

The display of guided missiles showed significant growth, a trend that would continue indefinitely. The eye-catchers were the American

Martin TM-61C Matador and Northrop SM-62 Snark, both large trailer-launched tactical missiles. Others included high-altitude research rockets, antiaircraft rockets, and targets.

To justify its popular name, the "Paris Air Show" was just that: daily displays of a wide variety of manned aircraft, with weekend extravaganzas, heavy on the French machinery, to convince the French people that their industry was leading the world, even if it wasn't quite doing so.

A crowd of official visitors mills around the SO 4050 Vatour, a French all-weather fighter that had just flown in the air show. It had been in production for a year in this version and as a two-seat bomber. With two SNECMA Atar engines, it could attain 580 miles per hour in level flight, and was the first French twin-engined airplane to exceed the speed of sound in a dive. Flight International

One of several impressive light planes from Czechoslovakia that achieved good sales in the West, the Super Aero 45 could carry four or five passengers at 140 miles per hour for 1,000 miles on the power of a pair of 105-horsepower Walter Minor air-cooled straight-four engines. More than 100 were being used by Aeroflot, the Soviet airline, for local service. Pierre Gaillard

This Dornier Do.27B utility airplane was one of the smallest from this veteran manufacturer, first flying in 1955. With a 290-horsepower Lycoming engine, fixed wing slots, and double-slotted flaps, it had a speed range of 35 to 155 miles per hour, one of the best to be found. It was also available with skis or floats. Pierre Gaillard

1959 PARIS AIR SHOW

The 23rd Salon International de l'Aeronautique was held from June 12 through 21. Since the last one, the world had entered the space age. The Soviets launched the first earth-orbiting satellite—Sputnik—in October 1957. The United States followed with Explorer in March 1958. In 1959 both space "powers" shot probes that missed the moon but pointed the way. And in February 1959 the United States launched the first of a long string of Discoverer satellites that were later revealed to have spying functions.

The rise of America at Paris and the decline of France were the hallmarks of the 1959 show. The U.S. military displayed complete ballistic missiles: the Convair Atlas, which would become the primary launch vehicle for civilian satellites and probes; the Douglas Thor-Able; and the Chrysler Redstone. Along with these were what appeared to be battle-ready examples of Nike antiaircraft missiles, batteries of which dotted the American landscape.

When considered alongside military airplanes ranging from small jet trainers to huge jet tankers, it was a very military display that the United States staged.

On the other hand, the French backed off from their usual array of late-model fighters and attack jets, and prototypes of more advanced designs. Financial considerations had forced them to drastically scale back their usual elaborate displays. Moreover, the growing antinuclear feeling of the DeGaulle government was pushing American NATO units out of France.

This may have played a role in the sharp response of the builders of the Mirage series of

The future can frequently be seen at display booths in the form of models. As often as not, so can ideas that never progress beyond this stage. In this case, a model represents a new type, the Armstrong Whitworth AW.650 Argosy, which had just flown for the first time a few months earlier. Multiple uses are easy to show. Flight International

delta-winged jets to the German choice of Lockheed F-104 Starfire interceptors to equip its air force. What had been behind-the-scenes rivalry was breaking out into the open with surprising animosity.

In the developing rivalry among nations for the market in airliners, the American charge to the fore was symbolized by a steady stream of regularly scheduled transatlantic PanAm 707s in and out of Le Bourget with loads of passengers. The French seemed unable to capitalize on their earlier success with the shorter-range Caravelle twin-jet.

The Soviets again displayed a Tupolev Tu-104 jet airliner that was more form than substance. An airline pilot friend of the author once described a take-off in a Tu-104 that required full power for 30

Neatly paved ramp area was still in short supply as the Le Bourget facility was expanding. Here, a Swedish SAAB J-35 Draken is parked on perforated landing mat. As the Draken was designed to operate off marginal surfaces, the mat proved no problem. Flight International

At last, a replacement for the immortal DC-3? Lockheed's C-130 Hercules looks as if it will be around for a long time, thanks to its ability to fill many roles. Since the first deliveries in late 1956, over a thousand have come off the assembly lines. At gross weight, it will clear a 50-foot barrier after a take-off run of 4,500 feet. Pierre Gaillard

On the sporting side, this Zlin 326 Trener-Master was about the best in the world for serious aerobatic flying, long popular in Europe. Power was a 160-horsepower Walter Minor six-cylinder engine, which gets it off the ground in less than 800 feet. Pierre Gaillard

minutes to reach 10,000 feet. But at a distance, and performing under ideal conditions (minimum fuel, no passengers), it suggested that Soviet technology was at least equal to that of the West.

A close-up inspection by an engineer of the large and generally well-built Soviet Tu-114 turboprop airliner revealed signs of design problems. There were a great many small fatigue cracks in the skin and the engine nacelles showed buckling due to heat, and signs of damage from hard landings. Soviet aircraft, more than those from other countries, demanded a very close look.

Sweden joined the ranks of the few nations capable of producing first-line military airplanes, demonstrating its SAAB Draken (Dragon) delta-winged jet fighter. Despite some of the worst flying weather in years, its pilot was able to show off

The USSR's Tuplev Tu-114 is the airline version of the Tu-20 Bear bomber. Claims include enough range to carry 120 passengers from Moscow to New York almost as fast as a pure jet. It is powered by four 12,000-horsepower Kuznetsov turboprop engines, each driving a pair of four-bladed contra-rotating propellers. Pierre Gaillard

the neat airplane's impressive maneuverability, especially in roll. While few Drakens were sold outside Scandinavia, it established Sweden as a major player.

Another highly maneuverable supersonic fighter displayed for the crowd was the English Electric P.1B, later to be called Lightning. With two after-burning turbojets stacked vertically, and the most sharply swept wings of any production fighter, it blasted through a series of tight, high-G turns.

Formation team flying was becoming an increasingly popular part of the air shows, though national teams had yet to appear. France offered a group of nine Dassault Mystere 4A fighters from an active squadron, while the RAF contributed 14 all-black Hawker Hunter Mk.6s which operated in two groups, one of which was always in front of the spectators.

In just a few years, the Paris Air Show had escaped the severe limitations of the ornate Grand Palais and had firmly established itself at Le Bourget. It was growing rapidly and overtaking rival industry shows.

aéronautique espace

32ᵉ SALON INTERNATIONAL DE PARIS LE BOURGET 3-12 JUIN 1977

A poster from the 1977 show illustrates the aviation-themed graphics that year.

CHAPTER 6

SPACE AND SUPERSONIC SUPREMACY

The 24th Salon International de l'Aeronautique was held from May 26 through June 4, 1961. Since the last Salon, the disastrous Bay of Pigs invasion of Cuba had embarrassed the United States. The World Speed Record was raised to 1,606 miles per hour with a McDonnell F4H Phantom II.

The heavily French atmosphere was giving way to an event that was increasingly international (10 countries had displays) and multilingual (dozens of languages and dialects). It was the first of the series to include

This Convair B-58 Hustler was the first of its kind to be seen in Europe, when it completed a flight from Fort Worth that included a New York–Paris run in 3 hours, 20 minutes. It followed the route of Charles Lindbergh in 1927, taking just one-tenth as long. At times, the Mach 2 bomber cruised at 1,300 miles per hour over the North Atlantic. Pierre Gaillard

actual space hardware. Since the last Salon, man had entered space with the one-orbit flight of Yuri Gagarin in the USSR's Vostok I spacecraft just a few weeks earlier.

American domination of the Salon continued, though without the aggressive array of military missiles that had formed the skyline of the 1959 event and had drawn considerable disapproval. This time, the centerpieces were a collection of Mach 2 fighters and the Mach 2 B-58 Hustler bomber. The latter had crossed the Atlantic in under 3 hours at an average of over 1,100 miles per hour. Sadly, during a flying display, it rolled into some clouds and shortly thereafter crashed.

Once again, the value in studying models of proposed aircraft was illustrated by a large model of what was called the "Super Carravelle," a delta-winged Mach 2 transport that would eventually emerge as the Franco-British Concorde SST. Fifteen years into the future, it would be in service, crossing the Atlantic as fast as the B-58.

While it may have been the Soviets who first conquered space, it was the Americans who brought it to Paris for the world to see. The U.S. "Space for Peace" exhibition featured the Mercury capsule in which Alan Shepard made a 12-minute suborbital flight just three weeks before the Salon

opened. Visitors were allowed to touch it and thus to take home a personal experience with the still-new space age.

Adding to the American display of advanced technology were the Mach 2 fighters on the ground and in the air: the U.S. Navy's F4H Phantom II and F8U-2 Crusader and A3J Vigilante attack-bomber, and the Air Force's F-104 Starfighter and F-105 Thunderchief. All were painted in flashy colors, adding to the feeling of openness, in stark contrast to the Soviets' general secretiveness.

The Salon's continuing growth could be seen in the opening of yet a third exhibition hall in just the fifth year at Le Bourget. Perhaps in reaction to negative comments about the limited displays they had mounted in recent Salons, the British expanded theirs with a collection of very large airplanes. The RAF produced Vulcan and Victor bombers, a Javelin interceptor, and an Argosy transport, while the civilian side was represented by a Britannia and a Herald airliner.

The limited Soviet display was dominated by the huge Tupolev Tu-114 four-turboprop airliner with its contra-rotating four-bladed props. Like many Soviet airliners of the period, it had a glassed-in nose like a bomber, suggesting it was meant to be converted to military use on short notice.

Light airplanes continued to play a major role at Paris. The United States fielded planes from Beech (Bonanza, Twin Bonanza, Baron, Debonair, and the experimental turboprop Baron called a Marquis), a variety of small Cessnas, and Pipers (Cherokee, Super Cub, Comanche, and Aztec). The spread of American personal planes throughout Europe was as much a demonstration of American salesmanship as it was of superior aircraft design.

Among the "native European" light planes were the Bolkow Junior, a German-built Swedish design that had begun life as an American home-built, the Andreasson BA-7. More truly European was the growing line of Rallyes, currently being built by Morane-Saulnier, and offering STOL performance at the expense of top-end speed that is not so important for the typical European private pilot.

The helicopter collection continued to reveal the growing extent of international cooperation.

The brand-new experimental Agusta 115 was an attempt to jump into the next generation of helicopters, using the Agusta-Bell 47J Ranger as the starting point. Agusta modified a French Astazou turboshaft engine to produce 320 horsepower and married it to a 47G rotor, 47J transmission and landing gear. It reportedly will lift its full load from fields more than 13,000 high.
Flight International

Agusta of Italy and Bell of the United States expanded their line. Development of the Sikorsky S-64 Flying Crane was continuing with Weser-flugzeugbau of Germany. The Boeing-Vertol 107 tandem-rotor machine was approaching service with New York Helicopter Airways. And for comic relief, a group of U.S. Army Bell H-13s performed a square dance routine, and one of them played with the world's largest yo-yo.

The final two days of the Salon featured public-oriented air shows from morning until late afternoon. Formation aerobatics was the key, with groups including nine English Electric Lightnings from the RAF and four Supermarine Scimitars from the Royal Navy with grayish purple, green, and yellow smoke trails. The U.S. Navy offered a quartet of Douglas A3D Skywarriors, direct from the carrier USS *Forrestal*. France not only displayed the 12 Mystere IVAs of its Patrouille de France team, but also a dozen Air Force Mirage IIIs.

A pair of research airplanes kept the large crowd fascinated. The French Nord Griffon blasted past on the power of its huge turbo-ram-jet engine. And the little British Short SC.1 showed off some of the novel capabilities of a true jet-lift VTOL airplane.

Hardly as spectacular as all the flying, but certainly as significant, were the engines displayed in the three halls. The spotlight was on Pratt & Whitney's JT-11, the commercial version of the military's J-58. Unlike the Mach 3 rated, 40,000-pound version, the new one was a tame 23,000 pounds of thrust, aimed at a new generation of larger, faster airliners.

The displays of rockets and missiles were the largest yet, with examples from France, Great

France's first first-line jet airliner, the Sud Caravelle. It had entered service two years previously and had been ordered by airlines in at least seven countries. The exceptionally clean noses of many Caravelles were originally built for British Comet airliners, but when accidents reduced the demand, DeHavilland sold complete noses to Sud Aviation. Pierre Gaillard

A typical indoor display, this by Dornier. Models predominate because of space limitations; in the center is a missile, while to the right atop a pyramid is the Do.31 VTOL airplane. Shades of 1911: Note the potted plants. Chairs are for the staff who answer questions, while there is usually a place behind the scenes for serious talking. DaimlerChrysler Aerospace

Britain, and Sweden. But they were upstaged by the American show of space projects, equipment, and actual hardware, such as the recovered capsule from a Discoverer satellite and SNAP nuclear power generators.

1963 PARIS AIR SHOW

The 25th event, June 7 through 16, was the first to be called a "Salon International de l'Aeronautique et de l'Espace," in recognition of the rapid growth of space-related hardware, models, and ideas. In a clearly political move, the USSR launched the first woman, Valentina Tereshkova, into space on the opening day.

Since the last Salon, the Cuban missile crisis had been "won" by the United States, the World Speed Record had been raised to 1,666 miles per hour by a Soviet pilot in an experimental E-166, and the World Distance Record had been stretched to 12,533 miles by the crew of a U.S. Air Force B-52 bomber.

Two subjects occupied much of the interest of the technical and managerial types at the Salon, and would continue to do so in varying degrees for many years to come: combat VTOL airplanes and supersonic airliners. There were models and futuristic paintings and innumerable intense discussions, but not all that much hardware to be seen.

The supersonic transport race was at this stage a rivalry between the Anglo-French cooperative and the United States—British Aircraft Co. and Sud Aviation in Europe, and North American Aviation and Boeing on the other side of the Atlantic.

The Anglo-French "Concorde," as it was now called, had gotten a huge boost in prestige with an order from PanAm World Airways, one of America's pioneering airlines. The design, as revealed (or concealed) by a model, had undergone few changes since the 1961 Paris Air Show, remaining a delta wing.

North American, on the other hand, had two basic designs on display in model form: a delta with a canard surface near the nose and fold-down outer wing panels a la the B-70 and a swing-wing (variable sweep) airplane. It appeared that North American was well behind its European rival, though it was looking at a

At Paris for the first time was this Nord 262 Fregat (Frigate), a turboprop feeder liner that began life as the Max Holste Super Broussard. *Powered by two Turbomecca Bastan engines rated at 1,000 horsepower, it would be one of the first European transports to enter the American market.* DaimlerChrysler Aerospace; Flight International

This Pilatus PC-6 Porter is a Swiss design meant for mountain flying from short fields, where its high aspect ratio wing would pay off. With a 340-horsepower Lycoming engine, it can lift 1,000 pounds from short, high-altitude fields. Later versions would have turboprop engines and even better performance. Flight International

larger airplane, which would stand a better chance of carrying enough passengers to pay its way than the small Concorde.

There were at least a half-dozen VTOL designs at Paris, several of them being serious enough to have warranted at least the beginnings of prototype construction. The British Hawker Siddeley Kestrel was flying so successfully that operational testing would soon begin, but none was on display. The futuristic-looking West German VJ 101, developed from the canceled Bell XF-109 with swiveling turbojet engines on its wingtips, had hovered free and was on its way toward cancellation. A second West German design, the Dornier Do 31 with separate lift and cruise engines, would not fly for another year.

From Italy came plans for a VTOL G.95 version of its standard NATO G.91 ground-support fighter planned for Rolls-Royce engines. But it was France that offered the Kestrel/Harrier its greatest competition. Dassault-Sud was flying the first Balzac prototype, and was confident enough in its vertical takeoffs and landings to demonstrate it at Paris.

This Sikorsky S-60 Flying Crane, built on license by Weser in West Germany, had no trouble lifting a large truck, which was simply driven under it and hooked up. With a maximum payload of more than 11,000 pounds, it can cruise at just over 100 miles per hour. Flight International

Military formation aerobatics are a major part of the Paris Air Shows, and a big draw for the nonindustry spectators. These four McDonnell F-4 Phantom IIs were part of the U.S. Navy's Blue Angels flight demonstration team. The British, French, and others have their own teams, which share the sky north of Paris. Pierre Gaillard

But it was the Dassault Mirage III V that was attracting the greatest interest. In appearance, a fairly standard Mirage delta-winged fighter, it had lift engines mounted vertically in the fuselage and was expected to become the first VTOL Mach 2 airplane to fly. The supersonic version of the Harrier, called the P.1154, was a popular topic of conversation, but never saw the light of day. In fact, the world is still waiting for its first production supersonic VTOL airplane.

While the practical desirability of supersonic airliners was a matter of debate, there was far less doubt about the eventual success of VTOL aircraft. The military's need for combat VTOL was clear, while the need of more than a few airline passengers for Mach 2 speed was still to be established.

Among the other military airplanes at the Salon, the one having the greatest impact was the Belgian-built F-104G Starfighter. Test pilot Bernard Neefs flew it from Brussels to Paris—about 150 miles—in just under 10 minutes, with almost half the flight at Mach 2, over a route that had been at least a week's journey by horses and wagons barely 100 years ago.

Halfway between conventional and VTOL aircraft are the STOL (Short Take-Off and Landing) types that were proliferating, even though no one seemed certain what it took to qualify an airplane as STOL. Many of the designs, such as the French Breguet 941 and the proposed Canadair CL-84, used the latest technology and potent turboprop engines to get them off and back down again. But when one realizes that the likes of Piper Super Cubs and Rallyes have very short take-off and landing qualities, the meaning of the term becomes hazy.

The first serious effort from the old Dutch firm Fokker appeared in the form of a small twin-turboprop airliner aimed at the regional market. If it got beyond the model stage, it would be in competition with the Douglas DC-9, on which construction of a prototype had just begun. But technology is just part of the success formula; Britain's new Hawker Siddeley Trident was in the same class as Boeing's 727, but the former is now all but forgotten.

One of the most promising new categories of airplanes was the small, 6-to-10-passenger executive

jet, of which more seem to appear annually. Hawker Siddeley's 125, the Aero 1121 Jet Commander, West Germany's HFB 320 Hansa, and the Dassault Mystere 20 (later to be called the Falcon 20 to aid American sales) all were on the horizon.

Helicopters were more prevalent and considerably more sophisticated, with a wide variety of aids to the type's legendary lack of stability being shown or at least claimed. Several companies were pushing rigid rotors for simplicity and greater maneuverability, but this idea was far from being perfected.

The gradually growing power of turbojets was about to take a big leap. Engines for the Concorde were announced as four 29,000-pound-thrust Bristol Olympus, while much larger engines were being proposed for whichever American SST advanced the furthest.

1965 PARIS AIR SHOW

The 26th Salon International de l'Aeronautique et de l'Espace was held from June 11 through 21. Shortly before the opening, a Lockheed YF-12A,

predecessor to the SR-71 Blackbird spy plane, set the first World Speed Record over Mach 3, with a pair of runs at 2,070 miles per hour. For reasons of intense security, this spectacular airplane was nowhere to be seen.

Since the 1963 Salon, both the United States and the USSR had achieved space walks outside orbiting spacecraft, and the U.S. Ranger VII had taken close-up photos of the moon. Winston Churchill had died, and President John Kennedy had been assassinated.

Most of 1963's trends continued, though at widely differing rates. International cooperation was building up steam, with Anglo-French efforts to create the Jaguar ground-attack fighter emblematic of the progress from licensed production to join research and development. The mushrooming cost of modern airplanes was forcing centuries-old rivalries, if not hatreds, into the background.

Among the VTOL projects, only the British project was gaining ground. A Kestrel forerunner of the Harrier was at Paris. But the much-trumpeted

Appearing for the very first time is France's largest helicopter, the Sud 3120 Super Frelon (Hornet). Powered by three 1,250-horsepower Turbomecca shaft-turbine engines, it could top 150 miles per hour while carrying 28 fully armed soldiers. This one was in the service of the French Navy. Pierre Gaillard

Mach 2 VTOL Mirage IIIV had been postponed indefinitely due to skyrocketing costs and the difficulties of getting such an airplane off the ground with a payload that would make it worthwhile. Engineers, as well as salesmen, were forced to view combat VTOL in practical terms, rather than simply an exciting challenge.

The supersonic airliner race had been refocused. The French/British Concorde was moving along, but the U.S. plans were mired in controversy about noise, air pollution, and the airlines' need for such an advanced craft. After years of rumors, the Soviets finally showed a model of their proposed Tu-144 SST, whose similarity to the Concorde could hardly have been a coincidence.

Present in all their aluminum glory were lots of Soviet airliners, most of them seen in the West for the first time. There was the Ilyushin Il-62, resembling Britain's Vickers VC-10 with its four engines at the tail. And the Tupolev Tu-134, a DC-9-like airplane with entirely too many large bulges for aerodynamic efficiency.

Both of them completely overshadowed the original Soviet Tu-104 that was also in the national grouping, alongside several turboprop

The Breguet 951, a genuine STOL (Short Take-Off and Landing) transport, used the deflected-slipstream method for increasing lift at low speed. The large propellers turned by four 1,250-horsepower turboshaft engines were spaced along the wing so they blast air over all of it. There was talk that McDonnell would build it on license. Pierre Gaillard

The Grumman E-2A Hawkeye is an airborne early warning center. The huge radar on top feeds information to a battery of on-board specialists, who use it to control fighters and ground support airplanes. It is powered by two 4,000-horsepower Allison turboprop engines. With an 80-foot wingspan, it is one of the largest to operate from aircraft carriers. Pierre Gaillard

transports and freighters. Of considerably greater economic potential were the rumors of a series of French Airbus designs.

Executive jets continued to grow in number and popularity. At Paris were examples of early-model Lear Jet 23, the Piaggio-Douglas PD.108, Dassault Fan Jet Falcon, Hansa HFB. 320, Hawker Siddeley 125 Jet Dragon, and Lockheed JetStar. Many were in series production, and the world's supply of such aircraft was rapidly growing.

The helicopter portion of the display was dominated by the huge Soviet Mil Mi-6 troop/passenger carrier and Mi-10 flying crane that were considered near the forefront of technology. These and the 20-passenger Mi-8 in Aeroflot airline markings could allegedly be ordered by foreigners, but there were serious doubts about their manufacturer being able to provide technical support at the same level as western builders.

The Hughes OH-6 small military helicopter was in large-scale production, and was to be followed by the Model 500 civil version. A trend toward making helicopters more like airplanes to

achieve higher speeds was illustrated by Lockheed's experimental XH-51A, with short wings and a turbojet engine, considered a compound helicopter.

Sikorsky offered a look at its S-61 passenger helicopter, whose Navy version, the CH-53A, was being prepped for a nonstop transatlantic flight. Agusta of Italy displayed a wide variety of the helicopters it was producing on license from Bell, while Boeing had both its tandem-rotor helicopters: the UH-46A Sea Knight and CH-47A Chinook.

This four-seat SIAI-Marchetti SF.250 is the latest beautiful light plane from the brain and pen of Stelio Frati, whose sleek two-seat Falco has long been one of the most graceful crafts in Italian skies. Military-style tip tanks add to the range while barely affecting the speed. Pierre Gaillard

The Tupolev Tu-134 airliner is representative of the second generation of Soviet airliners for the national airline, Aeroflot. It has better performance than the pioneering Tu-104, but retains suggestions of alternate military uses such as the glassed-in nose, reminiscent of the U.S. B-29. Pierre Gaillard

Strange looking and exceptionally loud, the Dornier Do31 VTOL aircraft performed its novel maneuvers, but reportedly could lift little more than the weight of its crew. Forward thrust was provided by the two conventional turbojets, while vertical lift was accomplished with several smaller engines mounted vertically inside the fuselage. DaimlerChrysler Aerospace

Previous Spread: The Mil V-10 was the largest Soviet helicopter yet seen at Paris. Similar in concept to Sikorsky's "Flying Crane," it can lift up to 33,000 pounds, including the bus as seen here. The six-bladed main rotor spans 115 feet, while the fuselage is 107 feet long. Pierre Gaillard

The Beagle Pup 100 might have signaled the rebirth of British light plane manufacturing, had it not run into organizational problems. It offered more speed, along with better aerobatic capability, than any comparable American two-seater. It eventually was used by the RAF as the Bulldog trainer. Pierre Gaillard

Among the engines from no fewer than 15 manufacturers, General Electric's huge GE4 mock-up overshadowed the rest: 6 feet in diameter, 25 feet long, and aimed at 50,000 pounds of thrust for the American SST. Just what would happen to it in the event the SST failed to materialize was not suggested.

The final day of the Salon featured a major air show aimed at the hundreds of thousands of Frenchmen and others who poured into Le Bourget. In the air were everything from a cute little 45-horsepower Tipsy Nipper from Belgium, through a wide variety of what were becoming known as "general aviation" aircraft, up to Mach 2 fighters from several nations and several dozen different types of helicopter. The show ran from 9 A.M. until 6 P.M.

Regardless of the effort placed on satisfying the needs of the public, the Salon was, first and foremost, a trade show where potential customers were softened up with the finest food and drink in a growing number of chalets or "hospitality suites." Paris was a place to do business in the most interesting and pleasant setting possible.

1967 PARIS AIR SHOW

The 27th Salon International de l'Aeronautique et de l'Espace was held from May 26 through June 4 at Le Bourget Aeroport. It was the rainiest and muddiest in memory and increased the demands of exhibitors for paving more of the display area. Since the last Salon, both the United States and the USSR had landed probes on the moon: Surveyor 1 and Luna 9.

SSTs appeared to be getting much closer to reality, even if the airlines' demand for them was less than overwhelming because of the initial cost and the limited possibilities of breaking even on their operations. The sole remaining American competitor was the Boeing variable-wing sweep design, which was in greatest peril from politicians and environmentalists.

The Concorde was at Paris . . . sort of. A full-size mock-up graced the static park, giving the attendees a clear picture of its imposing size and shape, if not its noise and grace. Claims that the prototype would fly early in 1968 were taken in stride by those accustomed to exaggerations.

There was little beyond rumors of the Soviet Tu-144, which was supposedly on schedule, whatever that meant. So much national prestige was wrapped up in the two SSTs that dates and specifications were automatically suspect. The Tu-144, for instance, was supposed to be able to cruise at 1,550 miles per hour for 4,000 miles with 120 passengers. Written guarantees were not available.

VTOL had made much more tangible progress since the last Salon. A preproduction Harrier was on show, and it was obviously the most advanced of all the wild variety of projects and schemes. The Chance Vought XC-142 turboprop-powered, tilt-wing research machine at Paris was one of two flying, and was said to cruise at more than 400 miles per hour.

Many of the VTOL aircraft ballyhooed at past Salons were nowhere to be seen. But the French did show off the neat little Nord 500. With its ducted fans, the Nord 500 at least looked like it might fly, though that phase of the program was still a couple of years off.

This was a big year for big cargo airplanes. The U.S. C-141 Starlifter was starting a long run as a standard type. The Soviet Antonov AN-22 was imposing, with huge contra-rotating propellers on its huge turboprop engines. The ugly duckling

Since the end of World War II, the Yak-18 had been a standard Soviet trainer. This 18T is the side-by-side seating conversion aimed at civilian training and touring, though that concept barely existed in the USSR. It is powered by the very popular 160-horsepower, five-cylinder radial M-11FR engine. Pierre Gaillard

This LTV XC-142 VTOL airplane is the prototype of a hoped-for VTOL military transport. The largest of VTOL test beds, it uses a tilting wing to achieve both horizontal and vertical flight. To get to Paris, it was shipped by aircraft carrier to Spain and flown the rest of the way.
Pierre Gaillard

more quickly, the 400-plus passenger Boeing 747 was not all that far from its first flight. As a purely self-financed project, it could well spell the difference between success and failure for the manufacturer.

Space, a part of the Salon for just a short time, had blossomed. The U.S. exhibit was slick and informative, with government and industry specialists ready to answer questions and take orders. Highlighting it was a mock-up of an X-15 rocket-powered research airplane that held the unofficial world records for speed (Mach 6.3 or 4,350 miles per hour) and altitude (67 miles or 354,000 feet).

The display of the Soviets was visually attractive, with actual spacecraft or high-quality mock-ups on show, but lacked meaningful written information or knowledgeable experts. A Vostok like those used for their first manned space flights was on display.

While large and very large airliners were in the spotlight, the opposite end of the scale was not being ignored. Feeder airliners, later called regional airliners, were growing in popularity. The first one to appear at Paris, however, was the 24-seat Yak-40, at a time when Soviet airliners were

was the Super Guppy, a Boeing Stratocruiser with an amazingly outsize fuselage for carrying large sections of airliners and space launchers.

Jumbo airliners were attracting considerable attention even though they were there in model form only. The British-French-German project was known as the A-300 Eurobus, but would soon become the now-familiar Airbus A300 and its stablemates. Starting later, but moving much

One of many versions and variants of the Dassault Mirage line, this Type III is a standard with the French Air Force, which is fully sold on delta wings. The prototype Mirage III exceeded Mach 2 on an early flight, and then climbed to 82,000 feet, marking it as a fighter comparable to any. Pierre Gaillard

A direct overhead view, shot from a Northrop RF-5 reconnaissance fighter on its arrival from the United States for the show. The black roofed building at right is the main display building, while the hangars across the top of the photo will soon become the home of the Musee de l'Air, one of the world's great air museums. Northrop, via the Air Force Association

not held in great repute by the western airlines that dominated the world's passenger business.

Of more long-term interest was the DC-9–like twin-turbojet Fokker F.28 Fellowship, the prototype of which had just flown. Others revealed at Paris in model form would not get much further. But at the smaller end were some that would succeed, including the boxy Short Skyvan and the STOL DeHavilland of Canada Twin Otter.

Among the limited number of light planes on display was the slick little Beagle Pup 100, a low-wing, tricycle-geared semi-sport-plane with true aerobatic qualifications. This, along with more versions of the French Rallye line, constituted much of the European effort to counter the growing domination of the Americans, who were flooding Europe with Cessna, Piper, and Beech

Nine Fouga Magister jet trainers of the French Patrol in perfect formation, showing off their skills and the usefulness of their airplanes. Each airplane can produce red, white, or blue smoke (the colors of the French flag) to emphasize their ever-changing formations. Don Berliner

products, though most of the Cessnas were built on license in France.

To keep things somewhat in perspective, both the United States and France tipped their hats to aviation's history. The U.S. pavilion featured a flying reproduction of Lindbergh's Ryan NYP *Spirit of St. Louis*, which had ended its epic flight at Le Bourget. And France moved Nungessor and Coli's hefty long-distance Breguet 19 from its museum home to the static aircraft park.

1969 Paris Air Show

The 28th Salon International de l'Aeronautique et de l'Espace ran from May 29 to June 8. It was marked by big, flashy grabs for publicity and sales.

Since the last Salon, three American astronauts had orbited the moon in Apollo 8 and two Mariner probes had sent back close-up photos of Mars. Communist Czechoslovakia had experimented with freedom, only to be invaded and squelched by its Soviet-inspired neighbors.

The unquestioned stars of the show were two Concorde SSTs, which posed in the static park and then flew carefully and well separated above Le Bourget. As one sat at the end of the runway, it was impossibly noisy, and a bit grotesque, thanks to the drooping nose that was necessary for pilot visibility. But once in the air, it was as graceful as anything seen in flight. With its broad delta wing and long, pointy nose, it was the obvious solution to a host of major technical problems.

The Soviet Tu-144 that had made its first flight before Concorde was nowhere to be seen. This led to a stream of rumors about mechanical and/or aerodynamic problems said to prove that the Soviets had tackled too big a challenge. There was little doubt that the Tu-144 faced even more serious economic problems than Concorde.

The other big event was the first appearance of Boeing's enormous 747 jumbo jet. Capable of carrying almost twice as many passengers as any other airliner, it towered over the static park and produced as many oohs and aahs as anything previously seen at Paris. If it lived up to Boeing's claims, it could revolutionize the airline business. If it failed, Boeing might cease to exist.

A novel little four-seat personal plane, decked out in uncharacteristic colors for something quite British. The Britten-Norman Nymph was designed to be built in England and then the assembly completed in small factories in under-developed countries to boost the local economies. Don Berliner

The other field of competition was space. The United States had a brilliantly prepared exhibit, with the actual Apollo 8 command and service module, which had been to the moon, and enough of its enormous Saturn V launch vehicle to awe the crowd. The USSR, on the other hand, had a very attractive hall full of spacecraft, but lacked any understanding of sales: There was no way to find out which was which, let alone what they were supposed to do.

VTOL aircraft had to take a back seat to these spectacular displays, even though there were more of them flying than ever. The British Harrier made the biggest splash with the news that the U.S. Marine Corps would buy a substantial number. This followed the first appearance in the United States by a Harrier after its pilot had won the novel, no-holds-barred Transatlantic Air Race.

From West Germany came the equally noisy but far less useful Dornier Do31 VTOL craft. It roared and slowly pirouetted in fine form, but was said to have a pay-load limited to its crew. The little French ducted-fan Nord 500 was undergoing flight tests, and its twin-fan follow-on, the military 501, was in model form and said to be capable of 370 miles per hour.

While the 747 towered over the airliner section of the static display park, there were more Soviet airplanes than ever before. With better paint jobs and fewer bombardier noses than previously, they made a better initial impression. But a journalist's

experience as a passenger in the Tu-154 and Il-62 would produce few words to be welcomed by the manufacturers' advertising departments, assuming they had any.

Among the fewer-than-usual light planes were two that attracted a lot of interest. The Fournier RF-4 powered glider had been flown across the Atlantic by Czech expatriate Mira Slovak. And the

A fairly typical display, among the growing hundreds in more and more permanent display buildings. In this case, the products produced by the sponsor lack the visual appeal of complete airplanes, so models of airplanes that use its equipment are prominently displayed. Don Berliner

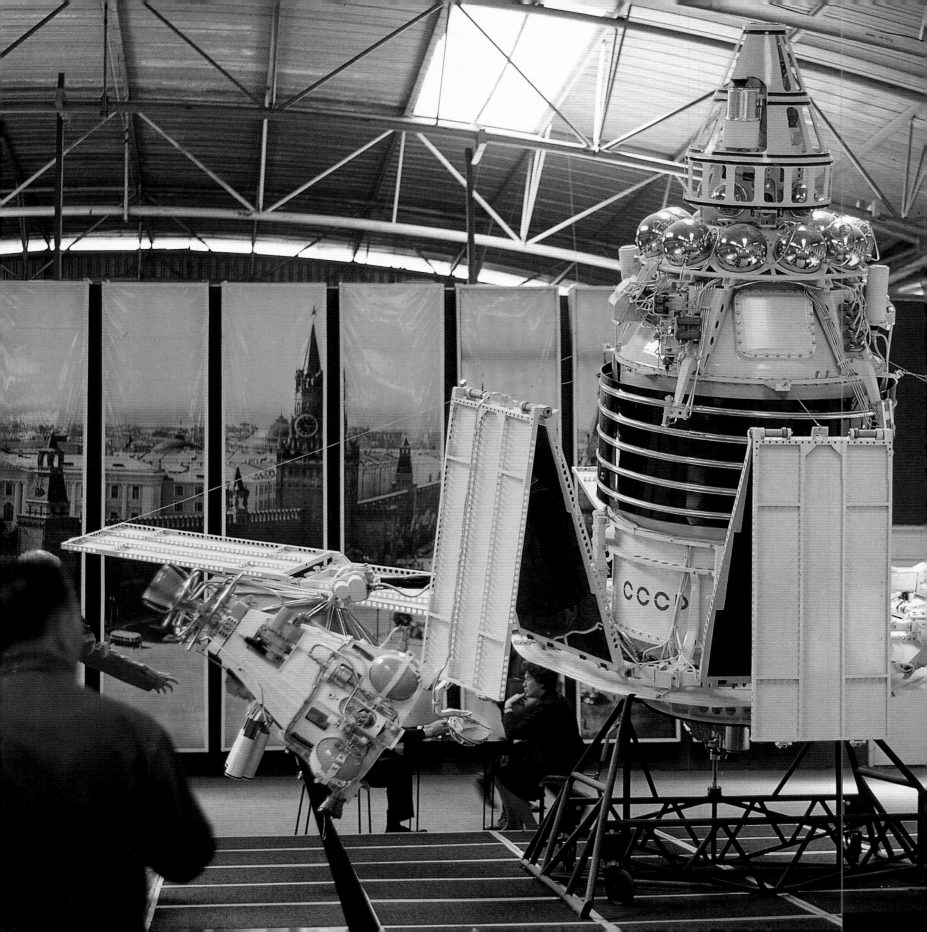

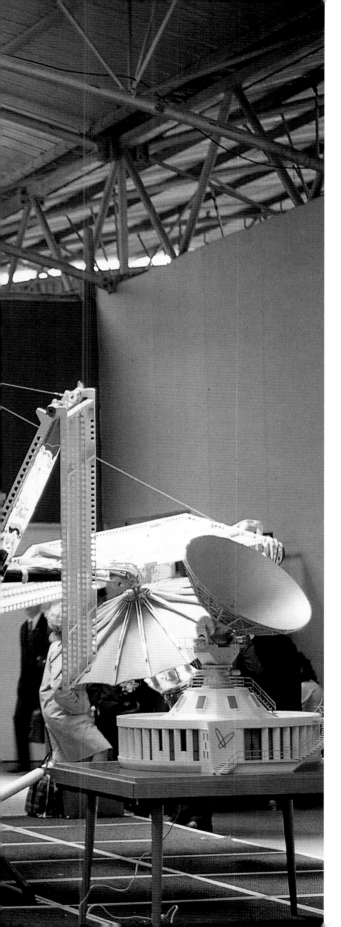

four-place Britten Norman Nymph, with its very un-British lavender-and-red color scheme, was meant for final assembly in third-world countries, as a boost to their aviation industries. A good idea that never took off.

The range and popularity of executive jets continued to grow. Sizable numbers of the Hawker Siddeley 125, Falcon 20, and several American types not only figured prominently in the displays, but occupied scores of parking places on the airport, having brought industry executives to the show.

The smallest airliners were more obvious than ever. From Czechoslovakia came the well-made LET L.410 TurboJet, whose pair of Canadian turboprop engines enabled it to carry up to 15 passengers. The similar Beriev Be-30 from the USSR claimed excellent short-field performance, but was looked upon with suspicion, as were all commercial products from that part of the world.

A larger STOL transport, the German-French Transall C.160, looked like a twin-engined version of the increasingly popular Lockheed C-130 Hercules. The C-160 would go on to have a long life in the service of several military air arms.

High-performance fighters attracted a lot less attention this year, due in no small part to the absence of the U.S. Department of Defense. But Sweden displayed its Mach 2 Viggen delta-wing, which was designed to operate from roads and could use its thrust reverser to back up, much to the glee of the crowd.

While primary attention was focused on the present and the future, the past was not totally ignored. A reproduction of the Vickers Vimy in which Alcock and Brown had become the first to fly the Atlantic nonstop in 1919 was flown over from England for the 50th anniversary of the epic achievement. And in the flying display was an accurate reproduction of the Bleriot monoplane in which Louis Bleriot had flown across the English Channel 60 years earlier.

International rivalries gained prominence in 1969. Among SSTs, it was the USSR vs. France and Great Britain. And in space it was the USSR vs. the United States. Just how much of the effort to lead the world was built on solid foundations of technology and how much was a grab for prestige would be seen in the years to come.

The space display of the USSR neared the peak of its size and completeness. The individual satellites and engines were of showroom quality, but there were no signs to distinguish one from another. Nor were there any brochures or multilingual experts on hand to answer questions.
Don Berliner

CHAPTER 7

RUSSIAN
FIASCOS

The 29th Salon International de l'Aeronautique et de l'Espace was held from May 27 through June 6, 1971. Once again, all previous statistical records were broken, as close to a million people examined the displays of 583 companies from 17 nations. Since the last Salon, six American Apollo astronauts had walked on the moon in history's most complex successful engineering project.

At Paris, the public finally got a look at the Soviet Tu-144 SST and could compare it with the Concorde. While their outward appearance was so similar as to cause suspicions that industrial espionage was involved, inside, they were

Lots of airplanes and lots of people. In the foreground is the Soviet collection of airliners: lower left, Il-62M; lower right, Il-76; center, 11-62; upper left, Concorde, and far right, Tu-144 SST. The smaller airplane at right is a Yak-42 feeder liner. Beyond the crowd of airplanes is one end of the chalet row. David Grove

from two different eras. The Concorde was designed with and flew with sophisticated computers to control, among other things, the variable-geometry inlet ramps.

The Tu-144—nicknamed the Concordski—was far less advanced and suffered from a lack of broad-based advanced technology. Once it was parked alongside the other airliners, there was no way to keep nosy westerners from a close-up inspection. This revealed tires that were threadbare; years later it was learned that they were good for just three landings before needing replacement.

But at the time, Soviet predictions of imminent airline operations at Mach 2 over long-haul routes was taken fairly seriously, if not believed outright. This was the first truly advanced Soviet airplane seen in the West, and it seemed to live up to its advance notices. Its American "rival," the Boeing 2707, had just been canceled by President Lyndon Johnson because of widely expressed concerns over air and noise pollution and the high cost of development and operations.

The second of the great competitions of the era—the race to the moon—had been won by the United States. To celebrate this, and no doubt to rub it in the Soviets' faces, the American pavilion included the actual Apollo 14 command module

that had orbited the moon while two of its crew hopped around on the surface, just a few months earlier. Along with it was a model of the Lunar Rover that would enable future moon explorers to drive around. Years later it was revealed that the complexity of a moon landing was far beyond Soviet technology, and the "race" had ended long before the United States' first Apollo flight.

Everything else had been pushed into the background, including VTOL efforts. The Harrier was now in RAF service as the world's first; a group of them made a formation take-off, suggesting a spectacular future for military formation aerobatic teams. The other VTOL projects showed little or no progress.

The era of the wide-bodied (two-aisle) airliner was in full swing, with Boeing explaining the lack of a huge 747 on display at Paris by the airlines' need to keep them flying and making money. Somewhat smaller types, such as Lockheed's L-1011 Tristar and the Douglas DC-10, were joining it, and leaving further behind the French efforts with the Mercure (which had just flown) and the first of the Airbuses, which was there only in mock-up form. The American domination of airliner manufacturing grew.

STOL was still big, though any meaningful definition of the term was made impossible by the demonstrations with the Lockheed C-5A Galaxy, the largest military transport/cargo plane in service and but by no stretch of the imagination an STOL design. With its weight held to the absolute minimum, a C-5A showed off its ability to take off in just 2,000 feet (eight airplane lengths), climb steeply, and then land in half that distance.

Among the very small airliners was the novel Britten Norman Trislander, a stretched version of the successful little Islander with a third engine protruding forward from the virtual stabilizer. It worked and went into production as a funny-looking exception to the old rule that "if it looks right, it will fly right."

Once again, there were more helicopters than ever, with the grand prize going to the Soviets' enormous Mil V-12. The span (of its outrigger rotor tips) was 220 feet, while it was 121 feet long, dimensions that previously had been limited to some of the largest of fixed-wing aircraft. It was

An Israeli Aircraft Industries' Arava light utility transport. This tiny country is starting to show its technical prowess, and the Arava would be the first indigenous design to sell internationally. It impressed the crowd with its ability to take off and land short, and with its low-speed maneuverability. Don Berliner

powered by a pair of 6,500-horsepower turboshaft engines that enabled it to claim a cruise of 150 miles per hour and lift a gross weight of 230,000 pounds. While it had already lifted almost 90,000 pounds of cargo, there was no sign of production orders.

There had always been a few sailplanes at Paris, and this year was no exception. What was a growing trend was powered sailplanes, though the soaring purists were not happy. But in fuel-expensive Europe, they make a lot of sense, offering self-launching capability and a much better chance of landing where you want than the long-popular sailplanes. Best known were the Fourniers, many with small Volkswagen car engines. And at the top of the line was the Caproni Vizzola A.21J Calif with its miniature jet engine on top.

Blurring the line between military trainers and combat airplanes were several "armed trainers," such as Yugoslavia's Galeb, Britain's BAC Strikemaster, the Italian MB-326, and the Spanish Super Saeta. Add to this the armed versions of such otherwise peaceful craft as Cessna's push-pull Skymaster, the Britten Norman Defender (a camouflaged Islander), and a Short Skyvan with mildly sinister intent.

Among the light twins good for executive transport or as small airliners were the very clean Partenavia P.68 Oscar, Israel's twin-boom Arva, the novel four-seat Wing Derringer, which hadn't been seen in years, and the unspectacular-but-logical Swearingen Merlin III.

On the final day of the Salon, the Soviets' Soyuz 11 manned spacecraft failed on reentry and its three-man crew perished.

Look to Lockheed for lunch! One of the better spreads was courtesy of Lockheed, which clearly knows how to influence potential customers and journalists. The food and drink were catered by one of the best restaurants in Paris, meaning one of the best in the world. Don Berliner

The VFW-Fokker 614 is unique in its placement of its engines on top of the wings. The prototype test program was just about completed, and some smaller airlines were starting to look at it. Designed to carry 40 to 44 passengers over legs as long as 600 miles, its low noise level could make it a good buy. Pierre Gaillard

1973 PARIS AIR SHOW

The 30th Salon International de l'Aeronautique et de l'Espace was held at Le Bourget Aeroport from May 24 to June 3. It was quite unlike anything Parisians had seen before.

A much improved version of the Tu-144 SST was on show and in flight. It had a more complex wing shape, similar to the Concorde, along with other improvements. On the final day of the Salon, it crashed, off the airfield but fully in view, killing the crew and eight people on the ground. At first, its pilot was blamed for trying to match the maneuvers of the Concorde and overstressing the airplane in the process.

Years later, it had become generally agreed that a specially instrumented French Mirage fighter had been trailing it, hiding in the clouds, while secretly recording technical data. The Tu-144 pilot, assured he had the sky above Le Bourget to himself, was apparently startled to see the Mirage through a break in the clouds. In trying to avoid the French jet, he pulled too many g-forces and his airplane broke up.

This effectively ended the rivalry between the Tu-144 and the Concorde, for whatever the cause of the crash, no airline would risk frightening its passengers by buying an airplane that had so publicly failed. When added to the long-term problems the Soviet aerospace industry faced—inability to meet delivery schedules, lack of product support, refusal to be sufficiently open about a myriad of technical matters—the crash spelled the end of the Tu-144 as a salable airliner, despite the protestations of innocence by the Soviets.

As for the Concorde, it was looking like a real airliner, rather than just an engineering marvel. It had been flown by pilots from 13 airlines that were considered potential customers. Unlike its eastern rival, it had achieved performance figures that most people believed: it had flown has high as 68,000 feet, as far as 3,900 miles nonstop, and as fast as 1,400 miles per hour or Mach 2.16.

For the first time in memory, some of the biggest newsmakers were indoors, rather than on the ramp or in the sky. Fewer meaningful new types of aircraft were on display than usual, while at the same time, many of the indoor displays and booths offered fascinating hints of the future of the aerospace industry.

One of the quietest "revolutions" in many years was beginning to show itself: composite materials. These expensive, sophisticated materials such as carbon-fiber and Kevlar, were combinations of materials especially selected to produce lower weight and greater strength than any of the finest of steels and aluminum alloys. But forming them into shapes that would withstand the rigors of years of regular use had given engineers some of their biggest headaches.

At long last, large components were being built of composite materials and examples could be seen. An actual production horizontal tail for a Grumman F-14 Tomcat was on display as proof that this new technique was maturing. What it promised was the freedom to design entire airplanes of any flamboyant shape without having to worry about the difficulties of mass producing parts having normal or reverse compound curves needed to achieve aerodynamic superiority.

Even light planes were starting to feel the impact of new materials. A series of German Wassmer personal planes built from fiberglass was on show, with the prospect of at least one of them

going into typically European limited production. Another series of small planes was emerging from Pierre Robin, all of them developments of Jodel homebuilts, but of more conventional mixed metal and wood construction.

While TriStar and DC-10 production was well under way, yet another generation of airliners seemed to be taking shape already. The first of what could be quite an extensive range of Airbuses was well on the way to certification, and was being followed by more smaller airliners. From Hawker Siddeley came the four-engined HS-146, which would later be known as the British Aerospace 146 Regional Jet, and would eventually be known as the Avro 146. And from Europlane came a 200-seat craft with engines at the rear and a T-tail; it would vanish without a trace.

Other small airliners included the feeder-liner version of the popular Falcon 30 and the VFW-Fokker 614. Neither would make more than a slight ripple. Nor would a twin-engined version of the DC-10, nor a new Boeing trimotored jet. Clearly, there was no shortage of ideas, as the airline business continued to show long-term growth.

A prototype Airbus A300B, which had made its first flight less than a year before. The hopes and dreams of European aviation rested on this design, which would make the first serious inroad into the American airline scene with the sale of a later version to Eastern Air Lines. Pierre Gaillard

The Rockwell Commander 112 in Swedish registry is the first light plane to be built by the successor to North American Aviation since the Navion in 1946. Much like the Navion, it failed to sell well, lacking the performance of several of its rivals, such as the Beech Bonanza.

The Dornier staff is waiting for customers, browsers, and the merely curious. Soon enough, hundreds will stroll through the arch to study the space age displays of both Dornier and Messerschmitt-Bolkow-Blohm. Satellites hang from the ceiling, while missiles are in glass cases at floor level. DaimlerChrysler Aerospace

Not much was shown of new ideas for combat airplanes, especially from the United States. Northrop did have a full-size mock-up of its F-17 Cobra fighter, which seemed to attract a great deal of attention from the Soviets, who were busy taking close-up photos and measurements. Did they realize the mock-up had been subtly modified to conceal any signs of classified advance design ideas? It probably didn't matter, as they had orders to bring back all the information they could, so that experts in Moscow could search it for items of interest.

After many days of rain and very low cloud decks, the finale air show was held in clear skies. Military formation teams swooped, leaving multi-colored smoke trails: France's Patroulle de France in its Fouga Magisters, and the RAF's Red Arrows in bright red Folland Gnats. Bob Hoover cavorted without peer in his familiar Shrike Commander and then in a Northrop F-5 Freedom Fighter.

Some of the demonstrations obviously were planned to show that properly designed airplanes could be fast without making a lot of noise. The new Cessna Citation business jet was one that flew past the crowd while making surprisingly little racket, unlike the Harrier and the SAAB Viggen, to name but two, that made the kind of noise that has always been happily associated with air shows but is increasingly frowned upon local authorities. The trend, obviously, is toward the latter.

1975 PARIS AIR SHOW

The 31st Salon International de l'Aeronautique et de l'Espace was held from May 30 through June 8 at Le Bourget Aeroport.

Since the last Salon, the Watergate scandal had led to the first resignation of an American president, three Skylabs had been orbited, and a Lockheed SR-71 Blackbird had flown from New York to London in under two hours. Henry Aaron (Hammerin' Hank) had broken Babe Ruth's career home run record of 714.

The biggest topic of discussion at Paris was the American coup of selling hundreds of F-16 Falcon fighters to several European countries, beating out domestic manufacturers with a combination of low prices and joint production. American-European rivalry continued to heat up.

The American ability to produce and deliver modern airplanes in less time than its rivals was an obvious advantage, as France, Germany, Great Britain, and other countries remained bogged down in outdated complications of nationality.

The subject next in popularity in the plush chalets was the big push by Boeing for its "100 percent certain" 7X7 series of airliners to replace aging 727 fleets. The new 200-seat airplanes had been placed on the back burner during the 1973–74 fuel crisis, but were now said to be headed for production. The rapid disappearance of the entire series makes one wonder about each year's crop of rumors and "sure things."

Yet another Tu-144 SST was on display, despite increasing suspicions that it had huge technical problems. The Soviets claimed the test models had racked up 1,000 flights, and announced that a total of 20 airplanes had been ordered. During its brief air show display, it was flown through the most modest of maneuvers of any airplane at the Salon.

More and more emphasis was being placed on space developments, with manned space laboratories being displayed by both the USSR and United States. The former's Salyut 2 and 3 had been orbited with crews, and had been serviced by ferry craft. The U.S. Spacelab was being built by a European consortium and would be sent up with the Space Shuttle in a few years. The transition from spectacular to serious science had been made by the major national space programs.

Other displays related to the forthcoming U.S. Apollo/USSR Soyuz orbital link-up, planned for later in the year, and to the Viking lander, which was intended to send back color pictures from the Martian surface. During the

One huge model of an Airbus A300 dominates the display, while below it, dozens of miniatures show off the colors of all the airlines that have ordered (or are considering ordering) the increasingly popular wide-bodied airliner. Flowers and little trees serve as natural walls, as well as decoration.
DaimlerChrysler Aerospace

To see it all at once without a mob getting in your way, take the high view of the center of the static display area. In the middle, in front of the main building, is a Concorde SST. At the very bottom is a B-17 Flying Fortress. In the upper right is one end of the expanding double row of chalets.
DaimlerChrysler Aerospace

A pair of Alpha Jet trainers, accompanied by enough bombs, rockets, fuel tanks, and electronics pods to overload a B-52. When carried in sensible numbers, they turn this trainer into a ground-support fighter. In the distant sky can be seen four Tiger Moths of the Tiger Club completing opposing loops. DaimlerChrysler Aerospace

Salon, the USSR successfully launched two Kosmos military reconnaissance satellites and a Molniya communications satellite, and sent a Venera space probe toward Venus.

New propeller-driven (both piston and turbo) military trainers were popping up all over the place. From Switzerland, the Pilatus PC-7 Turbo Trainer; from the United States, Beech's T-34C Turbo Mentor; from Scottish Aviation, the Bulldog development of the Beagle Pup; from Sweden, the SAAB Supporter, and from New Zealand, the CT/4 Air Trainer. It was generally agreed that some of these would have to fail because of the limited market.

About the only large military transport on display was the Ilyushin Il-76, using 1960s technology. It was hard to imagine that anyone outside

One of the most popular Paris planes of all time is the British Aerospace Harrier, which has long showcased its amazing talent to hover, fly backwards, and pirouette, complete with as much noise as any known airplane. This one is a rare two-seat trainer version, hovering with its landing gear down. Pierre Gaillard

the Soviet bloc would be willing to ignore the USSR industry's reputation for questionable workmanship and lack of economic efficiency enough to place any meaningful orders.

One of the more intriguing designs on display was the British-designed Lockspeiser LDA. 1, a tandem-winged (or canard), pusher-engined, small-scale prototype for which a wide range of centers-of-gravity was supposed to be possible. Its homely, almost old-fashioned lines would be in stark contrast to a sleek, futuristic airplane of similar layout being developed in California by an unknown designer named Burt Rutan.

Among the helicopters were Boeing and Sikorsky military multipurpose designs for the UTTAS competition, and Sikorsky's new civil S-76, its first completely new nonmilitary design in many years, and meant to compete with Bell's equally high-tech 222.

Agricultural airplanes have always played a role at Paris, though few have attracted much comment, being among the most utilitarian (and thus least glamorous) of flying machines. The Fletcher FU-24, designed in the United States and built in New Zealand, was a big airplane, with very long wings and a hefty 400-horsepower Lycoming engine. A low-cost ground-support version had also been developed.

The air show portion of the Salon was scaled back both in quantity and quality, thanks to increasing concern on the part of Le Bourget's neighbors after the Tu-144 crash, and to the proximity of the increasingly busy Charles DeGaulle International Airport to the east. Far fewer high-performance airplanes showed their stuff, leaving the skies available for more general aviation types. Czech Zlins, French Rallyes, CAPs, and especially the American Beech Turbo Mentor stole the show.

For those whose memories needed prodding, the Royal Air Force displayed a Hawker Hurricane and Supermarine Spitfire on the 30th anniversary of VE Day.

1977 Paris Air Show

The 32nd Salon International de l'Aeronautique et de l'Espace de Paris-Le Bourget was held from June 2 through 12. Since the last Salon, the

United States had celebrated its bicentennial, the Concorde SST had entered service, and almost 500 passengers had died when two Boeing 747s collided on the ground in the Canary Islands.

The show was the biggest yet, with more than 600 exhibitors crowding five halls, some 200 aircraft, and about 220 customer entertainment centers. Typically, the show was open to the public only on the weekends; it would otherwise be limited to trade visitors, or businessmen and women. But it's always amazing how many unaffiliated aviation enthusiasts manage to acquire whatever credentials are needed for admission to the display area and exhibit halls during the week.

The spotlight shone most brightly on a pair of odd-looking military cargo planes: Boeing's YC-14 and McDonnell-Douglas' XC-15. They were locked in a battle for a big contract to replace the ubiquitous Lockheed C-130 Hercules. In order to lift a heavier load off shorter runways, both prototypes had high-mounted turbojet engines that directed their exhaust blast over the wing, thus increasing lift substantially.

One of the odder agricultural airplanes seen at Paris: the WSK-Mielec M-15 from Poland. It was a mystery why something meant to fly low and slow had a turbofan engine, which works best high and fast. One possible explanation was that the real purpose of the airplane was to dispense poison gas. Flight International

Almost crowded out of the lower right corner of the picture is a refreshment stand, at Paris almost as important as airplanes and engines. Those who have finished eating and drinking are welcome to look at the Alpha Jet, its guns and tanks, and the U.S. Coast Guard Dassault Falcon behind it. Flight International

At left center is a Fokker F.27 Friendship, to its right is a VFW-Fokker 614 in the markings of a German airline. Behind it is an Airbus 300, all of them in white with red and black trim, despite their different origins. At right are a Fairchild A-10 and the nose of an elderly Constellation. Flight International

The Soviets continue to open up gradually. This is a mock-up of the giant Mir space station, with two major elements linked together, and acres of solar panels in the rear to provide power. The real Mir would be a vehicle for East-West cooperation via joint flights and joint crews. Flight International

This was just the latest in a long string of schemes to achieve boundary layer control over a wing, some of which had shown promise, but none of them going much beyond experimental status. While neither of these airplanes would enter production, a very similar machine would appear from the USSR in a few years. Accusations of industrial or military espionage would be hard to refute.

The extension of national coastal limits to 200 miles spawned new interest in maritime reconnaissance airplanes. The small airplanes, with their limited range, were headed for extinction, while types more along the lines of the older patrol bomber would soon be in favor.

The largest of the maritime designs seen recently at Paris was the Hawker Siddeley Nimrod,

A member of the support crew sits in the cockpit as a Swedish Air Force SAAB J-37 Viggen is prepared for display. The cockpit will remain open, so customers and the merely curious can see how a small company from a small country can produce a fighter that is up to world standards. Don Berliner

It's big, it's powerful, and it's flashy, but it doesn't go very fast, for it is a Grumman Ag-Cat. With a modern and somewhat incongruous (for flying farm machinery) Pratt & Whitney of Canada PT-6 turboprop engine of 550 to 750 horsepower, it can lift a heavier load of chemicals out of smaller fields.
Don Berliner

which had started out life as the beautiful DeHavilland Comet airliner and had steadily grown unattractive avionics bulges as DeHavilland was absorbed into Hawker Siddeley and then into the new British Aerospace Corp.

The Breguet Atlantique was another large antisub type, while the field seemed full of slightly smaller ones that had just recently looked a lot less militant. These included the Fokker F.27MA Maritime Enforcer, H.S. 748 Coastguarder, and two versions of the Nomad from Australia's Government Aircraft Factory. The trim little Partenavia P.68 was decked out in antisubmarine gear, as was the Dassault Falcon 20, which was in striking U.S. Coast Guard markings.

Some of the toughest competition was developing in the light strike/trainer category, where at least six countries showed off entries: the French Morane Saulnier Paris, German Dornier Alpha Jet, British Aerospace Hawk, Italian Macchi MB.339, Czech Aero L-39 Albatross, and the Polish WSK-Mielec Iskra. It's hard to imagine the worldwide market being sufficient to support production of all these, plus others expected shortly, and so the best should win out unless politics distorts the picture.

The SST race was over, though the Tu-144 refused to stay on the canvas even after having been knocked out. As the latest version of the Soviet SST arrived, an Air France Concorde

could be seen climbing away from DeGaulle Aeroport with a load of fare-paying passengers. The Tupolev was so fuel-hungry that it could never carry paying passengers, though a few "revenue" flights were made with nothing but mail. Talk of regular airline service by 1978–1980 was no more than vivid imagination in the service of the propaganda machine.

Several promising large airliners were being promoted by their builders: the Airbus A200, British Aerospace BAC X-11, and Dassault Mercure. All offered the advance aerodynamics that would be needed for a new generation of airliners, but the first two would get no further than the drawing board, and the Mercure would be a minor type when the story of the rapid growth of airliners was written.

None of the American wide-bodied airliners was on display, as they (747, L-1011, DC-10) were in large-scale production and worldwide service, and thus hardly needed a big sales effort. The Airbus A300 had not yet been quite so successful, and so one in Eastern Airlines markings was proudly shown off as the first of what would turn out to be a flood of American orders for the worthy French rival. The first Soviet Il-86 wide-body to be seen in the West offered the usual contrast: from a distance, it looked good, while up close it displayed the hallmarks of a late 1950s jetliner, including old-style turbojet engines that offered substandard fuel efficiency.

Quietly at first, and then more obviously, the list of important aerospace countries was growing beyond the United States, USSR, Britain, France, and Italy. New members included Argentina, Australia, Brazil, Czechoslovakia, Israel, and Poland. From hesitant beginnings, they were now running at a good clip, thanks to well-trained and creative engineers, and to countries willing to subsidize growth industries for long-term results.

The flying show, while tame by Paris standards (partly because of the crash of a U.S. Air Force A-10 "Warthog" on opening day), still gave the large audience a chance to see a lot of impressive aircraft, some of which were or would soon be major types. The Northrop YF-17 Cobra would soon emerge as the F-18 Hornet. DeHavilland of Canada's DHC-7 ("Dash 7") was one of the first of a stream of highly useful feederliners. And the

Kfir was a French Mirage with an Israeli engine and locally developed avionics. Several of them would become U.S. Air Force F-21 fighters.

1979 Paris Air Show

The 33rd Salon International de l'Aeronautique et de l'Espace de Paris-Le Bourget ran from June 9 through 17. The big news was an aeronautical achievement by Americans that could hardly have contrasted more with their country's reputation for doing big things. On June 12, Bryan Allen, a retrained racing bicyclist, pedaled an exotic, California-built airplane 22 miles across the English Channel. With wings as long as those of a DC-9 airliner, yet weighing just 75 pounds empty, the Gossamer Albatross proved that human-powered flight was more than just possible, though it was hardly practical.

The growing rivalry between Boeing and Airbus for the world's airliner orders had become one of the main issues facing the aviation community. Boeing's reputation and experience had produced so many orders that airlines wishing to wait less than five years for delivery began looking to the French manufacturer. Airbus' first major design, the A310, was a large, world-class airplane and finally gave European airlines a way to reduce their dependence on American industry.

The order books for both firms grew, with that of Airbus beginning to rival Boeing's: by the end of this year's Salon, it totaled many hundreds. This encouraged Airbus to look into the future with confidence and plan several new airplanes, including a four-engined version of the A300 that would look like a wide-bodied 707 and eventually emerge as the A340.

As for Boeing, its new twin-engined airplanes were moving toward flight and were in evidence in the form of components, photos, and models throughout the display buildings: the narrow-bodied 757 and its wide-bodied sister, the 767. There was even talk of a double-decked 747 that might carry 600 or more passengers.

With the Anglo-French Concorde SST in regular service, it was demonstrating its ability to operate effectively despite its speed, and to cost its operators embarrassing amounts of money. Nevertheless, a group drawn from British Aerospace and Aerospatiale was looking into a second

generation SST, which would carry 230 passengers and be only slightly slower, at Mach 1.8. By ignoring the huge development costs, it might even be economical enough to enable a few airlines to operate it without heavy government subsidies.

At the opposite end of the scale, more and more manufacturers were showing interest in commuter airliners capable of carrying 30 to 40 passengers for relatively short trips from minor markets. Canadian and Swedish companies introduced designs at the Salon, in hopes of getting into the international market without trying to challenge the big boys.

As evidence of the truth of the saying, "Old soldiers never die ...," the venerable Douglas DC-3 appeared in modernized form. With three powerful turboprop engines and wheels/skis, a prototype operated by Polair appeared ready to tackle the snow and ice of either of the earth's extremities. But the sweet sound of its radial engines was gone.

With the cost of military aircraft rising at a scary rate, there was rapidly increasing interest in low-cost replacements for conventional combat craft. One of the most intriguing ideas was the development of drones, many of them little more than large and rather sophisticated model airplanes equipped with a wide variety of surveillance devices.

Large numbers of Remotely Piloted Vehicles gave promise of real-time battlefield reconnaissance with no risk of human loss, and little of financial loss in case one was shot down. Moreover, there was no chance of repeating the national embarrassment that followed the Soviet downing of CIA pilot Gary Powers' U-2 spy plane over Russia in 1960.

A walk through the display buildings can produce the occasional surprise that doesn't take a doctorate in electronics to appreciate. Atop the Aeronautica Macchi stand sat a bright red airplane with twin floats and twin propellers at the front of its very pointy nose. It was the sole surviving Macchi-Castoldi M.C.72, and holder since 1934 of the World Speed Record for piston-engined water-based airplanes. In 1934 the open-cockpit craft was flown by Francesco Agello to an amazing 440.677 miles per hour. As of the writing of these words, the record has stood for over 65 years, or two-thirds of the history of the airplane.

Not all the men inspecting this quality mock-up of the Northrop F-17 Cobra are from potential customers. Some are intelligence agents from Soviet bloc nations. For their benefit, the airplane has been "modified" to conceal its true form. They probably get paid the same if they bring back good data or bad.
Don Berliner

8

DESIGNS
REFINED

*T*he 34th Salon International de l'Aeronautique et de l'Espace was held from June 5 through 14, 1981, at Le Bourget Aeroport. Since the previous shows, the Soviet Union had become bogged down in an unwinnable war in Afghanistan, which led to the American boycott of the 1980 Moscow summer Olympics. In April 1981, the Space Shuttle *Columbia* became the first successful aerospaceplane, landing like an airplane (OK, like a glider) after several days in earth orbit. Polish authorities began a crackdown on the independent labor union Solidarity.

Another Chinese fighter, the FT-7 trainer version developed from the Soviet MiG-21U. This one was fitted with a 23mm cannon in a gun pack. The FT-7 and the Ji-5 were the first Chinese military airplanes to be exhibited at Paris, and they indicated a strong interest in selling outside China. Presumably the lack of modern designs would be balanced out by low prices. Bernard Thouanel

Looking toward the airfield. At bottom are display buildings. At lower right, a prototype Concorde SST outside the Musee de l'Air. In front of the building is an Ariene space launcher, while across the center are the double rows of chalets. Beyond them is the actual airfield where Lindbergh completed his 1927 flight.
Flight International

In a year dominated by new-and-improved versions of established designs, Bell Aerospace's XV-15 tilt-rotor convertiplane stood out. After decades during which many companies tried to develop a combination helicopter/airplane using a wide variety of schemes, Bell apparently had pulled it off. At either tip of the XV-15's short wings was an engine and helicopter-like rotor that could be swiveled as a package. By tilting both rotors to be parallel with the ground, it could take off and land like a helicopter. Once in the air, it could tilt them forward, so they would act like airplane propellers. By avoiding the speed limitations of the conventional helicopter's advancing and retreating blades, it had far greater speed potential. It looked to have a bright future.

Airliner manufacturers Boeing, Lockheed, McDonnell-Douglas, and Airbus Industrie were busy trying to fill orders and plan for the future. Among the soon-to-be-successful ideas on display in the form of models were the advanced 747-300 with a stretched upper deck to provide additional passenger seating, rather than a lounge that produced no revenue, as in earlier 747s.

McDonnell-Douglas and Fokker were working together on a 150-seat MDF-100 that would go nowhere, though the designation would reemerge on the smaller Fokker F-100. Yet another dead-end scheme was a Boeing 727 with two engines in

place of three. But Boeing led the parade of new orders for new versions of its 737 and 767.

There was a decided lack of important new military aircraft in the static park, though France remained at center stage with delta-winged Mirages of various designations. The only new large military airplane was the U.S. KC-10 aerial tanker version of the standard DC-10 wide-bodied airliner. Visually it was rivaled only by the Soviet heavy-lift Mil Mi-26 helicopter, a primarily military machine that nevertheless appeared in Aeroflot airline colors and markings. Being claimed for it were a maximum payload of 44,000 pounds and cruising speed of 160 miles per hour.

The veteran Douglas A-4 Skyhawk, a U.S. Navy attack plane of the tailed-delta style, had gotten a thorough modernizing by the Israelis. But those in Israeli Air Force service are expected to be replaced soon by the indigenous Lavi, a single-engined, multirole fighter.

Italy's SIAI Marchetti showed off a new S-211 lightweight fighter that resembled several from other countries, and a turboprop version of its well-known SF.260 four-seat general aviation airplane.

The only new high-performance fighters were in the form of models and mock-ups. The Northrop F-6G Tiger Shark export fighter is expected to appear with high-tech avionics, though no customers had yet signed up. From Sweden came an advanced proposal to replace the SAAB Viggen with a canard-delta Fighter/attack/recco aircraft that would be called the Gripen.

Aerospatiale displayed an attack version of its Dauphin II helicopter. But most of what was new in the rotary area was in the equipment. Several firms showed off rotor mast-mounted avionics units that would enable a helicopter to aim and fire its weapons while remaining below the tops of sheltering trees.

One of the few categories offering a variety of new airplanes was general aviation. At the high end, Learjet flew one of its new winglet-equipped Longhorns nonstop from Newfoundland to Paris in just over 5 hours.

Other new general aviation types on display included a Cessna 425 Corsair, Mitsubishi Solitaire and Marquise, Swearingen Merlin IVC, and a Britten Norman Turbine Islander. Aerotalia

had a model of the turboprop version of its Partenavia AP.68TP Oscar, along with a model of a
proposed stretched version.

With fewer and fewer mass-produced American light planes being delivered, the French
increased their efforts to fill the void. Avions
Robin had the prototype of its all-metal, T-tailed
R3140 with a 140-horsepower Lycoming engine
and still some echoes of the original Jodels that
inspired its predecessors. Performance claims
included a cruising speed over 150 miles per hour,
and a maximum range of almost 1,000 miles.

*Big, impressive, and futile. Sitting atop the world's largest cargo plane, the six-engined Antonov AN-225, is the Buran, the USSR's answer to the American Space Shuttle. While the
external resemblance is almost total, the Soviet shuttle program never got as far as a manned flight.* Flight International

Another prototype attracted a different kind of interest. The Gyroflug Speed Canard from Germany was obviously under the influence of Burt Rutan and his Vari-Eze. It offered more room and higher speed than the popular homebuilt, and if it went into production could have a major impact on a segment of the aircraft industry that had so far resisted modernization, at least in the sense of radical design and structures.

While most of the new or improved helicopters were of the large, sophisticated sort, the little Robinson R22 offered a marked contrast. The first new piston-powered helicopter to appear in many years, it was simple and easy to maintain and would soon be seen in considerable numbers. Among the high-tech types, much of the talk was of Hughes' new tailrotor-less NOTAR version of its veteran 500. It would use a blast of air to create sideways lift to control torque and to turn the machine.

In the early days of the Paris Air Show, there were often new designs labeled "freaks," at least by journalists if not engineers. The term had long since faded out of existence, but not so the appearance of truly novel shapes. This year the prize went to the Australian Transavia Airtruk in its agricultural garb. With twin booms, a horizontal tail attached to each, and a central pod that defied description, it looked peculiar from every angle, but apparently worked. Almost as funny looking was the British Edgley Optica, with a bulbous nose like a two-seat Bell helicopter, a ducted fan behind the pilot, and twin booms. It offered unusually good visibility for pipeline patrol, aerial photography and other specialized functions.

Making its Paris debut was this one-of-a-kind, just-restored Maachi MC.205 Veltro. One of Italy's best World War II fighters, it was kept from fame by the general shortcomings of the Italian Air Force. Workmanship was the equal of any. Aermacchi

1983 PARIS AIR SHOW

The 35th Salon International de l'Aéronautique et de l'Espace was held at Le Bourget Aeroport from

A sunny day brings out the crowd. At left is a British Aerospace Corp. BAC-111 medium-range airliner. Beyond it is a Bae 125 executive jet, and at center right is a Bae Jetstream turboprop feeder liner. The large airplane at the rear with the "H" on its tail is a Short Belfast of Heavylift, a cargo hauler. Flight International

May 26 through June 5. Since the last show, U.S. President Ronald Reagan and Pope John Paul II had survived assassination attempts. An American Voyager probe had photographed Saturn, and two Soviet probes had landed on Venus. And Great Britain had won the brief little war with Argentina over the Falkland Islands.

The obvious star of the 1983 show was the boiler-plate Space Shuttle *Enterprise* that flew into Le Bourget atop its modified Boeing 747 carrier. Sadly, international terrorism had become so pervasive that the pair had to be parked on the far side of the field when not performing. And while flying around Europe on a tour, the 747 was equipped with countermeasure devices to fend off infrared missiles. Still, when it flew at Paris, the crowd loved it.

One of the other important items on display was not nearly so obvious. It was a new type of navigation with which a Rockwell Sabreliner flew across the Atlantic to stop within 25 feet of its planned parking spot using something called the Global Navigation System. Developed for the U.S. Department of Defense, it used a network of satellites to produce amazingly accurate location and speed information. Within a couple of decades, hand-held versions would be sold on the open market for less than $100, in a striking example of the impact of advanced technology on everyday life.

There was increased grumbling among the hundreds of aerospace firms that had been pouring hundreds of thousands of dollars into their displays and chalets. With other air shows forcing them to spread their resources, the common theme was, "Do we need all of this?" Some of them, such as Lockheed, McDonnell Douglas, and Pratt & Whitney, shifted their hospitality efforts to suites in downtown hotels. A few dropped out, only to be replaced by more. And most of them continued to spend and spend and spend.

Advanced concepts for fighters dominated parts of the show. British Aerospace Corp. was

The unquestioned star of the show: NASA's prototype Space Shuttle Enterprise, *flown across the Atlantic on its customized 747 carrier. The United States went all-out to impress the world with its space program, and with the potential of the Shuttle to greatly reduce the cost of orbiting satellites and conducting research.* Dan Hagedorn

If ever there was an airplane that shouldn't fly, this was it. The Guppy started out as the turboprop conversion of a Boeing C-97 Stratocruiser. The top was removed, and a great bulging upper deck was attached. With this, it could transport items so large that no other airplane could cope. Flight International

Two of Northrop's fighters: the gray RF-5E Tiger Eye and the red-and-white F-20 Tiger Shark. Many versions of the former were sold to small air forces, but efforts to establish the F-20 as a low-cost, high-performance answer to a lot of questions failed, despite ads featuring Chuck Yeager. Air Force Association

touting its Agile Combat Aircraft (ACA), able to launch a variety of missiles and thus replace the Tornado as the main RAF air defense airplane. The Tornado would, if the ACA entered service, become the first line of defense for North Atlantic convoys.

There weren't many new fighters on display, to the great displeasure of those who think the Paris Show should include as much noise as possible. Northrop's F-20 was there to try to stir up interest among some of the countries that operated its forerunner, the F-5, but little interest was shown. The French had yet two more Mirages: the 3NG with canard surfaces up front, and the 2000N two-seater equipped to deliver nuclear weapons.

Rockwell International displayed models of its advanced tactical fighter that stressed several futuristic concepts. It had a blended wing/body design,

with a delta wing having a curved leading edge. It was seen as capable of cruising at Mach 2 without afterburners. And the engines would have two-dimensional vectoring thrust nozzles to permit thrust vectoring in flight for enhanced maneuverability.

Northrop and Dornier had a joint design, the ND-102, with a highly tapered wing and no horizontal tail. It would rely on "tailerons" and vectored thrust for pitch control. Other German companies, however, had their own ideas, and no decision had yet been made on which direction to go.

There was more talk of airliners in the 100-seat range. Boeing and Fokker were looking at 100-seat variant of their big-sellers: Boeing of its 737 and Fokker of its F.28. At the same time, limited interest in the 150-seat A320 was pushing Airbus Industrie to take a second look at this range, the prototype of which had not yet flown.

Boeing was also talking stretches. The 737 would probably get a 10-foot fuselage extension to increase its capacity to 150 passengers. But there was less talk of a longer 747, as Boeing was expecting to concentrate on the 300 stretched-upper-deck version for the foreseeable future.

A major new player in the commuter market was DeHavilland of Canada, with its DHC-7 four-turboprop STOL airliner that could be stretched to carry 80 passengers. Along with it may well come the twin-engined DHC-8 with 30 seats, to compete with the SAAB-Fairchild 340.

Competition continued hot among firms building large engines for large airliners. For the Boeing 757, it was between the Rolls-Royce RB.211 and the Pratt & Whitney PW2037. For the 747-300, it was the P&W JT9D, the GE CG6, and the Rolls-Royce RB.211. All were in the 50,000 pounds of thrust range, which works out to around 80,000 horsepower at typical airliner cruising speed.

Not everything of interest at Paris was the latest design. The growing collection of enthusiast/replicator Jean Salis provided some

A view from a few hundred feet above the main entrance. At left is the original display building. At lower right are two of the four hangars containing the Musee de l'Air. In front of the left hangar is a Boeing 707 once flown by Air France. Beyond the double line of chalets is the airport. Flight International

unexpected flying thrills with its reproductions of the Deperdussin Monocoque that won the 1913 James Gordon Bennett Race and really introduced the world to streamlining. Along with it was a reproduction of a Breguet 14 single-engined bomber/long-distance record setter.

Not quite as surprising, but of far greater potential significance, were the homebuilt Piel CP.1320 and the modified Tampico, both using liquid gas for fuel and producing far less pollution than those pulping gasoline or kerosene.

1985 PARIS AIR SHOW

The 36th Salon International de l'Aeronautique et de l'Espace was held from May 31 through June 9 at Le Bourget Aeroport.

Since the last show, the Soviet Air Force had shot down a fully loaded Korean Airlines 747, insisting it had reason to think it was an American airplane on a reconnaissance mission. Later, two American astronauts "walked" outside their Space Shuttle completely free of tethers, thus becoming human earth satellites.

For what it's worth, the theme of the show was "The Aeronautical and Space Industry: A Trailblazer Industry for New Technologies." True enough, but the same could be said for the past few shows, and no doubt for the next few. Regardless, this was a big event, with more than 1,000 exhibitors from 33 countries occupying more than two million square feet of display space. To keep people and cars out of places someone thought they shouldn't be, they had erected almost 20 miles of fencing, to be patrolled by 20 miles of gendarmes.

As if to show that the Paris Air Show was still "le Salon," the French organizers all but shut it down on opening day to allow French President Mitterand to take a casual look at the displays. Those who were already on the show grounds had to stay put; those outside had to cool their heels until the presidential tour had ended. A lot of important people were unhappy.

The star of the week was one very large airplane, the Antonov An-124 Ruslan, a C-5 Galaxy look-alike with its own set of highly impressive statistics, or at least claims. Maximum take-off

Watercraft on dry land. In front is the Dornier Seastar multipurpose amphibian in white. Behind it, in yellow, is a Canadian CL-215 flying boat used mainly for fighting forest fires with water and chemicals. In back, flags identify the homelands of companies renting chalets.
Flight International

weight was said to be almost 900,000 pounds, and maximum payload 330,000 pounds. It was when one tried to find out its dimensions that confusion reigned. The length, according to various "authorities," was either 185 feet or 210 feet, while a brochure said about 220 feet. Could something so obvious be classified?

Among the serious technical types, the talk was mainly of exotic propellers: prop-fans, unducted fans, ultrahigh bypass engines. They featured many blades of wide chord and considerable curvature like scimitars. Among the claimed advantages were increased efficiency and reduced noise, the latter increasingly becoming a limiting factor, especially in Europe.

The fancy props were more than talk and sketches. Boeing announced it was ready to produce a medium-size airliner with turbofan engines driving unducted fans by the early 1990s. General Electric, in cooperation with France's Snecma, expected to have prototype engines ready for flight testing by Boeing in 1986 and by McDonnell Douglas a year later.

All the engine and propeller manufacturers had serious programs: P&W, Allison, and Hamilton Standard in the United States, leading a lot of people

to assume that a new era in aircraft propulsion was just around the corner. Others, who remembered past promises and predictions turning to dust, were more cautious. Airbus Industrie was one airframe manufacturer taking it easy, pointing to problem areas such as fatigue and de-icing, suggesting the state-of-the-art had not moved far enough forward to take the new propellers seriously.

One amazing device on display in the Soviet pavilion could easily have been included in the category of these new propulsors, but it was declared "just" an advanced propeller. It had a pair of contra-rotating, eight-bladed props with mildly curving blades made from some composite material. Was it a propaganda-driven effort to appear up to date? Or could it be a not-quite-so-high-tech scheme that just might work?

On a considerably higher plane, the U.S. Space Station had just become a truly International Space Station with the agreement with the European Space Agency (ESA) and with Japan for major contributions. ESA would design and build a laboratory module, a supply module and a service vehicle, while Japan would concentrate on materials and life sciences with a laboratory module and a free-flying experimental platform.

Delivery of materials and people to the Space Station would probably be handled by the Space Shuttle, though more advanced craft were in the design stage. British Aerospace had on display models of its HOTOL (Horizontal Take-Off and Landing) craft that looked like a cross between a Shuttle and a Concorde SST. It would take off from a runway and fly into orbit.

Power plants were also in the spotlight in the general aviation portion of the show. A Socata TB.16 had just received a modified Porsche engine based on the type in the 911 sports car. Pierre Robin showed off a DR.400 that had flown in to Le Bourget on a similar Porsche engine. And back at the engine factory, they had been flying a Mooney 231 on the same power for more than 100 hours. While scores of homebuilts have flown with converted auto engines, the manufacturing industry had shown little interest, despite the ready availability at lower cost, and the considerably greater mechanical sophistication when compared with traditional light plane engines.

A pair of Soviet trimotors. Nearer is a Yak-42 medium-range airliner. Behind it, a Tupolev Tu-154M that is in the same general class as a Boeing 727. In reality, the Soviet airliner only looks like a 727; the author can attest to its shortcomings as a passenger-carrier. But all shined up, they look great. Flight International

Teledyne Continental Motors, long the world's leading manufacturer of conventional horizontally opposed light plane engines, finally had something new: a series of liquid–cooled versions of its production engines. It also showed a series of Wankel (rotary combustion chamber) engines, but it would be one of those cooled mainly with ethylene glycol (antifreeze) that would help make history the next year.

In mock-up form, but not far from flight status, was Grumman's X-29 with its forward-swept wings. It had long been known that forward sweep has advantages over the popular rearward sweep. But it wasn't until the advent of practical, lightweight composite structures that the tendency of a wing to twist out of control in turbulence could be handled without an unacceptable increase in weight. If the research airplane was a success, production airplanes with forward-swept wings might become common.

Looking in the opposite direction, toward aviation history, there were two World War II airplanes of widely differing reputations. The French displayed a restored Dewoitine D.520 fighter of the 1939–40 period, when France's air force achieved so little. And the United States displayed a Boeing B-17G Flying Fortress, thousands of which bombed Germany's industries into rubble.

1987 PARIS AIR SHOW

The 37th Salon International de l'Aeronautique et de l'Espace was held at Le Bourget Aeroport from June 12 through 21.

Since the previous show, there had been two earth-shaking explosions: the nuclear reactor at Chernobyl in the Ukraine, and the Space Shuttle *Challenger* at Cape Canaveral. On a cheerier note, the Burt Rutan–designed *Voyager* had been flown around the world without stopping or refueling in

The wings sweep the wrong way! This full-size mock-up of Northrop's experimental X-29 features forward-swept wings. Theory says this is better than rearward sweep, but construction was too difficult prior to the advent of practical composite materials. Flight tests of the real thing seemed to bear out the theory. Flight International

The whole ball of wax. At the top, all the display buildings. At left, all the buildings of the Musee del'Air, and the hundreds of chalets. And in between, a couple hundred airplanes, helicopters, and sailplanes. Scattered around are, by actual count, a lot of people. Bernard Thouanel

One of several dozen radical airplanes designed by Burt Rutan. This Beech Starship went into production, but few were built, as its odd shape seemed to put off conservative corporation executives. Still, it was a foot in the door for efficient application of the laws of aerodynamics. Pierre Gaillard

the air, by Burt's brother, Dick, and Jeana Yeager. In the USSR, President Mikhail Gorbachev was shaking things up with his shocking demands for greater openness and democracy.

A lot of conversations on the ramp, in the chalets, and behind the scenes of the indoor displays concerned such matters as joint development and technology transfer, and the conflicts therein. The first referred to the increasing need for companies and even countries to cooperate on new projects, because of the costs. The second was a security concern: would the knowledge shared with a foreign partner for one high-tech project find its way into another for military hardware?

While the aerospace business had yet to come out of its long slump, it was hard to detect at Paris. Twenty-one countries displayed more than 230 types of aircraft, and the space rentals showed no drop over previous years' figures.

Probably the star of the show was the Rockwell B-1B swing-wing bomber that flew in from Texas in 11 hours, including 1 1/2 hours waiting for an arrival slot and clearance to make a low pass at Le Bourget. In the flying displays, the U.S. Air Force General Dynamics F-16C and McDonnell Douglas CF-18 showed they were the equals of everything, including prototypes of the French Rafale and the British Experimental Aircraft Program.

From other countries came versions of tried-and-true fighters. The Israeli Aircraft Industries upgraded F-4 Phantom II had more powerful P&W engines and was expected to grow canard surfaces. From China came the homegrown FT-7 interpretation of the MiG-19 and Ji-5 version of the MiG-21.

There were no major displays by the big American manufacturers of airliners, so the Soviets got more attention. Their Antonov AN-28 was a modern bush plane, available with skis and able to operate out of fields shorter than 2,000 feet. As an indication of the state of commuter airlines in that vast country, it was estimated by the Soviets that as many as 1,000 AN-28s were needed to replace a like number of AN-2s, radial-engined, fabric-covered biplanes with fixed landing gear.

At the opposite end of the scale, the USSR was planning its first modern production airliner, the Tupolev Tu-204 with a glass cockpit

and winglets. Even further into the future was a second-generation supersonic transport, despite the enormous cost in rubles and prestige of the failed Tu-144.

In the general aviation park were prototypes of the first two truly radical designs to go into production as executive airplanes. The Beech Starship, designed by Burt Rutan, and the Italian Piaggio P. 180 Avanti had their wings toward the rear, canard surfaces in the nose, and rear-facing and rear-mounted turboprop engines. The Starship used a great deal of composite materials in its construction, while the Avanti was conventionally aluminum.

There was a new category of single-engined general aviation airplane: the large, turboprop-powered craft meant for a variety of uses, especially freight hauling. Piper displayed its Malibu and

Cessna its Caravan. The spectacular Rutan *Voyager* round-the-world record setter was scheduled for display, but was bumped off a military cargo plane by a politician.

There was more space hardware on show than ever before, with the Soviets attracting the greatest interest with their full-scale mock-up of the new Mir space station. Included was the Kvant astrophysics research module, which was said to be able to carry commercial and foreign payloads into space for an advertised $15,000 per kilogram or $6,800 per pound.

France showed off a full-size model of its Hermes space plane, along with Germany's Columbus project for a manned free-flying laboratory meant to operate in conjunction with it. The Europeans were out to rival the American

A welcome from the representatives of mainland China. The Quiang Ji-5 is a ground-attack fighter developed from the Soviet MiG-19. It can carry air-to-ground weapons and air-to-air missiles, like the copy of the popular American AIM-9 Sidewinder heat-seeker.
Bernard Thouanel

The B-1 is one of America's front-line heavy bombers. It can carry a large payload of bombs and missiles for thousands of miles. This was the first appearance at Paris for the swing-wing bomber, and the crowds swarmed around it. Bernard Thouanel

From above. At left center, a row of Soviet airliners and the shuttle-carrying An-225. The smaller airplanes are on the far side of the wide parking area. At lower right can be seen a pair of American light twins taxiing out for take off. And at left in the far distance is Paris. Flight International

Space Shuttle as the International Space Station came closer to realization.

Private planes, of the two- and four-seat variety, had shown little change in the past couple of decades, but an Italian designer was out to change all that. Luigi Colani designed the airframe of the Cormoran CCE208, shown in mock-up. From its ultrasleek nose to the propeller mounted at the top-rear of its T-tail, it was clearly the work of an artist, not a practical engineer.

During the show, a prewar Lockheed 18 Lodestar completed an around-the-world flight from Paris to Paris in just 89 hours, beating the 91-hour record set in 1938 by Howard Hughes in a similar airplane. Even quicker was the 45-hour

flight around the world of a Gulfstream IV, also during the show.

1989 PARIS AIR SHOW

The 38th Salon International de l'Aeronautique et de l'Espace was held at Le Bourget Aeroport from June 9 through 18.

Since the last show, a PanAm 747 had been blown up over Scotland by terrorists, and *Voyager II* had taken close-up pictures of Neptune. But the big news was in Eastern Europe, where there were widespread rumblings of independence. During the month of the show, the Polish labor union Solidarity swept the Communists from parliament in the first free election since World War II.

The big visual hit of the show was the flying combination of the six-engined, twin-tailed Antonov AN-225 and its smaller friend, the Buran space shuttle. While the carrier was most impressive, and clearly the largest airplane currently in use, the shuttle was another matter. Nearly identical to the American Space Shuttle, it would never make a

A brightly painted Sukhoi Su-28 "Frogfoot" weapons trainer with its well-dressed pilot. It may actually have been an Su-25 that was displayed at Paris. Either way, it is a subsonic two-seater carrying a twin-barrel cannon, whose barrels can be angled downward by the pilot. Early versions were flown in Afghanistan. Bernard Thouanel

manned flight, ending its days as evidence of a major failure of the Soviet space program.

In general, the atmosphere at Paris was none too happy. Military budgets were being cut back everywhere, and forcing manufacturers and service organizations to reduce their staffs and operations. In order to stay in business, many of them were forced to resort to alliances with companies and countries long considered rivals.

Aerospatiale and Lockheed signed a "memorandum of understanding" during the show, agreeing to "identify, develop, and execute individual joint research and development, licensing, and/or production projects." Along with the merging of more companies, this suggested a serious drop in meaningful competition.

In addition, McDonnell Douglas and the French missile manufacturer Matra announced plans to jointly develop an air-to-air version of Matra's Mistral missile for helicopters. Rockwell

International and Panavia were looking into a Wild Weasel anti–aircraft version of the Tornado to replace the F-4.

The Soviets, meanwhile, were opening up in many ways. They adopted Western techniques that had long been symbols of "Western decadence," painting their airplanes in bright colors, distributing advertising brochures that actually included worthwhile information, and greeting potential customers with obvious pleasure. Only their lack of experience in marketing held them back.

In the sky, two Red Air Force fighters attracted unusual attention. The Sukhoi Su-27 was flown through some never-before-seen maneuvers by aerobatic ace Yevgeny Frolov, whose full control at extreme angles of attack stunned the crowd of knowledgeable observers. The crash of a MiG-29 dampened everyone's spirits, but the ability of its ejection seat to shoot the pilot out to safety from very low altitude was a great display of useful technology.

A camouflaged British Aerospace 146 commuter airliner, for which other uses are obviously being explored. Projected military uses include tactical airlift, parachute dropping, casualty evacuation, search and rescue, and even aerial refueling. Pierre Gaillard

A MiG-29 diving straight toward the ground after a major in-flight failure. The pilot has ejected and can be seen at left as his parachute starts to open. Thanks to an effective ejection seat and quick reactions, the pilot was not seriously injured, despite the low altitude at which he punched out. Bernard Thouanel

Airliners on display were mostly Soviet, as the big U.S. firms stayed away. The Tupolev Tu-204 looked as modern as anyone else's twin-engined airliner, with its glass cockpit (in which a few large cathode ray tubes replace dozens of little dials), and even winglets. The Ilyushin Il-96-300 four-engined wide-body appeared to be in the same class as Airbus' A340, but lacked much of the latter's sophistication.

The French had an A320 in the show, and announced healthy additions to its order book. Otherwise, it was smaller airliners being displayed. Czechoslovakia showed off the LET 610 development of its solid, successful LET 410 twin turboprop. Fokker had its turboprop F.27, now called the 50, along with its twin turbojet 100, formerly the F.28.

As further evidence of its willingness to work with its former foes, the USSR offered the use (for a price) of two flying laboratories to Western firms wishing to do research. A specially equipped Il-76 transport could be used for testing new engines with up to 27,500 pounds of thrust. It could fly them for as long as 8 hours, and as high as 15,000 feet. The An-124 (C-5A look-alike) was offered along with the necessary computer capability for analyzing transsonic air flow.

The most unusual machine among the many general aviation types was the Dornier Seastar, an amphibian with its two engines mounted in either end of a nacelle that was perched on struts above the fuselage. While much of the design was new, the engine arrangement had been seen at Paris a few decades before, but was not necessarily out of date.

BATTLE FOR MARKET SPACE

*T*he 39th Salon International de l'Aeronautique et de l'Espace was held at Le Bourget Aeroport from June 13 through 23, 1991. Between the 1989 and the 1991 shows, the world experienced some of the most drastic, yet peaceful changes in its history. The Berlin Wall was knocked down, and East and West Germany were reunified into a single Germany. The Cold War ended and the Warsaw Pact dissolved, leaving the nations of the old Soviet bloc independent. In South Africa, apartheid was outlawed, leading to majority rule for the first time. Only in Rumania was there any appreciable violence during the transition.

This is not a model airplane display, but the Paris Air Show. To squeeze thousands of airplanes and variants into the available space, extensive use must be made of scale models. These show current and future French fighters and transports in a way that people can get right up to them. Don Berliner

A modernized version of the classic big amphibian. This Beriev A-40 Albatross has a pair of advanced turbofan engines mounted high to keep them out of spraying water. A prototype set numerous world records, including lifting 10,000 kilograms to 33,000 feet. It was offered to wealthy westerners as a flying resort, but few showed interest.
Don Berliner

The brief, decisive Gulf War began and ended in a matter of days, as America demonstrated to Iraq and the rest of the world the overwhelming power of many of its most advanced aircraft, weapons, and electronic surveillance systems. In particular, the strange-looking Lockheed F-117 Stealth fighter slipped completely unnoticed through Iraqi air defenses, and then posed proudly on the ramp at Le Bourget for all to see.

A widespread recession was having a major impact on many aspects of the aerospace world, but this was hardly evident at Paris. A record 1,700 exhibitors from 21 countries had their products and services on view. And the line of expensive customer entertainment centers stretched for almost a mile.

Fear that the Gulf War would curtail the American and other countries' displays were all but forgotten when a wide variety of combat equipment was flown to Paris to form a victory exhibit. In the spotlight were U.S. Air Force, Navy, and Army fighters (F-14, F-15, F-16, F-18), attack bombers (A-10, AV-8B Harrier), and helicopters (AH-1W, CH-53E, SH-60B, CH-47D, and OH-58D).

Most of these aircraft had been seen at Paris before, and while that held true for the great majority of those on display, there were enough new types to maintain interest. The Russians (no longer the Soviets) were showing off the Ilyushin Il-114 60-passenger turboprop commuter airliner that would not have looked out of place or out of date on the ramp of any American airport.

The Beriev A-40 Albatross, on the other hand, was unlike anything shown at Paris in many years. It was a swept-wing, twin-turbofan amphibian with a wingspan of 137 feet and length of 128 feet. It was shown in its military version, with a nose-mounted refueling boom, but an airline version with a capacity of 100 passengers had a claimed cruising speed of 450 miles per hour and range of more than 3,000 miles. It was the most advanced such craft in the world, but any sales potential was hard to visualize.

Of even greater interest was the first publicly displayed MiG-31, a prototype of which had flown as far back as 1975. The 74.4-foot-long interceptor continued the line of high-tech MiGs that began with the MiG-25. With a pair of 34,000-pound turbofan engines, it had a claimed top speed of Mach 2.8 under unspecified conditions. More meaningful, if accurate, was the assertion that it could hit 1,865 miles per hour at 57,000 feet.

It was the most advanced Russian fighter known to be flying, and yet it was there, in a surprisingly sporty color scheme, for all the world to inspect, in stark contrast to the "old days" when the best were kept at home. For a while, the nose cone was off, revealing details of its electronically scanned, phased array fire control radar, said to be up to Western standards.

At the extreme opposite end of the scale, and unnoticed by most, was an accurate reproduction of the first airplane to fly in Europe, Alberto Santos-Dumont's type 14bis. The original was flown by the little Brazilian to the first World Air Speed Record (24.6 miles per hour) and Distance Record (720 feet) on the same day in 1906 in a park on the west side of Paris. The new 14bis was built by a Brazilian Air Force pilot who hoped to duplicate the flight after the air show. It was a wonderful reminder of how far aviation had come.

Everywhere one looked, so it seemed, there was Euro-this and Euro-that, as the emergence of the European Community was having a tangible impact on many phases of life. More and more rivals had become partners, in recognition of the difficulty in competing on even terms with the world-dominating United States.

Eurocopter was displaying its products: the Alouettes, Pumas, Gazelles, Dauphins, and other helicopters that long had gone under the Aerospatiale name. Bolkow, of Germany, was in the same boat. And there were new designs such as the Tigre and Panther ground-support helicopters.

Eurofighter was not yet so well developed, but was working hard on its first design, a Mirage-like delta wing with an under-fuselage air intake similar to that on the American F-16.

The American display, while it included more different types of aircraft than even the French, offered few that were of particular interest. Enstrom had an updated version of its Model 28 private helicopter. Swearingen's prototype SJ 30 four-passenger executive jet signaled the beginning of a new category of small biz-jets, many powered by the little Williams FJ turbojet that weighed 400 pounds and produced 500 pounds of thrust.

Perhaps most emblematic of the amazing changes in the old Soviet Union was the appearance of a slick little prototype three-seat light plane from the Yakovlev design bureau: the Yak-112. Using a lot of composite materials and powered by a 200-horsepower Lycoming IO-360 engine, it was to be certified to FAA standards so it could be sold in the United States. The Russians were eager to have foreigners inspect it at close range, and to answer questions with a previously unknown openness.

1993 PARIS AIR SHOW

The 40th Salon International de l'Aeronautique et de l'Espace was held from June 11 through June 20 at Le Bourget Aeroport.

Since the 1991 show, the USSR had been converted into something called the Commonwealth of Independent States, and its once-feared Communist Party outlawed. It may have been history's quietest major revolution, in stark contrast to the one that launched it in 1918. Now, Russia and the many former "republics" that made up the USSR could start to work on productive efforts, along with Poland, Hungary, Rumania, Bulgaria, and

This Egrett II is meant for high altitude research, using its wing of 103-foot span and sailplane-like aspect ratio of 27 to 1. With an 800-horsepower Garrett turboprop engine, it can climb above 45,000 feet and loiter for 10 to 12 hours at 200 miles per hour. This one is owned by the German branch of E-Systems and is used for classified work. Don Berliner

A Russian IL-96m in Aeroflot markings makes its first appearance at the 1993 show. Winglets combined with modern Western avionics and powerplants raised the standings of Ilyushin's flagship among its peers. Don Berliner

Fresh from its historic performance in the Gulf War, Lockheed's F-117 stealth fighter basks in the Bourget sun. After hearing about the futuristic craft with its curveless airframe, the Europeans got as close as Air Force guards permitted. Don Berliner

The French Dassault Rafale (Squall) is available in many versions, including a single-seat fighter for the Air Force and a two-seat interceptor and multirole fighter for the Navy. The Model D (for discreet, or stealthy) may or may not live up to its name. It has Mach 2 speed and is stressed to +9 and -3 1/2 g's. Bernard Thouanel

Czechoslovakia and the Baltic states of Estonia, Latvia, and Lithuania—once they figured out how to convert to democracy and capitalism.

Among the 22 nations displaying at Paris were first-timers Russia, Ukraine and the Czech and Slovak Republics that had just been created from Czechoslovakia. The Paris Air Show was among the first places for the world to see and feel the changes roaring through Europe.

Paris, of course, was concerned with the business of aviation and space, and this was where countries and their manufacturers found themselves allied with their foreign counterparts, regardless of decades or even centuries of hostility.

The rivalry between the United States and an increasingly united Europe was producing much-needed competition, and also some ill-conceived and doomed efforts. Money and brainpower were still going into efforts to replace the long-dominant Lockheed C-130 Hercules as the world's standard tactical transport, with the European future large aircraft. This, even though more than 2,000 of the American turboprops had been delivered to over 50 countries, and McDonnell Douglas was already flight testing an advanced turbojet tactical transport, the C-17.

But the main topic of conversation, if not of serious negotiations, was the grand effort of the Russians and other Eastern Europeans to modernize their industries with airframes powered by Western engines. On display was a prototype Ilyushin Il-96M wide-bodied airliner with Pratt & Whitney engines and Rockwell Collins avionics. Quite modern looking as it sat on the ramp, it would have to face the experience of Boeing (with its twin-engined 777 of similar size and performance) and the increasingly successful Airbus Industrie with its A340.

The manufacturers who thrive can usually trace their success to realistic advanced thinking. The latest objective of the big airliner builders was all the talk at Paris: the biggest airplane yet, a double-decked, 600-passenger airliner with a range of at least 8,000 miles. The expense of developing such a craft was clearly so large that Boeing and the Airbus countries were studying together, as well as separately.

In order to make such an airplane useful, even airports would have to be changed, as its estimated maximum take-off weight would be well over 1,000,000 pounds. It would require not the current engines rated at around 50,000 pounds of thrust, but an entirely new range of 90,000–100,000-pound engines. When Boeing launched its daring 747 in 1970, the world's largest builder of airliners risked everything. Now, an even larger program could risk the lives

of all the main manufacturers on the chance that airline traffic would grow for many years.

Of the 210 aircraft on display, few were new to Paris. Simple economics provided most of the explanation, as the cost of creating a new aircraft of appreciable size and complexity was zooming out of sight. Typical of the improved-rather-than-completely new were Israel Aircraft Industries modified Grumman Tracker and MiG-21 which displayed the ability of this smallest

The facility has grown every year, despite the ups and downs of the world's economics. This is almost the view a pilot gets as he approaches the main runway. At bottom center is a small portion of the VIP parking lot. Others are advised to arrive by excellent public transportation. Bernard Thouanel

143

The present and future of VTOL:
Bell/Boeing's sensational V-22 tilt-prop
convertiplane, and in the background, the
well-established British Aerospace
Harrier. Decades of development and
many millions of dollars have produced
aircraft that do anything a helicopter can
do, as well as anything an airplane can do.
Bernard Thouanel

One of France's and Europe's great hopes for the future: the wide-bodied Airbus A340 airliner. Almost as large as the popular Boeing 747, it is considered more of a pilot's airplane, having a user-friendly cockpit. For the passenger, it is as comfortable as any rival. Bernard Thouanel

To draw a crowd, slit the curtain of secrecy. At Paris, even the most blasé join the mob gawking at America's newest super airplane, Northrop's B-2 Stealth bomber. While the source of its ability to fool radar and infrared detection is mostly inside and still classified, the flying wing shape makes it very special. Bernard Thouanel

aerospace nation to compete effectively with the giants by not biting off more than it could chew.

A new category of very small transports/freighters was now established in the air as well as on display: the large single-turboprop. The amazing reliability of the turboprop engine, combined with its high power-to-weight ratio, made it ideal for commercial airplanes designed to carry 6 to 10 passengers. Pilatus of Switzerland displayed its prototype PC-12, Socata of France offered its XII TBM 700, and Cessna had a Grand Caravan alongside its Citation executive jets.

Encouraging growth was seen among sport aircraft. Brazil and France showed slick new motor gliders. There were almost 20 microlights, mainly from France but also from Belgium and the United States. The availability of a strong sponsor, in this case Breitling, the upscale Swiss watchmaker, led to daily demonstrations of modern competition aerobatics by pilots from the United States, Great Britain, Germany, and France, flying German Extra and French CAP high-powered monoplanes.

1995 PARIS AIR SHOW

The 41st Salon International de l'Aeronautique et de l'Espace was held at Le Bourget Aeroport from June 11 through June 18, two days less than in recent years.

Since the last show, the myopic Hubble Space Telescope had been repaired in space, a Russian cosmonaut had flown in the American Space Shuttle, and Britain and France had been connected by a 22-mile rail tunnel under the English Channel.

The air show was the biggest yet, with almost 1,600 exhibitors from 37 nations. On static display were around 200 different types of aircraft, including more truly unusual and interesting ones than in many years.

Attracting the bulk of the attention was the sinister looking Northrop Grumman B-2 stealth bomber. A huge flying wing, it combined Northrop's unequaled experience in creating all-wing airplanes, with the latest in stealth technology, most of which remained highly classified. If its appearance at Paris was intended to demonstrate American technological supremacy, it was a total success, as no other country's long-range heavy bomber could hope to match its radar-evading design.

Almost as unusual looking, though of considerably less significance, was the Airbus Beluga Super Transporter, the latest in a series of novel cargo haulers with great bulging fuselages. Starting several decades ago with Pregnant Guppy conversions of Boeing C-97 freighters, it had progressed to this Airbus A300 with an enormous upper deck to carry sections of airplanes and space vehicles that were too large for any other form of transport.

Hardly as flashy as either of these airplanes, but of considerable long-term significance, was Boeing's latest wide-bodied airliner, the 777, which entered service less than a week before the show opened. It offered improved passenger comfort, despite having as many seats as the latest Airbus A340, and almost as many as a 747, while being longer than its big brother. All on two engines, which gave it improved economy and what looked like a rosy future.

To place the Boeing-Airbus rivalry directly in front of the world, the latter had examples of its newest on display: the four-engined A340 and its twin-engined version, the A330. The former was starting to sell well, while the latter was lagging.

Still in the wings was the long-talked-about successor to the 747. The Airbus A3XX would have to be designed from scratch, while a two-deck 747 probably could be created more easily, cheaply, and quickly. All that held back design and production was the difficulty in determining if the airlines and their passengers were sufficiently interested to warrant one or even two of the largest and riskiest programs ever considered. Had the 747 failed in 1970, Boeing probably would have collapsed. Now, a super-747 could take several major companies with it if the demand failed to materialize. As a result, Boeing and Airbus were cautiously exploring some form of cooperation. The Russians, despite valiant efforts to jump into the mid-1990s, were unable to sell their best to airlines strapped for money and thus more conservative than ever.

French Mirage delta-winged jet fighters had been a staple of the Paris Air Shows since the mid-1960s, and there were both old and new ones on show, despite the redirection of efforts onto new lines. But this time, there was something a bit different in the way of Mirages: South Africa's Atlas

Denel Cheetah. The first of these converted Mirage IIIs were followed by more extensively modified machines, and they have been standard equipment for several SAF squadrons since the days of apartheid and boycotts.

The array of business airplanes was the most extensive ever, as the industrywide recession was easing. Some 30 types of turboprops and turbojets were parked in the ever-expanding Le Bourget ramp, with almost all being variations on familiar themes. But not all of them had familiar names, thanks to continuing mergers. What began life as the Hawker Siddeley 125 in 1965 had become the DeHavilland 125 and then the British Aerospace 125. It was now the Raytheon Beech Hawker Models 800 and 1000, to be built by Raytheon (formerly Beechcraft!) in Kansas.

Truly modern design was finally starting to make itself known among the light planes at Paris. Grob, of Germany, was displaying a prototype GF-200—a sleek four-seater with a structure of composite materials, center-mounted engine driving a pusher propeller in the tail, and a pressurized cabin. Its original Porsche engine had been replaced by a 270-horsepower, six-cylinder Lycoming airplane engine that was expected to produce a cruising speed of 245 miles per hour. If

It may look something like a blimp, but it's an airplane that can carry the bulkiest of loads. The special Airbus A300-Beluga can also climb at a surprisingly steep angle, at least when it is very lightly loaded. It is a custom-built airplane, as there is limited need for its special capabilities. Bernard Thouanel so, there might finally be a small airplane that could out-perform the venerable Beech Bonanza, which first appeared in 1946.

Most of the other light planes were of traditional design and construction, and even had non-retracting landing gear. Thus they continued to trail a long list of well-proven homebuilt designs in performance, efficiency, and visual appeal.

At the opposite end of the scale were the space displays, which continued to expand. The Russians, no doubt hoping for tie-ins with Western companies that would provide desperately needed financial support and sales know-how, came through with their best showing yet. At center stage were displays related to Russian participation in the International Space Station, the most expensive and complex program ever attempted. There were scale models of the complete modules that were scheduled to be launched into orbit for attachment to the first part of the station in 1998.

The French continued to struggle with their promising Ariane 5 launch vehicle which, if ultimately proven, could rival anything the United States had for economical orbiting of commercial payloads. A full-size Ariane launcher had been part of the Le Bourget skyline for many years.

The need for a new generation of fighters was yet another major topic of conversation at Paris. In the United States, where domestic requirements were sufficient to justify terribly expensive programs, the Lockheed (now Lockheed Martin) F-22 Raptor was flying, and prototypes were being built for a major competition to build the Joint Strike Fighter for the Air Force, Navy, and any foreign air arms with large amounts of cash.

Current top-of-the line fighters on the ground and in the air at Paris included the French Rafale, the Swedish Gripen, the Russian Sukhoi Su-35, and the American F-15E and F-16. All were actively being promoted to potential buyers as obviously superior to the others.

1997 PARIS AIR SHOW

The 42nd Salon International de l'Aeronautique et de l'Espace was held from June 15 to 22 at Le Bourget Aeroport.

Records were once again set: 1,860 exhibitors from 46 countries with 230 aircraft, 405 chalets/customer hospitality centers, and three million square feet of display space. A total of 286,000 visitors, while not a record, was nevertheless a lot of people from a lot of different places.

Since the last one, an American Space Shuttle had docked with the Russian Mir space station and NASA had apparently found evidence of ancient life in a meteorite from Mars. Boeing had merged with Rockwell International (née North American) and was about to join forces with McDonnell Douglas, leaving just three major American aerospace firms: Boeing, Lockheed-Martin, and Northrop-Grumman.

The talk among high-level executives from several countries was of cooperation vs. autonomy. There was a need to balance the economic and technical advantages of major firms working together, with the need, especially in Europe, of retaining some degree of independence. With national barriers falling throughout Europe, many feared the disappearance of whole countries in the rush to streamline business.

Hovering over all of this was the increasing world dominance of the United States. With no other super power as a military rival, the Americans were busy trying to lock up entire industries, or so it appeared to many Europeans. The mergers of aerospace manufacturers into a few mega-corporations promised greater efficiency that would be hard to challenge, especially when

This Blackjack is no game. It is the Tupolev Tu-160, Russia's top long-range strategic bomber. Equipped with variable-sweep wings and four 55,000-pound Samara turbofans, it has a claimed maximum speed close to Mach 2. With a range of more than 8,000 miles, it can reach most places on earth without refueling. Bernard Thouanel

The Rockwell X-31 continues a long and valuable tradition of research airplanes in the X-series. This one features enhanced maneuverability. Not aimed at production, its value will be in what is learned from test flights that can be incorporated into future fighters. Bernard Thouanel

promises of greater cooperation in Europe kept bumping up against the remains of national pride.

The most obvious rivalries concerned airliners. But these were being pushed down by the need to work together. The need to compete to see who would corner the market for super wide-bodies was tempered by the real fear that the market wouldn't be large enough to support more than one series of airplanes larger than a 747. Or maybe none. Nevertheless, Airbus continued to talk about an A3XX, and Boeing kept reviving its super-747. When the first 747 appeared in 1970, it seemed ridiculously large, but went on to be one of the industry's biggest money makers. With the chance that this could happen again, no one wanted to completely resign from the race as long as there was hope.

At another end of the scale, there were more and more pure-jet commuter airliners, and they were selling well. Leading the way was the EMB-145 from Brazil's EMBRAER, continuing to surprise those north of the equator with its corporate and design skills. Rivals included the Canadair Global Express. While among the turboprop commuters, Indonesia joined the fray with its IPTN N250 with American engines, British propellers, and 50 seats.

The smallest of the new airliners, and certainly the most revolutionary, was present in mock-up form. The Bell-Boeing 609 was the commercial version of its successful V-22 tilt-wing convertiplane. This one was envisioned taking off from a city park within walking distance of great office buildings, and whisking executives to meetings 200 miles away in less total time than the fastest of airliners or executive jets. It was worth keeping an eye on.

The military portion of the show was more talk than hardware. The American competition to develop a versatile, stealthy Joint Strike Fighter for all its air arms was clearly of interest to the

Even though Russia is deeply embedded in economic problems, it still designs and builds prototypes of advanced military aircraft, which it hopes to sell to other countries. This new Mil Mi-28N is an all-weather gunship loaded with French avionics and Russian weapons. India was apparently the most likely customer. Tim Senior via Robert F. Dorr

More first-rate airplanes from Brazil: the EMBRAER Super Tucano light jet trainer/ground support fighter-bomber. It is powered by a 1,600-horsepower P&W of Canada turboprop engine, driving an American Hartzell prop. It has attracted interest from many countries and is expected to become commonplace. Tim Senior via Robert F. Dorr

Europeans. If its Research and Development costs could be absorbed by hundreds of units produced, it could be cheaper than any comparable homegrown advanced fighter. The thought of such future reliance on Uncle Sam did not go down well with everyone, however.

The biggest new military machine on display was McDonnell-Douglas' C-17 Globemaster III, which fits between the C-130 Hercules and the C-5A Galaxy. It could lift at least three times the payload of a C-130, and almost as much as a Galaxy, even though it was considerably smaller.

An interesting example of international cooperation was on view as the Yak-130 light jet trainer that was being built jointly by Yakovlev and Aeritalia of Italy. It was obvious that the demise of the old USSR had resulted in a lot of unused capacity in factories and design offices, and this might keep some of that from being put to use in helping some unpopular but wealthy Middle Eastern states.

Among the largest of business jets, there was a healthy rivalry developing between Boeing, with

its executive version of the 737-700, and Airbus with a similar modification of its A319. The need for such large executive airplanes had been growing for several years. A far different need was addressed by the nifty-looking little Yak-58, a twin-boom six-seater with a shroud around its pusher propeller. One of its proposed functions was radio-jamming, which might make it of interest to highly competitive rock stations.

After many years out of production due to the high cost of liability insurance, new Cessna 172s and 182s were on display. Their price tags were the sort to stimulate the used airplane market. Israviation, of Israel, showed off its version of the Cirrus Design VK-30 homebuilt, called an ST-50. It boasted an exceptionally clean fuselage with a rear-mounted engine and pusher prop.

With the growth of already large twin-engined airliners, such as the Boeing 777 and Airbus A330, there came a need for very powerful engines, well beyond the 50,000–60,000-pound range used for many years. The call was answered by Pratt & Whitney with its PW4098, GE with its GE90, and Rolls-Royce with a new Trent. The first of these would probably go into the stretched, long-range 777-200X that would equal the 747 in size and thus need engines in the 110,000–115,000-pound thrust range.

Finally, there were airplanes at Paris that didn't quite fit the standard categories. Lockheed showed off its "flying hospital" conversion of a TriStar airliner. Airbus flew an A300 fitted out for microgravity and zero-gravity experiments. There was a Lockheed 10E like the one in which Amelia Earhart was lost, and which had just completed her flight. A new production Waco YMF open-cockpit biplane was offered those who like the wind in their hair, but were not up to building their own 1930s airplane from scratch.

1999 PARIS AIR SHOW

The 43rd Salon International de l'Aeronautique et de l'Espace was held from June 12 through 20 at Le Bourget Aeroport.

Since the previous show, ice had been detected at the Lunar poles, a balloon had finally been flown around the world after many failures, and NATO had added former Warsaw Pact nations

Hungary, Poland, and the Czech Republic over the muted protests of the Russians.

The show grounds exceeded two million square feet (49 acres) of display space, occupied by more than 1,750 exhibitors from 40 countries. The chalet rows included over 450 units in which companies large and small entertained potential customers with food and wine from some of the finest Paris restaurants and caterers. Despite the skyrocketing cost of developing new aircraft, there were some 200 on display, almost half of them also taking part in flying exhibitions.

The status of the overall aerospace industry was well stated by a reporter from the British weekly *Flight International*, "The speed with which the U.S. industry has acted to improve its long term survival and competitiveness just served to spotlight the indecision and inability within Europe to rise above its obsessions with national rivalry, egotistical leadership and governmental meddling."

As bad as that sounds, reality was actually better for the Europeans and worse for the Americans. The centuries-old obstacles faced in Europe were being overcome at a rate higher than anyone could have predicted, while American firms such as Boeing and Lockheed seemed to be frittering away their lead through questionable management and slipping quality control.

The most interesting military aircraft on display was a helicopter, the Boeing RAH-66 Comanche, the first seriously stealthy combat helicopter on its way to quantity production. The U.S. Army expects to use it for reconnaissance, ground support, and aerial combat. It was said to be the first fully fly-by-wire craft of its type.

Among the large military and/or civil aircraft, the most attention was directed at the Antonov AN-70, a hefty freighter powered by four turboprop engines, each driving novel contra-rotating propellers, in which the front prop had eight blades and the rear prop only six. One cannot help but wonder how large a bonus was required to find someone to hand-prop this contraption.

As has long been the case at American air shows, the most striking new design was from the fertile mind of Burt Rutan. His Proteus

A bevy of French private and executive airplanes. Closest is a TB.9 Club, F-GSAO is a TB.21, F-GLBJ is a TBM.700, F-GLBL is a TBM.700, F-WWRT is a TB.360 Tanagara, and F-GNHG at far right is a TB.200XL. All are in competition with similar American airplanes, which long had the market to themselves. SOCATA

A joint project between Yakovlev in Russia and Aer Macchi in Italy to design, build, and produce a light jet trainer. It is hoped that the Yak-AEM-130 will replace the Czech-designed L-39s long used to train Russian Air Force pilots. The blended wing-body design is for aerodynamic efficiency, not for stealth. Aer Macchi

One of the European Union's finer achievements, the Eurofighter EF.2000. This one is in Italian Air Force markings, but later ones will sport a variety of insignia. The crowd, dressed against the chill of mid-June, appreciates the sleek lines as it taxies past prior to its flight demonstration. British Aerospace

multipurpose high-altitude cruiser had a shape completely unlike anything previously seen at Paris or anywhere else. It wasn't there as a novelty, but rather as the prototype of a platform for lifting communications and research packages to high altitude for long periods of time.

As has been the case at Paris for quite a long time, much of the attention was focused on new airliners and new versions of older ones. A great batch of orders for EMBRAER, topping 100, was revealed at Paris, bringing the total for its Regional Jet 135s and 145s to more than 900. This is a figure previously associated with the major manufacturers, and gave a big boost in stature to the Brazilian firm.

What would you give to be able to listen in on their conversation? Are they studying weapons their airplanes or helicopters may carry in the future? Or are they worried that some future enemy may drop or fire these things at them? Could they be engineers spying on a rival's latest products? Don Berliner

Another entry in the medium-size airliner race was the Boeing 717 (previously known as the McDonnell Douglas MD-90, and before that the Douglas DC-9). Boeing was on a sales tour with it and expected to rack up orders. At the far end of its scale, the off-again-on-again 747-400X was back on.

Lightweight military jet trainers continued to appear, despite the presumably limited market. The latest was the Mako, from DaimlerChrysler Aerospace, which was touting a recent study suggesting a demand for more than 5,000 airplanes in its class over the coming 25 years.

Among the newer Russian airplanes was a Sukhoi Su-30MK destined for India. Like a MiG-29 10 years before, it crashed directly in front of the crowd, just after its two-man crew had ejected safely. They placed blame on the display organizers, who had insisted on a shortened flight demonstration for which they were unable to practice. This was generally accepted, and the ejection seat makers experienced a lot more traffic at their display booth.

While engines have always been a major part of the Paris Air Show, their very mechanical nature usually keeps them from the spotlight. This time, however, a giant GE90 high-bypass turbofan towered over nearby exhibits, making clear that it might well develop the 100,000–115,000 pounds of thrust claimed by its makers. The Boeing 777-200X was expected to be the first airplane to use this power plant.

The big space project, the International Space Station, was progressing slowly, in great part due to the inability of the Russians to come through with their vital early modules on time. Launch dates kept getting postponed, and more

This Boeing/Sikorsky RAH-66 Comanche was making its first visit to Paris. The two-seater is the most stealthy of all the known helicopters, and was generally kept at a distance from spectators, though superficial tours were given to the press. Don Berliner

and more doubt was being expressed about the long-term need for this most expensive project.

Alongside the Ariane 5 launcher from France was a new Anagara 1.1 launcher that the Russians hoped to market as a commercial vehicle. There was no explanation given for its being almost completely different from the Anagara previous displayed.

One group of airplanes stood out from all the rest, not because of their radical shapes or even the flashy promotion. Several World War II fighters appeared in Breitling colors (yellow noses) and performed in some of the daily demonstrations: P-51 Mustang, F4U Corsair, Supermarine Spitfire, Curtiss P-40, and an Hispano Buchon, which was a Rolls-Royce–powered Messerschmitt 109 built in Spain. They brought back memories to all the older show attendees, although the memories were not always pleasant.

Burt Rutan does it again. His umpteenth completely different, radical-design airplane was one of the centers of attention at Paris. The Proteus was built by Scaled Composites and carries Raytheon equipment on long flights at high altitude, where it serves as a platform for communications. Don Berliner

EPILOGUE

*I*n 90 years of Paris Air Shows, almost the entire history of aviation and the space age has been on display. Not just the hardware, but the ideas as well. Ideas that would lead to big jumps forward, and ideas that would die quickly and be forgotten.

Other shows have come and gone, but Paris carries on, continuing to grow despite the ups and downs of the economy. As the world has changed, so has the Paris Air Show. It has reflected the huge events in world history: World War I, the Great Depression, World War II, the Cold War, Korea, Vietnam, the Gulf War, and finally the fall of Communism.

Right from the start, there has been no better place to see the newest and the best and sometimes the oddest. If you had a product or a service to sell to the aviation community, or later the aerospace community, Paris was the place to show it off and to brag about its superiority.

If you wanted to meet important people in the industry and in the related agencies of every air- and space-minded government, Paris was the only place to be. If you were such a person, you had to be there, for all your rivals were sure to be on the scene, promoting their needs and their ideas and waving fistfuls of money in the faces of men and women who could have been your customers.

As for airplanes, no series of shows has ever offered the variety and the completeness: more than 2,700 different types and versions of airliners, military planes, general aviation planes, and helicopters. It was like a full set of *Jane's All the World's Aircraft* come to life.

Not only more kinds of airplanes seen at Paris, but more glasses of champagne and more sales brochures were handed out, and more film was exposed, than anywhere else in aviation history.

It began as the place to see airplanes, for few people had experienced anything of the sort prior to World War I. Today, while it is primarily a marketplace, it remains the place to see airplanes of all shapes and sizes and functions.

It is difficult to imagine the aerospace world without the Paris Air Show. For this, we must thank the French. While at times their nationalism seemed on the verge of going out of control, it was their clear vision of the need for such an event that has kept it in the forefront for almost the entire twentieth century. For this, we offer a toast in the finest of French champagne!

APPENDIX

Aircraft on display
Pre—World War II
Aero A.23 — 1928
A.I.R.9 — 1934
Airco — 1919
Albatross — 1911
Albatross ASS — 1928
Allar — 1938
Amiot 122 B.P.3 — 1928
Amiot 142 M — 1934
Ansaldo A.300T — 1921
A.N.T.35 — 1935
Antoinette — 1909
Arado two-seat biplane —1928
Arado Ar.69 — 1934
Armstrong-Whitworth Ajax — 1926
Armstrong-Whitworth Atlas — 1930
Armstrong-Whitworth Scimitar — 1934
Armstrong-Whitworth Siskin 5 — 1924
D'Artois flying boat — 1912
D'Artois torpille — 1912
Astra — 1911
Astra hydro biplane — 1912
Aubert P.A.20 Cigale — 1938
Aubert P.A.204 Cigale Major — 1938
Autoplane — 1909
Avia — 1909
Avia B.H.11 — 1926
Avia B.H.26 — 1926
Avia B.H.33 — 1928
Avia 51 — 1934
Avia 534 — 1934
Aviatik — 1911
Avimeta AVM 88 — 1926
Avions Atalante G.B.10 — 1938
Avions Gerard Club 145 — 1938
Avro 626 — 1934

Bathiat-Sanchez monoplane — 1913
Bathiat-Sanchez steel pusher — 1913
Bellanger — 1922
Benes & Mraz Be 555 Superbibi — 1938
Bernard twin — 1919
S.I.M.B. Bernard Type C — 1922
S.I.M.B. Bernard V.2 — 1924
Bernard (Ferbois) 15 C.1 — 1926
Bernard H.V.42 — 1930
Bernard H.52C.1 — 1934
Bernard 73S — 1930
Bernard 75 C.1 — 1932
Bernard 191 GR — 1930
Bernard 191 T — 1928
Bernard 200 TS — 1932
Bertin monoplane — 1912
Besson canard — 1912

Marcel Besson triplane — 1919
Besson H.6 — 1919
Marcel Besson M.B.35 Submarine Scout — 1926
Sanchez Beza biplane — 1912
Sanchez-Beza multiplane — 1921
Bleriot — 1909
Bleriot XI — 1909–13
Bleriot Popular — 1911
Bleriot cross-country — 1911
Bleriot racer — 1911
Bleriot two-seater XI-2 — 1911–13
Bleriot Aeronef — 1911
Bleriot monocoque — 1913
Bleriot hydro — 1913
Bleriot pusher — 1913
Bleriot-SPAD — 1919
Bleriot Mammoth 4-engine — 1919
Bleriot 45 — 1921
Bleriot-SPAD 34 — 1921
Bleriot-SPAD 51 — 1924
Bleriot-SPAD 61 — 1924–26
Bleriot-SPAD 81 — 1924
Bleriot-SPAD S.91 — 1928–30
Bleriot 165 — 1926
Bleriot 111 — 1930–32
Bleriot 125 — 1930
Bleriot amphibian — 1932
Bloch 80 — 1932
Bloch 91 — 1932
Bloch 92 — 1932
Bloch 131 — 1936
Bloch 151 — 1938
Bloch 162 B-5 — 1938
Bloch 211 BN4 — 1938
Borel monoplane — 1911
Borel two-seater — 1911
Borel hydro — 1912
Borel military two-seater — 1913
Borel military hydro — 1913
Borel military torpile — 1913
Borel S.C.I.M. — 1922
Boulton & Paul — 1919
Breda 15s — 1930
Breda 19 — 1932
Breda 25 — 1932
Breda 27 — 1934
Breguet double monoplane — 1911
Breguet biplane — 1912
Breguet monoplane flying boat — 1912
Breguet mono-float — 1913
Breguet float biplane — 1919
Breguet C2, type XVII — 1919
Breguet limousine — 1919
Breguet 14 T bis — 1921

Breguet 14 G.R. — 1926
Breguet XIV bis — 1922
Breguet XIX d'Oisy — 1924
Breguet 19A2 — 1921
Breguet 19 H — 1926
Breguet XXII Leviathon — 1922
Breguet 26 T — 1926
Breguet 28 T — 1926
Breguet 41 M4 — 1934
Breguet 46T Fulgur — 1934
Breguet 280 T — 1928
Breguet 270 A2 — 1930–32
Breguet 462 B4 Vultur — 1935
Bristol two-seater — 1911, 1912
Bristol two-seat military — 1913
Bristol Babe — 1919
Bristol Blenheim — 1936
Bristol Bulldog — 1930–32
Bristol Bullet — 1919
Bristol 143 — 1934
Bucker Bu.131 Jungmann — 1934

C.A.M.S. 30E — 1922
C.A.M.S. 33B — 1924
C.A.M.S. 37A — 1926
C.A.M.S. 53 — 1928
C.A.M.S. 55-6 — 1932
C.A.M.S. 80 — 1930
C.A.M.S. 160 — 1938
C.A.O. 200 — 1938
Caproni — 1919
Caproni 97 — 1932
Caudron biplane — 1911
Caudron monoplane — 1912
Caudron hydro biplane — 1912
Caudron hydro pusher — 1913
Caudron land plane — 1913
Caudron trimotor — 1919
Caudron trimotor biplane — 1921
Caudron C.27 — 1922
Caudron C.59 — 1922
Caudron C.60 — 1921
Caudron C.67 — 1922
Caudron C.68 — 1922
Caudron C.99 — 1924
Caudron C.104 G.R. — 1926
Caudron C.109 — 1928
Caudron C.140 — 1928
Caudron C.195 — 1930
Caudron C.232 — 1930
Caudron C.282 Super Phalene — 1932
Caudron C.460 — 1936
Caudron C.480 Fregate — 1934
Caudron C.520 Simoun — 1934
Caudron C.600 — 1934

Caudron — 1934
Caudron C.690 Rafale — 1936
Caudron C.714 — 1938
Caudron G.3 — 1922
Caudron trimotor — 1930
Caudron/Vizcaya P.V.200 — 1932
Chauviere — 1909
Cieva C.30A — 1934
Clement-Bayard — 1909, 1911
Clement-Bayard monoplane — 1912
Clement-Bayard three-seater — 1912
Clement-Bayard steel single-seater — 1913
Clement-Bayard steel two-seater — 1913
Louis Clement monoplane — 1919
Louis Clement triplane — 1919
Couzinet 20 — 1930
Couzinet 33 — 1932

Daspect — 1938
DeDion-Bouton — 1909
DeHavilland 80 Puss Moth — 1930
DeMonge-Buscaylet 52C 1 — 1922
Deperdussin school — 1911
Deperdussin military — 1911
Deperdussin two-seater — 1911
Deperdussin three-seater — 1911
Deperdussin 1912 racer — 1912
Deperdussin Gilbert record — 1913
Deperdussin 1913 Monocoque — 1913
Deperdussin hydro — 1913
Descamps A.2 — 1926
Dewoitine D.1.C.1 — 1925
Dewoitine D.7 — 1924
Dewoitine D.14 — 1924
Dewoitine D.27 fighter — 1930
Dewoitine D.27 trainer — 1930
Dewoitine D.30 — 1930
Dewoitine D.35 — 1930
Dewoitine D.412? — 1932
Dewoitine D.500 — 1934
Dewoitine D.510 — 1936
Dewoitine D.511 — 1934
Donet-Leveque hydro-biplane — 1912
Dornier D.S. — 1930
Dornier Do.17 — 1938
Drzeweicki canard — 1912
Santos-Dumont Demoiselle — 1909
Dutheil-Chalmers — 1909
Dyle et Bacalan D.B. 10 — 1926

L'Elytroplan — 1938
Esnault-Pelterie — 1909, 1911
R.E.P. hydro monoplane — 1912

Fairey Firefly II — 1932

Fairey Fox II — 1932
Farman — 1909
Maurice Farman — 1911
Maurice Farman headless hydro — 1913
Henri Farman — 1911
Henri Farman hydro — 1912
Henri Farman sesquiplane — 1913
Farman 2-engine Goliath — 1919
Farman school biplane — 1919
Farman 4-engine — 1921
Farman torpedo/Goliath — 1921
Farman 1-engine Goliath — 1922
Farman day bomber — 1922
Farman cabin monoplane — 1922
Farman Jabiru — 1924
Farman recco — 1924
Farman F.160 — 1926
Farman F.170 — 1926
Farman F.180 deLuxe — 1928
Farman F.190 — 1928
Farman F.200 — 1930
Farman F.224 — 1936
Farman F.231 — 1930
Farman F.301 — 1930
Farman F.355 — 1932
Farman F.360 — 1932
Farman F.393 — 1934
Farman F.400 — 1932
Farman F.403 — 1934
Farman F.404 — 1934
Farman F.431 — 1934
Farman F.2234 — 1938
F.B.A. 100-horsepower hydro — 1913
F.B.A. 130-horsepower hydro — 1913
F.B.A. 16 HE2 — 1922
Fernandez — 1909
Fiat — 1919
Fiat AS.2 — 1930
Fiat CR.20 — 1926
Fiat CR.30 — 1932
Fiat CR.32 — 1934
Fiat F.22 — 1928
Fiat G8 — 1934
Fiat TR.1 — 1930
Fieseler Fi. — 1934
Focke-Wulf FW.44 Stieglitz — 1934
Fokker — 1928
Fokker 1911 Spin — 1924
Fokker C.V. — 1926
Fokker C.VIII-W — 1930
Fokker D.XIII — 1924
Fokker D.23 — 1938
Fokker F.3 — 1921
Fokker F.VII-3m — 1926
Fokker F.IX — 1930

Fokker G.1 "Le Faucheur" — 1936

Galtier G.30 — 1938
Gangier — 1909
General Transaerienne — 1919
Gordou 832 — 1936
Goupy — 1911
Goupy hydro — 1912
Goupy tandem two-seater — 1913
Goupy single-seater — 1913
Gregoire-Gyp — 1909
Guillemin J.G. 40 Avion Sanitaire — 1930

Handley-Page — 1919
Handley-Page Hanley — 1922
Hanriot — 1909
Hanriot pursuit — 1922
Hanriot C.D. racer — 1921
Hanriot H.10 ED 2 — 1930
Hanriot H.D. 14 school — 1921–22
Hanriot H.34 — 1924
Hanriot H.31 — 1924
Hanriot H.35 — 1926
Hanriot H.41 — 1926
Hanriot H.41S — 1926
Hanriot H.180 — 1934
Hanriot H.180T — 1934
Hanriot 220 — 1936
Hanriot H.232 — 1938
Hanriot H.431 — 1928
Hanriot H.460 — 1928
Hanriot N.C. 510 T.3 — 1938
Lorraine-Hanriot L.H.13 — 1932
Lorraine-Hanriot L.H.21S — 1930
Lorraine-Hanriot L.H.130 — 1932
Hawker Fury — 1934
Hawker Hart — 1932
Hawker Hurricane — 1938
Heinkel He.5 — 1928
Heinkel He.70 — 1934

Junkers W.33 — 1928
Junkers Ju.52 — 1934

Kauffmann — 1911
Kellner-Bechereau cabin monoplane — 1932
Kellner-Bechereau double-wing — 1938
Klemm-Daimler — 1928
Koechlin — 1909
Koolhoven F.K. 31 — 1922–24
Koolhoven F.K. 35 — 1926
Koolhoven F.K. 55 — 1936

Latecore single engine — 1919
Latecore Trimotor — 1919
Latecore LAT.6 — 1922
Latecore F.15 — 1924
Latecore F.16 — 1924
Latecore F.17 — 1924
Latecore Lat. 28 — 1930

Latecore Lat.29 — 1932
Latecore Lat.350 — 1930
Letov S.231 — 1934
Letov S.528 — 1936
Levasseur — 1919
Levasseur torpedo — 1921
Levasseur school — 1921
Levasseur — 1922
Levasseur naval pursuit — 1924
Levasseur shipboard recco — 1926
Levasseur VI C.2 — 1926
Levasseur 7.T Limousine — 1926
Levasseur P.L.11 — 1930
Levasseur P.L.12 — 1930
Levasseur P.L.72 B2B — 1928
Levasseur P.L.151 — 1932
Levasseur P.L.200 — 1934
Lignel 20s — 1938
Lignel 31 Mistral — 1938
Loire 45 — 1938
Loire 46 — 1936
Loire 130 — 1938
Loire et Olivier — 1911
Loire et Olivier trimotor — 1919
Loire et Olivier float plane — 1922
Loire et Olivier flying boat — 1922
Loire et Olivier LeO H.18 — 1928
Loire et Olivier LeO 20 BN3 — 1928
Loire et Olivier LeO 21 — 1926
Loire et Olivier H.22 — 1930
Loire et Olivier LeO H.27 — 1930
Loire et Olivier LeO H.24 — 1934
Loire et Olivier LeO H.25 — 1932
Loire et Olivier LeO H.30 — 1932
Loire et Olivier LeO H.190 — 1926
Loire et Olivier LeO 203 — 1930
Loire et Olivier autogyro — 1936
Loire Gourdou Leseurre L.G.L. 32 C.1 — 1926
Loire Gourdou Leseurre L.G.L. 33 C.1 — 1926
Loire-Nieuport 250 — 1936

Macchi M.52 — 1928
Macchi MC.72 — 1934
Magni "Vale" — 1934
Marçay-Moonen — 1911
Edmond de Marcay cabin biplane — 1919
Mauboussin 112 — 1934
Mauboussin 120C — 1934
Messerschmitt M.35 — 1934
Messerschmitt Me.108 — 1934
Miles Monarch — 1938
Morane-Saulnier school — 1911
Morane-Saulnier racer — 1911
Morane-Saulnier military two seater — 1911
Morane parasol — 1913
Morane Garros replica — 1913
Morane standard two-seater — 1913

Morane-Saulnier single-seat parasol — 1919
Morane-Saulnier two-seat parasol — 1919
Morane-Saulnier cantilever
    monoplane — 1922
Morane-Saulnier M.S.35 E.P.2 — 1926
Morane-Saulnier M.S. 121 C1 — 1928
Morane-Saulnier M.S. 129 E.T.2 — 1926
Morane-Saulnier M.S. 130 E.T.2 — 1928
Morane-Saulnier M.S. 132 E.T.2 — 1926
Morane-Saulnier M.S. 140 — 1928
Morane-Saulnier M.S. 224 — 1930
Morane-Saulnier M.S. 225 — 1932
Morane-Saulnier M.S. 230 — 1930
Morane-Saulnier M.S. 275 — 1934
Morane-Saulnier M.S. 301 — 1930
Morane-Saulnier M.S. 315 — 1932–34
Morane-Saulnier M.S. 332 — 1932
Morane-Saulnier M.S. 341 — 1934
Morane-Saulnier M.S. 405 — 1936
Morane-Saulnier M.S. 406 — 1938
Morane-Saulnier M.S. 430 — 1936
Moreau monoplane — 1912
Moreau stability monoplane — 1913
Mureaux — 1919
Mureaux Express Marin — 1926
Mureaux M.4C.2 — 1928
Mureaux M.B.35 — 1928
Mureaux III R.2 — 1930
Mureaux 113 R2 — 1934
Mureaux 115 R2 — 1934
Mureaux 140-T — 1932
Mureaux 160-T — 1932
Mureaux 170 C.1 — 1932
Mureaux 180 C.2 — 1934
Mureaux 190 C.1 — 1936
Mureaux 200 A.3 — 1936

Nieuport school monoplane — 1911
Nieuport two-seater — 1911
Nieuport hydro monoplane — 1912
Nieuport-Dunne — 1913
Nieuport armed military — 1913
Nieuport racer — 1913
Nieuport tandem two-seater — 1913
Nieuport C.D. sesquiplane — 1921
Nieuport Astra cabin biplane — 1919–21
Nieuport Astra 29 — 1932
Nieuport-Astra 29C.1 — 1922
Nieuport-Astra 37C.1 — 1929
Nieuport-Delage 37C sesquiplane — 1922
Nieuport-Astra Delage 42 C2 — 1924
Nieuport-Astra 541 — 1930
Nieuport-Astra 641 — 1930
Nieuport-Delage 42 C.A. — 1926
Nieuport-Delage 48 C.1 — 1926
Nieuport-Delage twin — 1928
Nieuport-Delage metal sesquiplane — 1928
Nieuport-Delage 82 — 1930
Nieuport-Delage 590 — 1932

Nieuport-Delage long-range recco — 1932
Nieuport-Delage tail-less — 1932

Pander light monoplane — 1924
Paulhan-Train — 1911
P.N.A.E. L.2 — 1930
P.N.A.E. P.VI — 1930
Ponche and Primard — 1911
Ponnier rigid l.g. monoplane — 1913
Ponnier flex l.g. monoplane — 1913
Potez cabin biplane — 1919
Potez military two-seater — 1921
Potez limousine — 1921
Potez trimotor airliner — 1921
Potez S.E.A. IV P.M. — 1919
Potez Type VII sporting biplane — 1919
Potez VIII — 1922
Potez XVIII — 1922
Potez XI CAP2 — 1922
Potez 25 A.2 — 1926
Potez 28 G.R. — 1926
Potez 32 — 1928
Potez 35 — 1928
Potez 36 — 1930
Potez 39A2 — 1930
Potez 40 — 1930
Potez 43 — 1932
Potez 45 — 1932
Potez 49 — 1932
Potez 51 — 1932
Potez 54 — 1934
Potez 56 — 1934
Potez 58 - 1934
Potez 60 — 1934
Potez 63 — 1936–38
Potez 452 — 1936
Potez 662 — 1938
P.Z.L. P.VIII — 1930
P.Z.L. P.XI — 1932
P.Z.L. P.11c — 1934
P.Z.L. P.24 — 1934–36
P.Z.L. P.26 — 1934
P.Z.L. P.43 — 1936
P.Z.L. Elan — 1938
P.Z.L. Mouette — 1938
P.Z.L. Silure — 1938
P.Z.L. Wilk — 1938

R.E.P. single-seat monoplane — 1913
Raoul-Vendome — 1909
Ricci R.6 single-seat triplane — 1921
Ricci R.9 two-seat triplane — 1921
Romano R.80 — 1936
Romano R.82 — 1938
Romeo Ro.5 — 1930
Romeo Ro.5s — 1930
R.W.D.6 — 1932

S.A.B.C.A. S.47 — 1938

S.A.F.A. Koolhoven F.K.43 — 1932
Saint Nazaire Richard-Penhoet — 1926
Savary biplane — 1911
Savoia S.53 — 1922
Savoia-Marchetti S.55 — 1928
Savoia-Marchetti S.66 — 1932
Savoia-Marchetti S.80 — 1934
Schmitt tractor biplane — 1913
Schneider — 1922
Schneider twin-boom — 1924
Schreck 290 HM4 — 1930
Schreck F.B.A. 310 — 1930
S.E.C.M. Letece XX — 1921
S.E.C.M. 12 B.N. 2 — 1924
S.E.C.M. XXIII — 1922
S.E.C.M. fighter — 1928
S.E.C.M. Amiot 140 M — 1930
S.E.C.M. Latham 110 — 1932
Sloan biplane — 1911
Sommer biplane — 1911
SPAD-Herbemont S.27 — 1919
S.P.C.A. single-engine — 1932
S.P.C.A. trimotor — 1930
S.P.C.A. trimotor — 1932

Tampier roadable — 1921
Tampier T.2 — 1924
Tampier T.3 — 1924
Tampier T.4 — 1924
Tipsy cabin — 1938
Tipsy open — 1938
Train monoplane — 1911
Tubavion — 1912

Vickers Viking — 1919
Vickers Vimy commercial — 1921
Vickers Supermarine Spitfire — 1938
Vinet monoplane — 1911
Vintlon helicopter — 1909
Voisin canard — 1911
Vought V-156 Vindicator — 1938

Weymann two-seater — 1930
Wibault Wib. 121 — 1928
Wibault Wib. 170 — 1938
Wibault 280T10 — 1930
Wibault-Penhoet 282 T 12 — 1932
Wibault-Penhoet 365 T 7 — 1932
W.L.D. monoplane — 1909

Zodiac — 1911, 1912
Zodiac Mauboussin M.121 — 1932

Post–World War II
A-15 sailplane — 1965
ADEM Moldavia Favorite — 1997
Adventure Paramoteur — 1999
Aerfer Sagittario II — 1957
Aeritalia AP.68TP Spartacus — 1983

Aeritalia/Aerfer AM-3C — 1971, 1973
Aeritalia AMX — 1987
Aeritalia/Fiat G.91Y — 1971—73
Aeritalia/Fiat G.222 — 1971, 1975—81, 1987
Aermacchi AL.60 B2 — 1963—65
Aermacchi AL.60 F-5 — 1969
Aermacchi LA.60 military — 1965
Aermacchi S.211 — 1997
Aermacchi S.211A — 1999
Aermacchi SF.260E — 1997—99
Aermacchi M.290TP Redigo — 1997
Aermacchi MB.326 — 1963—65
Aermacchi MB.326G — 1969—73
Aermacchi MB.326K — 1971—79
Aermacchi MB.339 — 1975—79, 1985, 1993
Aermacchi MB.339A — 1981—85
Aermacchi MB.339B — 1987
Aermacchi MB.339C — 1987, 1991
Aermacchi MB.339CX — 1999
Aermacchi MB.339FD — 1997
Aermacchi MB.339K — 1981—87
Aermacchi MB.339PAN — 1983
Aero L.1 Blanik — 1959
Aero L-29A Akrobat — 1969
Aero L-39 Albatross — 1977—79
Aero L.40 Meta Sokol — 1959
Aero L.60 Brigadyr — 1959
Aero L-139 — 1993, 1999
Aero L-159 — 1999
Aero L-200D Morava — 1963
Aero L-410 Turbolet — 1969
Aero L-410 UPV Turbolet — 1979
Aero 45 — 1949
Aero Baroudeur — 1987
Aero Boero 115 — 1989
Aero Boero 180 — 1989
Aero Commander Grand Commander — 1963
Aero Commander 680T/Astafan — 1971
Aero Commander AC.1211 Jet Commander — 1963—65
Aerocentre Martinet — 1946
Aeroduc HLM-01 — 1987
Aeroduc RW-152 — 1987
Aero Kuhlmann Scub — 1995, 1999
Aeromere F.14 Falco — 1961
Aeromot AMT 100 Ximango — 1993
Aeromot AMT 200 Super Ximango — 1993
Aeroresources Super J-2 — 1973
Aerospacelines Guppy — 1983
Aerospatiale Caravelle — 1981
Aerospatiale Caravelle 12 — 1971
Aerospatiale Corvette — 1981
Aerospatiale (Nord) N.262 Fregate — 1971
Aerospatiale (Nord) N.262C Fregate — 1977
Aerospatiale SE.313B Alouette II — 1975
Aerospatiale SA.315A Lama — 1969—71
Aerospatiale SA.315B Lama — 1971—77

Aerospatiale SA 316B Alouette III — 1971, 1975, 1981
Aerospatiale SA.318C Alouette Astazou — 1969—71
Aerospatiale SE.319 Alouette III — 1971, 1975—77
Aerospatiale SA.319B Alouette III — 1973—75
Aerospatiale SA 319C Alouette II — 1969
Aerospatiale SA.321F Super Frelon — 1969
Aerospatiale SA.321G Super Frelon — 1975
Aerospatiale SA.321J Super Frelon — 1969—73
Aerospatiale SA.330 Puma — 1969, 1975—77, 1981, 1985—89, 1995
Aerospatiale SA.330 Mk.II — 1989
Aerospatiale SA.330BA — 1983
Aerospatiale SA.330C Puma — 1971
Aerospatiale SA.330F Puma — 1971, 1973
Aerospatiale SA.330G Puma — 1975
Aerospatiale SA.330J Puma — 1979
Aerospatiale AS.332 — 1979, 1983—84
Aerospatiale AS.332B — 1981
Aerospatiale AS.332C — 1983
Aerospatiale AS.332F — 1983
Aerospatiale AS.332L — 1983
Aerospatiale AS.332M1 — 1985—87
Aerospatiale SA.340 — 1969
Aerospatiale SA.341 Gazelle — 1969—75, 1983, 1989, 1995
Aerospatiale SA.341G Gazelle — 1975—77
Aerospatiale SA.342 Gazelle — 1975—77
Aerospatiale SA.342 HOT — 1987
Aerospatiale SA 342G Gazelle — 1977
Aerospatiale AS.342J — 1981
Aerospatiale AS.342L — 1981
Aerospatiale SA.342M/AS.342M Gazelle — 1979—87, 1995
Aerospatiale SA.350 Ecuriel — 1977, 1989
Aerospatiale SA.350B/AS.350B Ecureil — 1979—87
Aerospatiale AS.350B1 — 1987
Aerospatiale AS.350L1 — 1985—87
Aerospatiale SA.355 — 1985, 1989
Aerospatiale AS.355F Ecureil II — 1981—83
Aerospatiale AS.355F2 — 1985—87
Aerospatiale SA.360 Dauphin — 1973—75
Aerospatiale SA.360C Dauphin — 1977, 1981
Aerospatiale SA.361 — 1979
Aerospatiale SA.361H — 1977—79
Aerospatiale SA.361N — 1979
Aerospatiale SA.365 Dauphin — 1975—79, 1987—89
Aerospatiale AS.365C — 1981—83
Aerospatiale AS.365F — 1983—87
Aerospatiale AS.365M Panther — 1985—87
Aerospatiale AS.365N — 1981—85
Aerospatiale SN.600 Corvette — 1973—75
Aerospatiale SN.601 Corvette — 1975—79

Aerospatiale SE.1221 Djinn — 1975
Aerospatiale SE.3160 — 1969—71, 1985
Aerospatiale Socata TB-9 Tampico — 1981
Aerospatiale Socata TB-10 Tobago — 1981, 1985—89
Aerospatiale Socata TB.16 — 1985
Aerospatiale SocataTB.20 Trinidad — 1981, 1985, 1989
Aerospatiale Socata TB.21 — 1987
Aerospatiale Socata TB.21C Trinidad — 1985
Aerospatiale Socata TB.30 Epsilon — 1981, 1985—89
Aerospatiale Socata TBM 700 — 1989
Aerostar MiG-21 Lancer — 1997
Aerostructure Lutin 80 — 1983
Aerosud Avid Flyer — 1985
Aerotechnik L.13 SDM — 1995
Aerotek Hummingbird — 1993
Agstar microlight — 1989
Agusta A.106 — 1969
Agusta A.109 — 1973—75, 1979—83, 1987
Agusta A.109A — 1977, 1981, 1985
Agusta A.109 Mk.II — 1981—87
Agusta A.109 Mk.II Medevac — 1985
Agusta A.109 Mk.II Widebody — 1985
Agusta A.109 Power — 1995—97
Agusta A.109BA — 1993
Agusta A.109K — 1985—87
Agusta A.109K2 — 1993—95
Agusta A.109WB — 1987
Agusta A.109MAX — 1991
Agusta A.119 Koala — 1995
Agusta A.129 — 1985—87
Agusta A.129 HOT — 1987
Agusta HH-33F — 1981
Agusta-Bell 47G — 1955
Agusta-Bell 47G-3 — 1961, 1965
Agusta-Bell 47G-4 — 1965, 1969
Agusta-Bell 47J — 1957
Agusta-Bell 47J-3 Super Ranger — 1961
Agusta-Bell 47g-JZA — 1965
Agusta-Bell 102 — 1959
Agusta-Bell 105B
Agusta-Bell 204AS — 1971
Agusta-Bell 204B — 1961, 1965
Agusta-Bell 205 — 1965, 1969—73
Agusta-Bell 205A1 — 1969, 1971
Agusta-Bell 206 — 1977
Agusta-Bell 206A JetRanger — 1969—75
Agusta-Bell 206A-1 — 1973
Agusta-Bell 206B — 1975—77, 1985
Agusta-Bell 212 — 1971—77
Agusta-Bell 212ASW — 1975—77, 1983
Agusta-Bell 214 — 1981
Agusta-Bell AB.412 — 1983—87
Agusta-BoeingVertol CH-47C — 1977
Agusta-Finmeccanica A 109 Power — 1999
Agusta-Finmeccanica A 109 VIP — 1999
Agusta-Finmeccanica A 199 Koala — 1999

Agusta-SIAI S.211 — 1991
Agusta-Sikorsky AS.61N1 — 1985
Agusta-Sikorsky SH-3D — 1971—75
AI (R) ATR.72 — 1997
AI (R) ATR.72-210A — 1997
AI (R) Avro RJ — 1995
Airbus Industrie A300B — 1973—75, 1979
Airbus Industrie A300B2 — 1977
Airbus Industrie A300B2 (zero-g) — 1997
Airbus Industrie A300B4 — 1981
Airbus Industrie A300B4 Freighter — 1995
Airbus Industrie A300-300 — 1995
Airbus Industrie A300/600 — 1985
Airbus Industrie A300/600 ST Beluga — 1999
Airbus Industrie A310 — 1983, 1993—95, 1999
Airbus Industrie A319 — 1997
Airbus Industrie 319J — 1999
Airbus Industrie A320 — 1987—91, 1999
Airbus Industrie A321 — 1993, 1999
Airbus Industrie A330 — 1993
Airbus Industrie A330/200 — 1999
Airbus Industrie A340 — 1999
Airbus Industrie A340-200 — 1993
Airbus Industrie A340-300 — 1993—97
Air Creation XP.5825 — 1993
Airmas 386 — 1987
Airship Industries Skyship 500 — 1983
Airship Industries Skyship 600 — 1985
Airspeed Ambassador — 1969
Airtech (CASA-Nurtaneo) CN-235 — 1985
Airtech CN235-100 — 1991
Airtech CN-235QC — 1991
Airtrainer CT/4A — 1975
Alpavia D2 Rabouyt Heliplane — 197
Alpavia RF33 — 1965
Ambrosini S.7 — 1951—53
Ambrosini S.110 Grifo — 1949
American General AG-5B Tiger — 1993
American Jet Industries T.610 Super Pinto — 1971
AMX — 1985, 1989—91
AMX-T — 1991
Antonov AN-2 — 1997
Antonov AN-12 — 1965
Antonov AN-22 — 1969
Antonov AN-24 — 1965
Antonov AN-24RT — 1969
Antonov AN-26 — 1971—75
Antonov AN-28 — 1979, 1987
Antonov AN-30 — 1975
Antonov AN-32P — 1993
Antonov AN-38 — 1995
Antonov AN-70 — 1999
Antonov AN-72 — 1979—81
Antonov AN-74 — 1987
Antonov AN-74T — 1991
Antonov AN-74TK — 1997
Antonov AN-74 TK 200 — 1999

Antonov AN-124 — 1985—87
Antonov AN-124-100 — 1999
Antonov AN-225 — 1989
Armstrong Whitworth AW. 52G — 1946
Armstrong Whitworth AW.650 Argosy — 1959
Armstrong Whitworth AW.650 Argosy C.1 — 1961—63
Arsenal AIR 100 — 1949
Arsenal AIR 102–1953
Arsenal Ars-4-111 — 1949, 1953
Arsenal V.B.C.1 — 1946
Arsenal VG 70-01 — 1946
Atlas Denel Cheetah — 1995
ATR 42 — 1985—93
ATR 42-500 — 1995
ATR 42-MP — 1999
ATR 72 — 1989—93
ATR 72-210 — 1993—95
ATR 72-500 — 1999
Paul Aubert PA-204 Cigale-Major — 1953
Auster — 1953
Averso AX-02 — 1995
Averso Snoopy — 1995
Avia — 1946
Avia 14 — 1957
Aviamilano F.8 Falco — 1957
Aviastar microlight — 1989
Aviasud Albatross — 1995—97
Aviasud Albatross 6.SEV — 1993
Aviasud Albatross 80.EV — 1993
Aviasud Mistral — 1987
Aviasud Mistral 6.SEV — 1993
Aviasud X-Pair — 1993
Aviatika 890 — 1993
Aviatika 890U — 1993
Aviatika 900 — 1993
Aviatika Locafly — 1995
Aviatika Locafly Duster — 1995
Aviation Farm J5 motor glider — 1993
Aviette man-powered — 1977
Avione Craiova IAR 99 SOIM — 1999
Avions Moniot APM20 — 1995
Avions Moniot Lionceau — 1995
Avro Anson — 1999
Avro Shackleton — 1953
Avro 707A — 1953
Avro Vulcan — 1955, 1963—65
Avro Vulcan B-2 — 1959—61
Avro RJ85 — 1995
Avro Canada CF-100 — 1955

BAC Jet Provost T.5 — 1969, 1977
BAC Lightning F.1A — 1965, 1969, 1971
BAC Lightning F.6 — 1971
BAC Lightning F.53 — 1969
BAC H 126 — 1965
BAC 167 Strikemaster — 1969, 1975—77
BAC 167 Strikemaster B4 — 1971
BAC 111 — 1971, 1977

BAC 111-201AC — 1979
BAC 111-400 — 1975
BAC-Sud Concorde — 1969, 1997
BAC-Vickers VC-10 — 1963
BAC Super VC-10 — 1965
BAe 125 — 1989
BAe 125/700 — 1981—83
BAe 125-800 — 1987
BAe 125-800B — 1985, 1991—93
BAe 146 — 1989
BAe 146-100 — 1983—85
BAe 146-200 — 1985
BAe 146-200A — 1987
BAe 146-300 — 1987—91
BAe 146 RJ70 — 1991
BAe 1000 — 1993
BAe ATP — 1987—93
BAe EAP — 1987
BAe (Percival) Jet Provost T.5 — 1979
BAe (Hawker-Siddeley) HS.748 Srs. 2A — 1989
BA3 (Hawker-Siddeley) HS.748 Srs. 2B — 1981—83
BAe (Hawker-Siddeley) HS.748 Multirole — 1981
BAe Hawk T.1 — 1981—83
BAe Hawk 100 — 1991, 1999
BAe Hawk 200 — 1987—89, 1997—99
BAe Jetstream 31 — 1983—85, 1989
BAe Jetstream 41 — 1995
BAe Nimrod AEW.3 — 1981—83, 1999
BAe Harrier GR.5 — 1987—89
BAe Harrier GR.7 — 1995—99
BAe Sea Harrier FRS.1 — 1981—85
BAe Tornado — 1999
BAF Dragon — 1983
Beagle-Auster Airedale — 1961
Beagle Bassett — 1965
Beagle Pup 150 — 1969
Beagle (BAE) Bulldog — 1969, 1979
Beagle 206 — 1963—65, 1969
Beagle 206S — 1969
Beagle B 242 — 1965
Bede BD-5 — 1973
Bede BD-5J — 1977
Beech D.18 — 1963, 1975
Beech A23 Musketeer II — 1965
Beech A.24R Musketeer Super R — 1971
Beech 33 Debonair — 1961
Beech 33 Debonair 285 — 1969
Beech B33 Debonair — 1965
Beech F.33A Bonanza — 1971—73, 1987
Beech 35 Bonanza — 1961
Beech S5 Bonanza — 1965
Beech A.36 Bonanza — 1969, 1977—81, 1991, 1995
Beech A.36 Turbo Bonanza — 1987
Beech G.50 Twin Bonanza — 1961
Beech 55 Baron — 1961, 1973
Beech 58 Baron — 1971, 1975—79

Beech 58P Baron — 1977
Beech Duke — 1975
Beech Queen Air 70 — 1969
Beech 76 Duchess — 1979—81
Beech 80 Queen Air — 1965, 1969
Beech 90 King Air — 1965
Beech C90 King Air — 1971, 1975, 1979, 1991
Beech C90A King Air — 1991
Beech E90 King Air — 1973
Beech F90 King Air — 1981
Beech D95A Travelair — 1965
Beech 99 — 1969, 1987
Beech A100 King Air — 1973
Beech C100 King Air — 1971
Beech Super King Air 200 — 1975—83, 1987
Beech Super King Air 200 T — 1985
Beech King Air 300 — 1985—89
Beech King Air 300AT — 1993
Beech Super King Air 350 — 1991—95
Beech Super King Air 350AT — 1993
Beech 400 Beechjet — 1987—89
Beech 400A Beechjet — 1991—95
Beech 1900 — 1983—85, 1989, 1993
Beech 1990D — 1995
Beech 2000 Starship — 1987—89
Beech 2000A Starship — 1993
Beech C-12C — 1979
Beech YT-34C Turbo Mentor — 19757
Beech T-34C Turbo Mentor — 1979, 1987
Beech Seminole — 1965
Beech Pilatus PC-9 Mk. II — 1995
Belgian Aerospace M 80 Masquito — 1999
Bell 47 — 1953
Bell 47D-1 — 1951
Bell 47G — 1969, 1971
Bell 47G-2 — 1955
Bell 47H — 1955
Bell 204 — 1959
Bell 206 Jet Ranger — 1999
Bell 206A Jet Ranger — 1969, 1973, 1981
Bell 206B Jet Ranger — 1989—91
Bell 206B Jet Ranger III — 1997
Bell 206L Long Ranger — 1977, 1981, 1987
Bell 206L-4 Long Ranger IV — 1997
Bell 206LT Twin Ranger — 1993
Bell 206NTH Jet Ranger — 1993
Bell 212 — 1973
Bell 214B — 1975—77
Bell 214ST — 1983—85
Bell 222 — 1977, 1981, 1987
Bell 222A — 1985
Bell 222B — 1987
Bell 222UT — 1983
Bell 230 — 1993
Bell 406 Combat Scout — 1985
Bell 407 — 1997—99
Bell 412 — 1981, 1997—99
Bell 412 EMS — 1995

Bell 412EP — 1997
Bell 412SP — 1985—89
Bell 427 — 1999
Bell H-13 Sioux — 1961
Bell TH-57A — 1969
Bell OH-58 — 1987—89
Bell OH-58D — 1995
Bell AH-1F — 1987, 1991
Bell AH-1S — 1977
Bell AH-1W — 1991, 1995—99
Bell UH-1B Iroquois — 1963
Bell UH-1D — 1965
Bell UH-1G Huey Cobra — 1969
Bell UH-1H Huey — 1993
Bell UH — 1HP Huey II — 1993
Bell XV-15 — 1981, 1995
Bell Agusta Aerospace AB 139 — 1999
Bell Agusta Aerospace BA 609 — 1999
Bell-Boeing XV-22 — 1995
Bell-Boeing 609 — 1997
Bellanca 7GCBC Citabria — 1975
Bellanca 8GCBC Scout — 1975
Bellanca 8KCAB Decathalon — 1975
Bellanca Super Decathalon — 1997
Bellanca Turbo Viking — 1975
Beriev A-40 — 1991
Beriev Be-30 — 1969
Beriev Be-32 — 1993
Bertin Terraplane — 1965
Besneux P70-B — 1973
Beta Air (Beriev) BE 200 — 1999
Biman Flexwing — 1995
Blackburn NA.39 Buccaneer — 1959
Blackburn Buccaneer S.1 — 1963
Bleriot XI (Reproduction) — 1969
Bleriot XI-2 — 1973
Boeing 707 — 1979
Boeing 707-138B — 1981, 1991
Boeing 707-321B tanker — 1997
Boeing 707-323C — 1981
Boeing 707Q — 1985—87
Boeing 707 Phalcon AEW — 1993
Boeing 717-200 — 1999
Boeing 727-100 — 1983—85
Boeing 727-2D6 — 1971
Boeing 727-30 — 1981
Boeing 737-300 — 1991
Boeing 737-700 — 1997
Boeing 747 — 1969
Boeing 747 Shuttle Carrier — 1983
Boeing 747-200 — 1973
Boeing 747F — 1975
Boeing 767 — 1983
Boeing 777 — 1995—97
Boeing B-17G Flying Fortress — 1985
Boeing YC-14 — 1977
Boeing E-3A AWACS — 1977, 1983—85
Boeing E-3F AWACS — 1991—93
Boeing T-43A — 1977
Boeing QSRA — 1983

Boeing UH-46A Sea Knight — 1965
Boeing CH-46C Chinook — 1969
Boeing CH-47 Chinook — 1995
Boeing-Vertol CH-47A Chinook — 1965
Boeing-Vertol CH-47D Chinook — 1991, 97—99
Boeing-Vertol 107 — 1961
Boeing-Vertol 179 — 1975
Boeing Stratocruiser — 1953
Boeing KC-97G — 1957
Boeing KC-135 Stratotanker — 1963
Boeing B-47 Stratojet — 1957
Boisavia B-60 Mercurey — 1951—53
Bolkow Bo 105 — 1969, 1971
Bolkow 207 — 1965
Bolkow Junior B — 1965
Bolkow 208 Junior — 1983
Bolkow Bo 208C Junior — 1961, 1969
Bolkow LFU-205 — 1969
Bolkow MHK-101 — 1969
Bolkow Bo 209 Monsun — 1969
Bolkow Phoebus — 1969
Bombardier Learjet 31A — 1999
Bombardier Learjet 60 — 1999
Bombardier Learjet 45 — 1999
Bombardier Challenger 604 — 1999
Bombardier Global Express BD.700 — 1997—99
Bombardier Canadair CL 415 — 1999
Bombardier DASH 8 400 — 1999
Brasov IS.28B2 — 1975
Brasov IS.28E3 — 1975
BredaNardi BN.300C — 1975
BredaNardi NH.500 — 1975
BredaNardi NH.500C — 1975
Breezy RLU.1 — 1975
Breguet 11E — 1946
Breguet 763 Deux-Ponts — 1953—57
Breguet 900 — 1949, 1953
Breguet 940 STOL — 1961
Breguet 941 — 1963—65
Breguet 941S — 1969, 1971
Breguet 960 Vultur — 1953
Breguet 965 — 1955
Breguet 1050 Alize — 1955—57
Breguet 1100 Taon — 1957
Breguet 1150 Atlantique — 1963—65, 1969—1977
Breguet 1150 Atlantique ATL 2 — 1983, 1989, 1995
Breguet XIVB (reproduction) — 1983
Breguet 19GR Super Bidon — 1971
Breguet Mercure — 1977
Bristol 171 Sycamore — 1951, 1957
Bristol 192 — 1959
Bristol Britannia — 1955, 1959
Bristol Britannia C.1 — 1961
Britten Norman BN-2 Islander — 1965
Britten Norman BN-2A Islander — 1969—75, 1979

Britten Norman BN-2AAA-6 Islander — 1971
Britten Norman BN-2A Defender — 1977
Britten Norman BN-2A-7 Defender — 1971, 1975, 1979
Britten Norman BN-2A-8 Defender — 1973
Britten Norman BN-2A-10 Islander — 1971
Britten Norman Turbo Islander — 1977
Britten Norman BN.2T — 1989
Britten Norman BN-2A Mk.III Trislander — 1971—79
Britten Norman BN-3 Nymph — 1969

C.A.B. Minicab — 1953
Calvel-Piel Zef — 1977
Campbell Cricket — 1971
Campbell Cougar — 1973
Canadair C.114 — 1965
Canadair CF-5D — 1995
Canadair CL-28 Argus — 1965
Canadair CL-41R Tutor — 1963
Canadair CL-44 — 1963
Canadair CL-215 — 1973, 1979, 1985
Canadair CL-215T — 1991
Canadair CL-415 — 1995—97
Canadair Challenger — 1979—81
Canadair Challenger 600 — 1983
Canadair Challenger 601 — 1983—87, 1993—95
Canadair Challenger 601-3A — 1991
Canadair Challenger 604 — 1993, 1997
Canadair Regional Jet — 1993—97
Cantineau-Betemps — 1951—53
Caproni Vizzola A.21J Calif — 1971—73
Caproni Vizzola A.21SJ — 1977—79
Caproni Vizzola C.22J — 1981—85, 1987
Carmam JP.15-36 — 1975
Carmam JP.15-36NIS — 1977
Carmam JP.15-36AR — 1977
CASA C.101 Aviojet — 1979—85
CASA C.101CC Aviojet — 1985—89
CASA C.101DD — 1991
CASA C.212 Aviocar — 1971—79, 1983—95
CASA C.212 Aviocar Srs. 200 — 1981
CASA C.212-200 Aviocar — 1997
CASA C.212-400 Aviocar — 1997—99
CASA CN-235 — 1987—89, 1993—97
CASA C-235-300 — 1999
CASA C-295 — 1999
CASA HA.200 Super Saeta — 1971—73
CASA Pilan — 1983
CASA/IPTN CN-235 — 1997
Castel Maubossin CM-100 — 1949
Castel CM.25S — 1953
Castel CM.310P — 1953
CATIC K8 — 1999
Caudron G.III — 1971—73
Caudron C.600 Aiglon — 1973
Caudron C.800 — 1953
Caylus gyrocopter — 1997

Centre Air C.A.620 Gaucho — 1963
CEA DR.253B Regent — 1969
CEA DR.315 Petit Prince — 1969
Centrair C.201 Marianne — 1985—89
Centrair Parafan 1 — 1985—87
Centrair Parafan II — 1987
Centrair Pegase B — 1985
Centrair Pegase 101 — 1983, 1987
CERVA CE-43n Guepard — 1973
Cessna L-19 Bird Dog — 1987, 1995
Cessna T-41A — 1965
Cessna 150 — 1965
Cessna 150M — 1975
Cessna 152 — 1983, 1997
Cessna 152T — 1983
Cessna 172 — 1963, 1983, 1997
Cessna 180 — 1953
Cessna 182 — 1979
Cessna TR182 — 1979
Cessna 182M Skylane — 1969—71
Cessna 182P Skylane — 1973—75
Cessna 182S — 1997
Cessna 185 — 1977
Cessna 188 — 1977
Cessna 188 Agwagon 300 — 1969
Cessna A.188B Agtruck — 1975
Cessna 195 — 1953
Cessna U.206 — 1977
Cessna U.206E Stationair — 1971
Cessna TU.206F Stationair II — 1975
Cessna T.206 Stationair 6 — 1981
Cessna TU.206 Turbo Stationair 6 — 1979,
    1987
Cessna 207 Skywagon — 1975—77,
    1989
Cessna 207 Turbo Skywagon — 1969
Cessna 208 Caravan I — 1985—89, 1995
Cessna 208B-GC Caravan I — 1991
Cessna 210 — 1977
Cessna P.210 — 1993
Cessna 210D Centurion — 1965
Cessna P.210N — 1985
Cessna T.210E Centurion — 1969—71
Cessna T.210L Centurion II — 1975
Cessna 210N — 1979
Cessna P.210N Centurion II — 1979—81
Cessna 310P — 1969
Cessna 310Q — 1971—73
Cessna 310R — 1979
Cessna 310-II — 1975
Cessna 337 Skymaster — 1963
Cessna 337 Super Skymaster — 1965
Cessna P337 — 1979
Cessna 340 — 1973
Cessna 340A — 1979
Cessna 340-II — 1975—77
Cessna 401A — 1969
Cessna 402 — 1973
Cessna 402B II — 1977
Cessna 402C — 1979

Cessna 404 Titan — 1977—79, 1985
Cessna 404MP — 1983
Cessna 404 Omni Turbo Titan Courier —
    1985
Cessna 406 Grand Caravan — 1999
Cessna 411 — 1965
Cessna 414 — 1971—77
Cessna 414A Chancellor — 1979, 1985
Cessna 421B Golden Eagle — 1975—77
Cessna 425 Corsair — 1981
Cessna 441 Conquest I — 1977—85
Cessna 441 Conquest II — 1983—85
Cessna 500 Citation — 1973—79
Cessna 525 Citationjet — 1993—99
Cessna 550 Citation II — 1981, 1987
Cessna 550 Citation S II — 1985
Cessna 560 Citation V — 1989, 1993
Cessna 560 Citation V Ultra — 1995—97
Cessna 601 — 1989
Cessna 650 Citation VI — 1985—89, 1993
Cessna 650 Citation VII — 1995—97, 1999
Cessna Citation III — 1983
Cessna Citation Bravo — 1997—99
Cessna Citation Excel — 1999
Cessna Citation X — 1995—99
CFM Streak Shadow — 1993
Chance Vought F8U Crusader — 1959
Chance Vought F8U-2 Crusader — 1961
Chance Vought TF-8A Crusader — 1963
Chapeau Le Levrier — 1946
Charcoal Raven X — 1987
Christen AI Husky — 1989
Columban MC.11B Cri-Cri — 1977
Columban MC.12 Cri-Cri — 1981
Conair F-27 Firefighter — 1987
Conroy CL-44D-4 — 1973
Conroy DC-3TP — 1969
Consolidated PBY Catalina — 1999
Contrair ASW.20FP — 1981
Convair B-36 — 1951
Convair B-58 Hustler — 1961
Convair C-131A — 1959, 1963
Convair F-102 Delta — 1959
Convair 880 — 1977
Convair 990 — 1977
Chudzik — 1987
Czech Super Aero 45 — 1957
Czech Aero 145 — 1959
Czech L.40 Meta-Sokol — 1958
Czech Ld.60 Brigadyr — 1957

Dassault MD.450 Ouragan — 1949—51,
    1955
Dassault MD.452 Mystère — 1951
Dassault MD.452 Mystere IV — 1953, 1991
Dassault MD.452 Mystere IVA — 1957
Dassault MC.452 Mystere IVN — 1955
Dassault Mystere XXII — 1955
Dassault Super Mystere B1 — 1955—57
Dassault Super Mystere B2 — 1965

Dassault Alpha Jet — 1975, 1981, 1985,
    1991, 1997
Dassault Balzac V 001 — 1963—65
Dassault Falcon 10 — 1969—77, 1981,
    1987
Dassault Falcon 10F — 1985
Dassault Falcon 10MER — 1975, 1979,
    1985
Dassault (Mystere) Falcon 20 — 1963—65
Dassault Falcon 20 — 1971—75, 1979,
    1983—85, 1989, 1995
Dassault Falcon 20C-5 — 1995
Dassault Falcon 20FR — 1985—87
Dassault Falcon 20H — 1981
Dassault Falcon 30 — 1973
Dassault Falcon 50 — 1977—93
Dassault Falcon 50EX — 1995—99
Dassault Falcon 100 — 1983—85
Dassault Falcon 200 — 1983—85
Dassault Falcon 900 — 1985—91, 1995
Dassault Falcon 900B — 1991—93, 1997
Dassault Falcon 900C — 1999
Dassault Falcon 900EX — 1995—99
Dassault Falcon 2000 — 1993—99
Dassault Guardian 2 — 1985
Dassault Guardian — 1979—83
Dassault Hirondelle — 1969
Dassault Mercure — 1971, 1975
Dassault Mirage III — 1963, 1971—75
Dassault Mirage III BE — 1971—73
Dassault Mirage III C — 1961, 1965
Dassault Mirage III E — 1965, 1969—73,
    1977
Dassault Mirage III NG — 1983
Dassault Mirage III R — 1965, 1969, 1973
Dassault Mirage III RD — 1971
Dassault Mirage III T — 1965
Dassault Mirage IV A — 1963—65,
    1969—71
Dassault Mirage IV P — 1985
Dassault Mirage V — 1969, 1973, 1993
Dassault Mirage F.1 — 1969—75,
    1979—83, 1987
Dassault Mirage F.1B — 1977, 1985
Dassault Mirage F.1C — 1975—77, 1983
Dassault Mirage F.1CG — 1977
Dassault Mirage F.1CH — 1979
Dassault Mirage F.1CR — 1983—87, 1991
Dassault Mirage F.1E — 1975
Dassault Mirage G — 1969
Dassault Mirage G.8 — 1971—73
Dassault M.5E2 — 1983
Dassault Mirage Milan — 1971
Dassault Mirage 50 — 1975, 1979—81
Dassault MBage 50M — 1987
Dassault Mirage 2000 — 1979—85, 1995
Dassault Mirage 2000B — 1981—85, 1993
Dassault Mirage 2000B5 — 1997
Dassault Mirage 2000C — 1983, 1987—91,
    1999

Dassault Mirage 2000D — 1991, 1997—99
Dassault Mirage 2000N — 1983—87,
    1991—93
Dassault Mirage 2000S — 1989, 1993
Dassault Mirage 2000-5 — 1991,
    1995—97, 1999
Dassault Super Mirage 4000 — 1979—83,
    1987
Dassault-Breguet Atlantique ANG — 1979
Dassault Breguet Atlantique ATL2 —
    1985—87, 1991—93, 1997
Dassault Etendard IV — 1957
Dassault Etendard IV M — 1973
Dassault Etendard IV P — 1961
Dassault Super Etendard — 1979—91,
    1995—97
Dassault Super Etendard E — 1987
Dassault Alpha Jet — 1977, 1983, 1989,
    1993—95
Dassault Alpha Jet II — 1987
Dassault Alpha Jet E — 1987
Dassault Rafale — 1987—89, 1995—97
Dassault Rafale A — 1991
Dassault Rafale B — 1993, 1999
Dassault Rafale C — 1991—93, 1999
Dassault Rafale M — 1993, 1997
Dassault Vatour — 1965
Marcel Dassault MD-311 Flamant — 1991
Marcel Dassault MD-312 Flamant — 1991
Datwyler MD-3-160 Swiss Trainer — 1985,
    1991
Dechaux Helicop-jet — 1975, 1981
deHavilland 106 Comet 1A — 1953
deHavilland 114 Heron 2 — 1961
deHavilland 121 Trident — 1963
deHavilland 125 — 1963
Robert Denize RD.105 — 1977
Deperdussin B — 1973
Deperdussin 1913 (reproduction) — 1983
Dewoitine D.412 — 1932
Dewoitine D.520 — 1985
Dewoitine D.520C — 1973
DHC-3 U-1A Otter — 1961
DHC-4 Caribou — 1961—63
DHC-5 Buffalo — 1965, 1969, 1983—85
DHC-5D Buffalo — 1977
DHC-6 Twin Otter — 1977—79, 1985
DHC-6 Twin Otter 200 — 1969, 1971
DHC-6 Twin Otter 300M — 1983, 1993
DHC-6 Twin Otter 300S — 1973, 1981
DHC-7 Dash-7 — 1977—85
DHC-7 Transporter — 1979—81
DHC-8 Dash 8 — 1985—87, 1993
Boeing-DHC Dash 8-300 — 1991, 1995
DHC CC-142 — 1987
Diamond Katana DV-20 — 1993, 1997
Diamond Katana DV-20S — 1999
Diamond DA40 — 1997—99
Diamond HK36 Super Dimona TTC — 1997
Dinfia Guarani II — 1965

Dornier Do 27B — 1957
Dornier Do 28 Skyservant — 1959, 1965,
    1975, 1979
Dornier Do 28B Skyservant — 1963
Dornier Do 28D-1 Skyservant —
    1969—1973, 1977
Dornier Do 31E-3 — 1969
Dornier Do 32 — 1963
Dornier Do 128-2 — 1981
Dornier Do 128-6 — 1981
Dornier Do 228-100 — 1981—85
Dornier Do 228-101 — 1987—89
Dornier Do 228-200 — 1983—85,
    1991—93
Dornier Do 228-201 — 1987
Dornier Do 328 — 1993
Dornier Do 328-100 — 1995
Dornier Seastar — 1985—89
Dornier Turbosky — 1979
Douglas A-26 Invader — 1953
Douglas A-4 Skyhawk — 1963
Douglas A4E Skyhawk — 1965
Douglas C-124 Globemaster — 1957
Douglas C-133A Cargomaster — 1961
Douglas B-66 Destroyer — 1957
Douglas C-9A Nightingale — 1969
Douglas F4D-1 Skyray — 1961
Douglas DC-3 — 1987
Douglas DC-3C — 1991
Douglas DC-6B — 1953
Douglas DC-8 — 1963
Dragon Fly — 1995
Dragon Fly helicopter — 1997
Druine D.3 Turbulent — 1953
Druine D.5 Turbi — 1953, 1977
Durable RD.02 Edelweiss — 1977
Durable Edelweiss RD.05 — 1983
Dyke Delta — 1977
Dynali Chickinox — 1991
Dynali Chickinox Tandem — 1993

Edgley Optica — 1981—85
EH Industries EH101 — 1997
Eipper Quicksilver GT — 1987
EMA.124 — 1971
EMA/Boeing CH-47C — 1971
EMBRAER EMB-100 Bandierante — 1977
EMBRAER EMB-110P1 Bandierante —
    1979—83
EMBRARER MBA 110P2 Bandierante —
    1979
EMBRAER EMB-111A — 1979
EMBRAER EMB-120 Brasilia — 1985—89,
    1993
EMBRAER MBA-121 Xingu — 1977,
    1981—83
EMBRAER EMB-121A — 1979
EMBRAER CBA-123 — 1991
EMBRAER ERJ-135 — 1999
EMBRAER EMB-145 — 1997—99

EMBRAER EMB-312 Tucano — 1981–89, 1993–97
EMBRAER EMB-312H Super Tucano — 1997
EMBRAER Tucano F — 1993
Emouchet SA.104 — 1953
ENAER Avion Liviano — 1989
ENAER T-35 Pillan — 1985–89, 1993
ENAER T-35 Turbo-Pillan — 1991
English Electric Canberra — 1953
English Electric P.1B Lightning — 1959, 1963
Enstrom F.28A — 1973
Enstrom F.28A-F — 1975
Enstrom F.28F — 1989–91
Enstrom F.180C Shark — 1977
Enstrom F.280C — 1981
Enstrom F.280FX — 1991–99
Enstrom F.480 — 1993–99
Enstrom F.480FX — 1997
Epervier ATL — 1991
Escopette Emouchet — 1951
Estivals ED-3 — 1977
Eurocopter SA.330B Puma — 1991
Eurocopter AS.332 Super Puma — 1997
Eurocopter AS.332L2 Puma — 1993
Eurocopter AS.332S Puma II — 1991
Eurocopter AS.332 Mk.II Super Puma — 1999
Eurocopter SA.332UL Puma — 1995
Eurocopter SA.342 Gazelle — 1993
Eurocopter SA.342M Gazelle — 1991
Eurocopter SA.350 Ecureil — 1997
Eurocopter AS.350B Ecureil — 1997
Eurocopter AS.350BA Ecureil — 1995
Eurocopter AS.350B1 Ecureil — 1993
Eurocopter AS.350B2 Ecureil — 1993
Eurocopter AS.350B3 Ecureil — 1997–99
Eurocopter AS.352 Cougar — 1991, 1993
Eurocopter AS.352UL Cougar — 1997
Eurocopter AS.352U2 Cougar — 1997
Eurocopter AS.355F Ecureil II — 1991
Eurocopter AS.355M Ecureil II — 1991
Eurocopter AS.355N Ecureil II — 1993–95
Eurocopter AS.365 Dauphin — 1993, 1997
Eurocopter SA.365C1 Dauphin — 1991
Eurocopter SA.365N Dauphin — 1993
Eurocopter EC.505 — 1993
Eurocopter AS.532 Cougar — 1995, 1999
Eurocopter AS.532U2 Cougar — 1995
Eurocopter AS.550 Fennec — 1993, 1997
Eurocopter AS.550C2 Fennec — 1993
Eurocopter AS.565AA Panther — 1993
Eurocopter AS.535SA Panther — 1995
Eurocopter AS.565UA Panther — 1991
Eurocopter Bo. 105 — 1997
Eurocopter Bo.105 CBS — 1993
Eurocopter Bo.117 — 1997
Eurocopter Bo.117 B1 — 1993
Eurocopter Bo.117 C1 — 1993–95, 1999
Eurocopter EC.120 — 1997

Eurocopter EC.120B Colibri — 1999
Eurocopter EC-135 — 1995–99
Eurocopter EC-135B — 1999
Eurocopter NH 90 — 1999
Eurocopter Tiger — 1991, 1995–99
Eurocopter Gerfaut — 1993
Eurofighter EF.2000 — 1995–99
Eurofighter Typhoon — 1997
Extra EA 230 — 1993
Extra EA 260 — 1991
Extra EA 300 — 1991–93
Extra EA 300F — 1995
Extra EA 300S — 1993–97

Fairchild C-82 Packet — 1953
Fairchild C-123 — 1957
Fairchild A-10A Thunderbolt II — 1977–81, 1991
Fairchild Hiller FH.1100 — 1969
Fairchild Merlin 300 — 1985
Fairchild Metro III — 1985
Fairchild-Dornier 328J — 1997–99
Fairchild-Dornier 328TP — 1999
Fairey Firefly IV — 1946
Fairey Rotodyne — 1959
Fauvel A.V.36 — 1953
FFVV Planeur Swift — 1999
Fiat G.46 — 1949–51
Fiat G.59 — 1949
Fiat G.59-4B — 1951
Fiat G.82 — 1955
Fiat G.91T — 1965
Fiat G.91Y — 1969
FFA AS.202 Bravo — 1969, 1979–83, 1989
FFA AS.202-18A Bravo — 1977
FFA AS.202-18A-1 Bravo — 1987
FFA AS.202/18A4 Bravo — 1991
FFA AS.202/26A Bravo — 1985
FFA Diamant — 1969
FFT Eurotrainer 2000A — 1991
FFT SC-OIB-160 Speed Canard — 1991
Fiat G.91 — 1959
Flag Euro Shadow — 1993
Fletcher FU-24/950 — 1975
FMA IA 58 Pucara — 1977–79, 1991
FMA IA-63 Pampa — 1985–91
Focke-Wulf FW-190 (reproduction) — 1983
Fokker S.11 — 1949
Fokker S.12 — 1949
Fokker S.14 — 1951
Fokker F.25 Promotor — 1946
Fokker F.27 Friendship — 1957–59
Fokker F.27 Friendship 400 — 1973–75
Fokker F.27 Friendship 600 — 1971–73
Fokker F.27 — 1989
Fokker F.27M — 1979
Fokker F.27MP Friendship — 1983
Fokker-VFW F-27MPA — 1977
Fokker F.27 Maritime Enforcer — 1985

Fokker F.28 Fellowship — 1969, 1975, 1979, 1983
Fokker F.28 Fellowship 1000 — 1973
Fokker F.28 Fellowship 2000 — 1971
Fokker F.28-6000 Fellowship — 1975–77
Fokker VFW-614 — 1973, 1977
Fokker 50 — 1987, 1991–95
Fokker 70 — 1993–95
Fokker 100 — 1987–93
Folland Gnat T-1 — 1965, 1973
Forward Aircraft FK 60 Utility — 1999
Fouga C.M.7 — 1949, 1953
Fouga C.M.8-R 13 Cyclone — 1949
Fouga C.M.82R Lutin — 1951
Fouga 90 — 1979
Fouga CM.170 — 1957
Fouga CM.175 — 1957
Fouga CM.170-R Magister — 1953–55
Fournier RF-4D — 1985
Fournier RF-5 — 1987–89
Fournier RF-6B — 1975
Fournier RF-6B-100 — 1977–79
Fournier RF-6B-180 — 1977
Fournier RF-8 — 1973–75
Fournier RF-9 — 1977–79
Fournier RF-10 — 1983
Fournier RF-47 — 1993–95
Fuji FA-200-160 — 1973
Fuji FA-200-180 — 1971, 1975
GAF Jindivik 3B — 1973
GAF Nomad — 1975–77
GAF Nomad 24A — 1979
Galaxy Aerospace Astra SPX — 1997
Gatard AG.02 Poussin — 1977
Gazuit Valladeau GV.103L — 1969
Gazuit Valladeau GV.1020 — 1969
Gazuit Valladeau GV.1031 — 1971
Geiser Moto Delta — 1975, 1979
Geiser Moto Delta G.11 — 1981
General Avia F.22B Pinguino — 1993
General Avia F.22C Sprint — 1993
General Avia F.22R — 1993
General Dynamics B-58 Hustler — 1965
General Dynamics YF-16 Falcon — 1977
General Dynamics F-16 Falcon — 1975, 1979
General Dynamics F-16A Falcon — 1981, 1985–87
General Dynamics F-16C Falcon — 1985–91
Generalavia F.20P Condor — 1983
Giles G.222 — 1997
Glaser-Dirks DG-500T — 1995
Gloster Meteor IV — 1946
Gloster Meteor IV record — 1946
Gloster Meteor NF-11 — 1955
Gloster Javelin — 1959
Gloster Javelin FAW.9 — 1961
Gobe 82 — 1983
Goodyear Airship — 1973, 1985
Greyhound — 1946

Grob Speed Astir — 1979
Grob Asw-20F — 1979
Grob Twin Astir — 197
Grob G.103C — 1993
Grob G.109B Ranger — 1983–85, 1989–91
Grob G.115A — 1987–91
Grob G.115C — 1995
Grob G.115D — 1993–95
Grob G.115D-2 — 1995–97
Grob G.115E — 1999
Grob G.115T — 1995
Grob G.115TA — 1999
Grob GF-200 — 1995
Grob Twin Two Aero — 1985
Grob Egrett-2 — 1991
Grob Strato-1 — 1991
Grillon 120 — 1985–87
Grinwald G.802 Orion — 1983–85
Grumman Widgeon — 1953
Grumman Ag-Cat — 1979
Grumman Turbo Ag-Cat — 1979
Grumman Turbo Mallard — 1995
Grumman A-6E — 1991
Grumman EA-6B — 1991
Grumman SA-17 — 1953
Grumman C-20G — 1995
Grumman E-2A Hawkeye — 1965
Grumman E-2C — 1977, 1991, 1995
Grumman F-14A Tomcat — 1973–75, 1991
Grumman F-14D Tomcat — 1997
Grumman AO-1F Mohawk — 1961
Grumman OV-1 Mohawk — 1963
Grumman G-111 Albatross — 1963, 1981
Grumman Gulfstream I — 1961
Grumman Gulfstream II — 1969, 1973
Grumman S2F-3 Tracker — 1993
Grumman S-2T Turbo Tracker — 1993
Grumman WF-2 Tracer — 1961
Grumman-Agusta S-211 — 1995
Grumman-American AA-1 — 1975
Grumman-American AA-5 Traveler — 1975
Grumman-American AA-5A Cheetah — 1977
Grumman-American AA-5B Tiger — 1975–77
G.A. Gulfstream 1C — 1981
G.A. Gulfstream IISP — 1995
G.A. Gulfstream III — 1981–87
G.A. Gulfstream IV — 1987–91
G.A. Gulfstream IV SP — 1993–99
G.A. Gulfstream V — 1997–99
G.A. Gulfstream SRA-1 — 1985
G.A. Gulfstream C-20G — 1997
G.A. Fanjet 1500 — 1983
G.A. Peregrine — 1983
G.A. Commander 900 — 1983
G.A. Commander 1000 — 1983
Guerchais-Roche 35 — 1946
Guerchais-Roche 39 — 1946
Guizhou FT-7 — 1987
Gyrodyne XRON-1 — 1961

Gyro Club ULM Charentais Autogyre Magni — 1999
Gyro Club ULM Charentais Autogyre Magni M5 — 1999
Gyro Club ULM Charentais Jibaru — 1999
Gyroflug Speed Canard — 1981, 1987–89

Hamburger Flugzeugebau HFB.320 Hansa — 1965
Handley Page HP.115 — 1965
Handley Page Herald — 1957
Handley Page Dart Herald — 1959, 1977
Handley Page Victor — 1955–59
Handley Page Victor B.1 — 1961
Handley Page Jetstream Mk.1 — 1969, 1971
Handley Page Jetstream, Srs. 200 — 1971
Hanriot H.D.1 — 1973
Hansa (MBB) HFB.320 Hansa — 1969–1973
Harbin Y-12 — 1987
Hawker Hurricane IIC — 1971, 1975
Hawker Hunter — 1953–55, 1959
Hawker Hunter 6 — 1957
Hawker Hunter T.7 — 1957, 1961–63
Hawker Sea Fury X — 1946
Hawker Siddeley P.1127 Kestrel — 1963–65
Hawker Siddeley Andover C.2 — 1969
Hawker Siddeley Andover MF — 1965
Hawker Siddeley Argosy — 1969
Hawker Siddeley Argosy C.1 — 1971
Hawker Siddeley Buccaneer S.2 — 1969–71
Hawker Siddeley Dominie T.1 — 1969–71
Hawker Siddeley H.S.125 Jet Dragon — 1965, 1969
Hawker Siddeley H.S. 125, Srs. 400B — 1971, 1975
Hawker Siddeley H.S.125/600B — 1973
Hawker Siddeley H.S.700 — 1979
Hawker Siddeley H.S.125 700B — 1977
Hawker Siddeley H.S.748 — 1969, 1977
Hawker Siddeley H.S.748, Srs. 2A — 1971–73
Hawker Siddeley H.S.748 Coastguarder — 1977
Hawker Siddeley Harrier — 1977
Hawker Siddeley Harrier GR.1 — 1969–71
Hawker Siddeley Harrier T.1 — 1975, 1979
Hawker Siddeley Harrier T.2 — 1969–71
Hawker Siddeley Harrier T.4 — 1973
Hawker Siddeley Harrier T.50 — 1979
Hawker Siddeley Harrier T.52 — 1979
Hawker Siddeley Sea Harrier FGS.1 — 1979
Hawker Siddeley Hawk — 1975, 1979
Hawker Siddeley Hawk T.1 — 1975
Hawker Siddeley Hawk T.50 — 1975
Hawker Siddeley Heron — 1969
Hawker Siddeley Nimrod MR.1 — 1971–73
Hawker Siddeley Trident 1E — 1969

Heli Avia Skyarrow 500 TF — 1999
Hiller helicopter — 1953
Hiller FH 1100 — 1965
Hiller 12E-4 — 1961
Hiller military — 1953
Hiller UH-2E — 1985
HL helicopter — 1987
Hindustan HTT-34 — 1985
Hispano HA-200-D — 1965
Hispano HA-200-R1 Saeta — 1957
HOAC F.15F — 1995
HOAC Katana — 1995
HOAC Super Dimona — 1995
Hoffman H.36 Dimona — 1981—87
Hoffman H.36-II Dimona — 1987
Hoffman H.40 — 1989—91
Max Holste MH.52 — 1946
Max Holste MH.260 Super Broussard — 1961
Max Holste MH.1521 Broussard — 1953, 1957, 1969
HTM Skytrac 1 — 1973
HTM Skyrider — 1973
Hughes OH-6A — 1965
Hughes 269 — 1975, 1981
Hughes 269C — 1979
Hughes 269C/300 — 1971—73
Hughes 300 — 1969, 1987
Hughes 300C/269 — 1977
Nardi-Hughes 269 — 1977
Hughes 369/500 — 1971
Hughes 369D — 1981
Hughes 369HE/500 — 1971
Hughes 369HS (NH500) — 1973
Hughes 500 — 1969
Hughes 500D — 1977—81
Hughes H.500E — 1983—87
Hughes 500 MD — 1981
(Nardi) Hughes 500M-D — 1977—79
Hughes 500 MD/ASW — 1979
Hughes Defender — 1979
Hughes YAH-64 — 1983
Hughes AH-64 Apache — 1987—89
Hunting Percival Jet Provost — 1959
Hurel-Dubois H.D.10 — 1951
Hurel-Dubois H.D.31 — 1953
Hurel-Dubois H.D.32 — 1955
Hurel-Dubois H.D.34 — 1957, 1961, 1997
Hurel-Dubois H.D.35 — 1955
Hydroplum Amphibian — 1987

IAI Arava — 1971, 1981
IAI Arava 201 — 1973—75
IAI Arava 202 — 1977
IAI 1123 Commodore Jet/Westwind — 1971—75
IAI 1124 Westwind — 1977—79
IAI 1125 Westwind 2 — 1981
IAI 1125SP Astra — 1991—93
IAI Astra SPX — 1995

IAI Huey 800 — 1995
IAI Kfir C2 — 1977
IAI Scout RPV — 1981
IAI Seascan — 1979
IAI Super Phantom — 1987
IAI Super Searcher — 1999
IAR 83 Pelican — 1985
IAR 99 Soim — 1991, 1997
IAR 109 Swift — 1993
IAR 316B Alouette III — 1973
IAR 317 Airfox — 1985
IAR 330 Puma — 1985, 1997
IAR 824 (IS-24) — 1973
IAR 826 — 1973
IAR 827A — 1981
IAR 831 Pelican — 1983
IAR IS.28B — 1973
IAR IS.28M2 — 1977, 1993
IAR IS.29G — 1973
IAR IS.32 — 1977
Ibis Quicksilver MXL2 — 1987
ICA-Brasov IS.28B2 — 1991
ICA-Brasov IS.28M2 — 1981, 1991
IRMA IAR.823 — 1975—77
IS.28MA — 1983
IS.28M2 — 1983
IS.29DW Club 29 — 1981
IS.30 Metallique — 1981
IS-46 — 1993
Ilyushin Il-18 — 1965
Ilyushin Il-62 — 1965, 1969
Ilyushin Il-62M — 1973
Ilyushin Il-62M-200 — 1971
Ilyushin IL-76 — 1973—75
Ilyushin Il-76MF — 1997
Ilyushin Il-76T — 1979
Ilyushin Il-76TD — 1993
Ilyushin Il-86 — 1979—81
Ilyushin Il-96M — 1993—95
Ilyushin Il-96-300 — 1989—91
Ilyushin Il-96M0 — 1999
Ilyushin Il-96T freighter — 1997
Ilyushin Il-103 — 1995, 1999
Ilyushin Il-114 — 1991
Ilyushin Il-114-100 — 199
Ilyushin Il-114T — 1997
Ilyushin Il-203 — 1997
IPTN CN235 MPA — 1993
IPTN N250 — 1997
IRMA BN-2A Islander — 1973
Israviation ST-50 — 1997
Issoire APM.01 Lionceau — 1997
Issoire APM.20 — 1997
Issoire Siren PIK 20E.11F — 1983
Issoire Siren PIK 20E.78 — 1983
Italair F.I20 Pegaso — 1973

Jaen AJ-1 Serrania — 1991
Jaguar — 1981
Jaguar International GR.1 — 1981

Jodel D.11 — 1977
Jodel D.18 — 1985
Jodel D.92 — 1977
Jodel D.111 — 1953
SAN-Jodel DR.1051 Ambassadeur — 1961
Jodel-Wassmer D.120 — 1955
Jupiter light helicopter — 1987
Jurca Sirocco — 1977
Jurca Tempete — 1977

Kaman H-43B Huskie — 1961
Kaman UH-2A Seasprite — 1963
Kamov Ka-26 — 1969—75
Kamov Ka-32 — 1985, 1991
Kamov Ka-32A — 1993
Kamov Ka-50 — 1993, 1997
Kuffner WK-1 — 1983

Lake LA-4 — 1979, 1983
Lake LA-4-200 Buccaneer — 1973, 1981
Lake LA-250 Renegade — 1987
Lake Turbo 270 — 1989
Lake Seawolf — 1985
Languedoc — 1946
Lanot Sagittaire — 1987
Latecore 235 — 1985
Lazair microlight — 1983
(Gates) Learjet 23 — 1963—65
(Gates) Learjet 24 — 1975
(Gates) Learjet 25 — 1969
(Gates) Learjet 25B — 1971—73
(Gates) Learjet 25C — 1971—73
(Gates) Learjet 31 — 1991
(Gates) Learjet 31A —1993—95
(Gates) Learjet 35 — 1975, 1987
(Gates) Learjet 35A — 1977, 1991
(Gates) Learjet 60 — 1993—95
(Gates) Learjet C-21A — 1989
Leduc 010 — 1946
Leduc 021 — 1955
LET 59 — 1991
LET L.410 TurboLet — 1971, 1975
LET L.410A TurboLet — 1973
LET L.410UVP TurboLet — 1983, 1987
LET L.410UVP-E TurboLet — 1985, 1989
LET L.410UVP-E-20 — 1993
LET L.410UVP-E20B — 1991
LET L.610 — 1989—91
LET L.610G — 1993, 1997
Lockheed 10E — 1997
Lockheed 18 Lodestar — 1987
Lockheed L.1049G Super Constellation — 1953
Lockheed P2V-6 Neptune — 1955
Lockheed C-5A Galaxy — 1971
Lockheed C-130 Hercules — 1957—59, 1983
Lockheed HC-130B Hercules — 1969, 1971
Lockheed C-130C — 1961
Lockheed C-130C.1 Hercules — 1975

Lockheed C-130E Hercules — 1963, 1999
Lockheed C-130H Hercules — 1995
Lockheed C-130 HTTB — 1985
Lockheed C-130J — 1999
Lockheed CP-140A — 1991
Lockheed C-141 Starlifter — 1965
Lockheed JetStar — 1963—65, 1969
Lockheed JetStar II — 1977
Lockheed L-100-20 Hercules — 1977
Lockheed L-100-30 — 1981
Lockheed L-1011 TriStar — 1971—75, 1997
Lockheed (General Dynamics) F-16 Falcon — 1993—95
Lockheed Martin F-16C Falcon — 1997—99
Lockheed F-104 Starfighter — 1959, 1963
Lockheed F-104C Starfighter — 1971
Lockheed F-117A — 1991
Lockheed XH-51A Aerogyro — 1965
Lockheed P-3A Orion — 1963—65
Lockheed P-3C Orion — 1971—73, 1991, 1995, 1999
Lockheed P-3F Orion — 1975
Lockheed S-3A Viking — 1975
Lockheed Macchi Santa Maria — 1961
Lockspeiser LDA.01 — 1975
LTV A-7D Corsair II — 1971—73
LTV A-7E Corsair II — 1975
Aer Lualdi L.59 — 1961
Lucas L.5 — 1987

Macchi MC.205V Veltro — 1981
Macchi MB.308 — 1949—51
Macchi MB.323 — 1953
Macchi MB.326 — 1959—61
Macchi-Castoldi M.C.72 — 1991
Marco J5 — 1987
Marmande Microjet 200B — 1987
Martin B-57 Canberra — 1957
Mathis biplane — 1946
Maule M.5 — 1981
Maule M.7-235 — 1987—89
MBB Bo 105 — 1973, 1977, 1983, 1989
MBB Bo. 105 (PAH-1) — 1987
MBB Bo. 105C — 1975, 1981
MBB Bo. 105C Argos 1 — 1987
MBB Bo..105CB — 1985
MBB Bo.105CB-3 — 1991
MBB Bo.105CBS-4 — 1991
MBB Bo.105L — 1979
MBB Bo.105LS — 1985
MBB Bo.105P PAH-1 — 1979—81
MBB Bo.105S — 1985
MBB Bo.105/PAH-1 — 1985
MBB Bo.106 — 1979
MBB Bk.107 — 1981
MBB Bo.108 — 1991
MBB Bk.117 — 1983—91
MBB Bk.117A-3 — 1985—87
MBB Bk.117B-1 — 1991
MBB/Bo 209 Monsun — 1971

McDonnell Douglas AV-8B Harrier — 1991, 1997
McDonnell Douglas TAV-8B Harrier II — 1993
McDonnell F4H-1 Phantom II — 1961
McDonnell Douglas F-4B — 1963—65, 1973
McDonnell F-4J Phantom II — 1969
McDonnell RF-4C Phantom II — 1969
McDonnell F-4K Phantom II — 1969
McDonnell F-101 Voodoo — 1963
McDonnell Douglas Combat Explorer — 1995
McDonnell Douglas DC-8-62 — 1975
McDonnell Douglas DC-8-72 — 1983
McDonnell Douglas DC-9-81 — 1981
McDonnell Douglas MD-90-30 — 1993
McDonnell Douglas DC-10 — 1971
McDonnell Douglas DC-10-30 — 1973
McDonnell Douglas KC-10 — 1981
McDonnell Douglas YC-15 — 1977
McDonnell Douglas C-17A — 1995—97
McDonnell Douglas F-15A Eagle — 1977—81
McDonnell Douglas TF-15 Eagle — 1975
McDonnell Douglas F-15C Eagle — 1991
McDonnell Douglas F-15E Eagle — 1991—97
McDonnell Douglas CF-18 Hornet — 1987
McDonnell Douglas CF-18A Hornet — 1989
McDonnell Douglas F/A-18A Hornet — 1991
McDonnell Douglas TF-18A Hornet — 1981
McDonnell Douglas F/A-18C Hornet — 1993—97
McDonnell Douglas F/A-18D — 1995
McDonnell Douglas EF-18A Hornet — 1997
McDonnell Douglas (Hughes) OH-58D — 1991
McDonnell Douglas AH-64 — 1995
McDonnell Douglas (Hughes) AH-64A — 1991—93, 1997
McDonnell Douglas AH-64D — 1997—99
McDonnell Douglas (Hughes) MD-520N — 1993, 1997
McDonnell Douglas MD.600N — 1997
McDonnell Douglas MD.900 — 1997
M.D.G. — 1946
MD Helicopter MD Explorer — 1999
Meridionali CH-47C — 1975
Messerschmitt 109 (Hispano Ha.1112) — 1999
Microturbo 200 — 1979
Microturbo Microjet 200B — 1981—85, 1989
MiG-21MF-2000 — 1993
MiG-21-93 — 1995
MiG-29 — 1989, 1995, 1999
MiG-29M — 1993
MiG-29SE — 1993
MiG-29SM — 1997
MiG-31 — 1991

MiG AT — 1995—97
Mignet HM.18 — 1985
Mignet HM.293 — 1987
Mil Mi-2 — 1979
Mil Mi-8 — 1969—71, 1975
Mil Mi-6 — 1965
Mil Mi-8MB — 1997
Mil Mi-8T — 1973
Mil V-8 — 1965
Mil V-10 — 1965
Mil V-12 — 1971
Mil Mi-17 — 1981, 1989
Mil Mi-17M — 1993
Mil Mi-17MD — 1995
Mil Mi-26 — 1985, 1989
Mil Mi-26TM — 1993
Mil Mi-28 — 1993
Mil Mi-28N — 1997
Mil Mi-34 — 1993
Mil Mi-35M — 1995
Miles Gemini — 1946
Miles H.D.M.105 — 1957
Mistral — 1989
Mitsubishi Mu.2 Marquise — 1981—83
Mitsubishi Mu.2B Marquise — 1969, 1971, 1985
Mitsubishi Mu.2B-36A — 1977
Mitsubishi Mu.2B-40 Solitaire — 1981—83
Mitsubishi Mu.2B-60 — 1979
Mitsubishi Mu.2L — 1975
Mitsubishi Mu-300 Diamond — 1983
Mitsubishi Mu-300 Diamond 1A — 1985
Molniya A-1 — 1995
Mooney Super 21 — 1965
Mooney M20E — 1987
Mooney M.20F Executive — 1969
Mooney M.20J (201) — 1979, 1985, 1989, 1993, 1997
Mooney M.20J-ATS — 1991
Mooney M.20J-MSE — 1991
Mooney M.20K (231) — 1981, 1985—89
Mooney M.20L — 1989
Mooney M.20M Bravo TLS — 1991, 1997
Mooney M.20R Ovation — 1995—97
Mooney 231 Turbo — 1983
Mooney 252TSE — 1987
Mooney MSE — 1995
Morane Saulnier MS.130Et.2 — 1973
Morane Saulnier MS.230 — 1971
Morane Saulnier MS.472 P-2 — 1946
Morane Saulnier MS.474 — 1949
Morane Saulnier MS.701 — 1949
Morane Saulnier MS.731 — 1951
Morane Saulnier MS.760 Paris III — 1961, 1965
Morane Saulnier MS.880 Rallye — 1961
Morane Saulnier MS.880B Rallye Club — 1969—73
Morane Saulnier MS.883 Rallye — 1969
Morane Saulnier MS.885 Rallye — 1961

Morane Saulnier Rallye 100 — 1977
Morane Saulnier Rallye 100S — 1975
Morane Saulnier Rallye 100ST Galopin — 1975, 1981
Morane Saulnier MS.889 Rallye 125 — 1973—75
Morane Saulnier MS.892 Commodore — 1965
Morane Saulnier MS.892A — 1969
Morane Saulnier MS.892E Rallye 150GT — 1973
Morane Saulnier Rallye 150T — 1975—77
Morane Saulnier Rallye 150ST — 1975—77
Morane Saulnier MS.893A Rallye Commodore 180 — 1969—75
Morane Saulnier MS.893E Rallye 180 — 1973, 1977
Morane Saulnier Rallye 180GT — 1975, 1981
Morane Saulnier Rallye 180T — 1981
Morane Saulnier MS.894 Rallye — 1969
Morane Saulnier MS.894A Rallye Minerva 220 — 1971—75
Morane Saulnier MS.894C Rallye — 1969
Morane Saulnier MS.894E Rallye 220 — 1973
Morane Saulnier Rallye 235C — 1977, 1981
Morane Saulnier Rallye 235E — 1981
Morane Saulnier Rallye 235G Guerrier — 1977, 1981—83
Morane Saulnier Rallye 235GT — 1975
Morane Saulnier Alcyon — 1987
Moynet Jupiter — 1963
Mudry H101 — 1977
Mudry CAARP CAP-X — 1989
Mudry CAP-XS — 1983
Mudry/CAARP CAP-10 — 1973
Mudry/CAARP CAP-10B — 1973—75, 1979, 1983, 1989—97
Mudry/CAARP CAP-20 — 1971—75
Mudry/CAARP CAP-20L — 1977—79
Mudry/CAARP CAP-20LS/200 — 1979—81
Mudry/CAARP CAP-21 — 1981—83, 1989
Mudry/CAARP CAP-231 — 1989—93
Mudry CAP 231 EX — 1993—95
Mudry CAP-231MX — 1997
Mudry CAP 232 — 1995—99
Myasischev M-55 — 1995
Myasischev M.101T Gzhel — 1997

Nanchang A-5M — 1987
Nardi F.N.333 — 1957
Nardi-Hughes NH-300C — 1981
Nardi-Hughes NH-500MD — 1981
NC 211 Le Cormorant fuselage — 1946
NC 589 — 1949
NC 853 — 1949, 1953
NDN Firemaster 65 — 1991
NH Industries NH90 — 1997
Nieuport-Delage XI — 1973

Nieuport-Delage 90 "Colonial" — 1932
Nord Cadet — 1965
Nord Norecrin — 1949, 1953
Nord 262 — 1963—65
Nord 262A — 1969, 1975
Nord 262C — 1969, 1973, 1977, 1987
Nord 500 — 1969
Nord N.C.856 Norvigie — 1955
Nord N.C. 1203 II Norecrin — 1955
Nord N.C. 1405 Gerfaut — 1957
Nord N.C. 1500 Noreclair — 1946
Nord N.C. 1500-02 Griffon 2 — 1961
Nord N.C. 1750 Noralpha — 1955
Nord N.C. 2501 Noratlas — 1955—57, 1987, 1997—99
Nord N.C. 3202 — 1961
Nord N.C. 3400 — 1961
Nord Transall C-160 — 1965
Norman NDN Firecracker — 1977
North American Navion — 1949
North American A3J-1/A-5A Vigilante — 1961—63
North American F-86 Sabre — 1957
North American F-86F Sabre — 1955
North American TF-100 Super Sabre — 1989
North American F-100D Super Sabre — 1957
North American TF-100F Super Sabre — 1957, 1991
North American P-51D Mustang — 1999
North American OV-10A Bronco — 1969
North American-Rockwell Shrike Commander — 1969
North American-Rockwell Hawk Commander — 1969
North American-Rockwell Sabreliner — 1971
North American T-39A Sabreliner — 1961—63
Northrop F-5 Freedom Fighter — 1965
Northrop RF-5A — 1969
Northrop F-5E Tiger II — 1973—77
Northrop RF-5E Tiger Eye — 1979, 1983
Northrop F-5F Tiger — 1975, 1985
Northrop YF-17 Cobra — 1977
Northrop F-20 Tiger Shark — 1983
Northrop T-38A Talon — 1961
Northrop Grumman B-2 — 1995
Northrop Grumman E-2C Hawkeye — 1997
Northrop Grumman E-8 — 1995
Northrop Grumman E-8C Jstars — 1997

Omnipol Prague Dauphin — 1965
Opus 280 — 1995

Panavia Tornado — 1977—85, 1989
Panavia Tornado F.2 — 1981
Panavia Tornado GR.1 — 1981, 1991, 1995—97
Panavia Tornado IDS — 1991
Partenavia P.64 Oscar — 1965

Partenavia P.64B Oscar 180 — 1971
Partenavia P.66B Oscar 150 — 1971
Partenavia P.68 — 1981
Partenavia P.68B Victor — 1975—79
Partenavia P.68C-TC — 1979
Partenavia P.68TC — 1981—83, 1987
Partenavia AP.68TP — 1979
Partenavia AP-68TP-300 Spartacus — 1985
Partenavia AP-68TP-600 Viator — 1985
Partenavia P.68 Observer — 1977—79, 1983—85
Partenavia (Aercosmos) P.68 Observer II — 1993
Partenavia (Aercosmos) P.68C — 1993
Partenavia (Aercosmos) AP.68 TP.600 Viator — 1993
Partenavia P.68 Victor — 1971—73, 1989
Partenavia P.68OBS — 1981
Partenavia P.68R — 1977—79
Pauchard Mobycoptere — 1987
Paumier MP.20 — 1977
Payen PA 49 Katy — 1955
Percival Prencitce — 1946
Percival Provost — 1953
Peregrine 600 — 1981
Periera Osprey — 1987—89
Piaggio P.136 — 1949
Piaggio P.137-L — 1959
Piaggio P.148 — 1951
Piaggio P.116 — 1961
Piaggio P.166CL2 — 1973—75
Piaggio P.166DL3 — 1977—81, 1987
Piaggio P.180 Avante — 1987—89, 1993, 1999
Piaggio-Douglas PD.808 — 1963—65, 1969—75
Piasecki HUP-2 — 1955
Piel CP.70 Beryl — 1977
Piel CP.1320 — 1983
Pik 20C — 1979
Pik 30 Siren — 1985—87
Pilatus B.4 — 1975
Pilatus B.4 — PC 11 — 1977
Pilatus P.2 — 1949
Pilatus P.4 — 1949
Pilatus PC-6 Porter — 1961
Pilatus PC-6 Turbo-Porter — 1979, 1983, 1987—89, 1993
Pilatus PC-6A Turbo-Porter — 1963—69
Pilatus PC-6B Turbo-Porter — 1969—75, 1981, 1985
Pilatus PC-6/B1-H2 — 1973
Pilatus PC-6/B2-H2 — 1977
Pilatus PC-6/B2-H4 — 1991
Pilatus PC-7 Turbo-Trainer — 1975—91
Pilatus PC-9 — 1985—93, 1999
Pilatus PC-9B — 1991
Pilatus PC-11 — 1973
Pilatus PC-XII — 1993, 1997
Pilatus PC-XII Eagle — 1997

Pilatus PC-12 Executive — 1999
Pilatus Britten Norman Islander — 1983—87
Pilatus Britten Norman Turbine Islander — 1983—85
Pilatus Britten Norman Defender — 1985—87
Pinguin BM.1 — 1973
Pioneer Flighstar — 1983
Piper PA-24 Comanche C — 1969
Piper PA-25-260 Pawnee 260C — 1971
Piper PA-27 Aztec D — 1969
Piper PA-27 Aztec 250E — 1971
Piper PA-28 Cherokee — 1961
Piper PA-28 Archer II — 1981
Piper PA-28 Archer III — 1997
Piper PA-28-161 Warrior II — 1983—85, 1989
Piper PA-28R-180 Cherokee Arrow 180 — 1969
Piper PA-28R-200 Cherokee Arrow 200 — 1969, 1971
Piper PA-28RT Arrow IV — 1981
Piper PA-31 Comanchero — 1985
Piper PA-31 Navajo — 1969
Piper PA-31P Navajo — 1971—73
Piper PA-32-300 Cherokee Six — 1969—71
Piper PA-32R Saratoga SP — 1981—83
Piper PA-34 Seneca — 1979
Piper PA-34-220 Seneca — 1985
Piper PA-34 Seneca III — 1981—83
Piper PA-34 Seneca V — 1997
Piper PA-38 Tomahawk — 1979—81
Piper PA-39 Twin Comanche C — 1969
Piper PA-42 Cheyenne III — 1981—83
Piper PA-42-100 Cheyenne 400LS — 1985
Piper PA-42-720 Cheyenne IIIA — 1985, 1989
Piper PA-42-1000 Cheyenne 400LS — 1987
Piper PA-44 Seminole — 1981
Piper PA-46 Malibu — 1995
Piper PA-46-310 Malibu — 1985—89
Piper PA-46-350P Malibu Mirage — 1997—99
Piper (Smith) PA-60 Aerostar 601P — 1975
Piper PA-61 Aerostar 602 — 1981
Pitts Special S-1S — 1983
Pitts Special S-2A — 1973—75, 1979
Pitts Special S-2B — 1989—95
Polyt 5 — 1971
Potez 75 — 1957
Potez 94 — 1965
Potez CM.170 Magister — 1969—71
Potez 840 — 1961
Potez 841 — 1965
Potez-Heinkel CM.192 — 1961
Pottier P.70S — 1977
Pottier PA 15-34 Kit-Club — 1977
Pottier P2305 — 1993
Praga — 1946
Procaer F.15B Picchio — 1961

Procaer F.15C Picchio — 1965
Procaer F.15E Picchio — 1973
Procaer P.400 Cobra — 1961
Promavia Jet Squalus — 1987–89
P.Z.L. H-3 Kolibrie — 1959
P.Z.L. M-2 — 1959
P.Z.L. M-15 — 1977
P.Z.L. M-18 Dromader — 1977–79
P.Z.L. Mi-2 — 1977
P.Z.L. SZD.30 Pirat — 1975
P.Z.L. SZD.38A Jantar — 1975
P.Z.L. SM-1 — 1957–59
P.Z.L. TS-8 Bies — 1957–59
P.Z.L. TS-11 Iskra 00 1866
P.Z.L. Wilga 35 — 1975
P.Z.L. 101 — 1959
P.Z.L. 102 Kos — 195
P.Z.L. 110 Rallye — 1977
P.Z.L. 110 Koliber — 1979
P.Z.L. 130 Orlik — 1985
P.Z.L. M.20 Seneca — 1987
P.Z.L. Swidnik PW.5 Swift Cobra — 1993
P.Z.L. Swidnik W-3 Sokol — 1991–93
P.Z.L. Mellec An.28 — 1993
P.Z.L. Mellec M.20 Mewa — 1993
P.Z.L. Mellec M.26 Iskierka — 1993
P.Z.L. Sokol — 1995
P.Z.L. SW-4 helicopter — 1997

Rans Airaile S.12 — 1993
Rans Airaile S.14 — 1993
Rans Coyote II — 1993
Rans Sakato S.10 — 1993
Rapetout gyrocopter — 1997
Raytheon Beech Hawker 125-800 — 1995
Raytheon Beech Hawker 800XP — 1997–99
Raytheon Beech Hawker 125-1000B — 1995
Raytheon Beech PC.9 Mk.II — 1997
Raytheon Beech King Air 200 — 1997–99
Raytheon Beech King Air 350 — 1997–99
Raytheon Beech 400A Beechjet — 1997–99
Raytheon Beech 1900D — 1997–99
Raytheon Beech T-6A Texan II — 1999
Reims Cessna F.150J — 1969
Reims Cessna F.150L — 1971–1973
Reims Cessna F.150L Aerobat — 1971
Reims Cessna F.150M — 1977, 1997
Reims Cessna FRA.150M — 1977
Reims Cessna F.152-II — 1979–81
Reims Cessna F.172H — 1969
Reims Cessna F.172K — 1971, 1979
Reims Cessna FR.172KXP — 1977
Reims Cessna F.172M — 1973, 1975
Reims Cessna F.172N — 1977–79
Reims Cessna FR.172E Rocket — 1969
Reims Cessna FR.172G Rocket — 1971
Reims Cessna FR.172J Rocket — 1973–75
Reims Cessna F.172R Rocket — 1999
Reims Cessna F.172 Skyhawk II — 1981

Reims Cessna F.177RG Cardinal — 1971–1977
Reims Cessna F.182Q — 1977
Reims Cessna F.182S — 1999
Reims Cessna F.337 Super Skymaster — 1969
Reims Cessna F.337C Super Skymaster — 1971
Reims Cessna FP.337G — 1977
Reims Cessna FT.337 — 1973
Reims Cessna F.337GP — 1975
Reims Cessna FT.337GP — 1973
Reims Cessna FTB.337 —1977, 1981
Reims Cessna FTB.37G — 1975
Reims Cessna FTB.337GA — 1979
Reims Cessna F.337 Milirole — 1971
Reims Cessna F.406 Caravan II — 1983, 1987–91, 1995, 1999
Reims Cessna F.406 Caravan II Vigilant — 1991, 1997
Rein Flugzeugbau RW.3 Passat — 1961
Republic P-47 Thunderbolt — 1963
Republic F-84 Thunderjet — 1953
Republic RF-84F Thunderjet — 1957
Republic F-105 Thunderchief — 1959–61
Rex Composite APM 20 Lionceau — 1999
Rex Composite APM 21 Lionceau — 1999
RFB FK.3M — 1969
(VFW-Fokker) RFB Fanliner — 1977
RFB Fantrainer — 1979, 1983
RFB Fantrainer 400 — 1987–89
RFB Fantrainer 600 — 1981, 1987, 1993
RFB MFI-10(M) — 1993
Riley 400 Dove — 1965
Robin ATL — 1983–85, 1989
Robin ATL Azur — 1991
Robin ATL60 — 1987
Robin HR.100/200 — 1971
Robin HR.100/210 — 1973
Robin HR.100/235 — 1975
Robin HR.100/285 Tiara — 1973–75
Robin HR.200/100 — 1975
Robin HR.200/100S Standard — 1975
Robin HR.200/120 — 1993
Robin HR. 200/120B Club — 1975, 1997
Robin HR. 200/125 — 1973
Robin HR. 200/160 Acrobin — 1973
Robin DR 250/100 President — 1977
Robin DR.300/108 — 1971
Robin DR.315X Petit Prince — 1975
Robin DR.400 Dauphin — 1989
Robin DR.400/4+2 — 1975
Robin DR.400 Regent 80 — 1985
Robin DR.400/100 Cadet — 1987, 1995
Robin DR.400/120 Dauphin — 1981, 1993, 1997
Robin DR.400/125 Petit Prince — 1973, 1995
Robin DR.400/140 Major — 1975, 1993
Robin DR.400/140B — 1977

Robin DR.400/160 Major 80 — 1979
Robin DR.400/180 — 1987, 1991–93
Robin DR.400/180R — 1979, 1983
Robin DR.400/180RP — 1985–87
Robin DR.400/185V6 — 1995
Robin DR.400/2001 — 1997
Robin R 200/120B — 1995
Robin R 1180T — 1979
Robin R 1180 — 1977
Robin R 2100 — 1977
Robin R 2112 — 1979
Robin R 2160 — 1977, 1995
Robin R 2160M — 1997
Robin D 3000 — 1985, 1989, 1993
Robin R 3000/V6 — 1991
Robin R 300/160 — 1991, 1995–97
Robin D 3100 — 1987
Robin DR.3120 — 1983
Robin R 3140 — 1981, 1985
Robin 80 — 1981
Robin Cadet — 1989
Robin X-4 — 1991
Robinson R22 — 1981, 1987–89, 1999
Robinson R22M — 1991
Robinson R44 — 1999
Rockwell Sabreliner — 1985
Rockwell Sabreliner 40A — 1973
Rockwell Sabreliner 60 — 1975–77
Rockwell Sabreliner 65 — 1979, 1983
Rockwell Sabreliner 75 — 1977
Rockwell Sabreliner 75A — 1975, 1979
Rockwell Sabreliner 700 — 1979
Rockwell Shrike Commander 500S — 1975, 1987
Rockwell Shrike Commander 690 — 1973
Rockwell Thrush Commander — 1975
Rockwell S-2 Thrush Commander 800 — 1977
Rockwell Turbo Commander 685 — 1973
Rockwell Turbo Commander 690A — 1975
Rockwell Turbo Commander 690B — 1977–79
Rockwell Commander 980 — 1981
Rockwell Commander 1000 — 1981
Rockwell Commander 112 Super Sport — 1973
Rockwell Commander 112A — 1975
Rockwell Commander 112TC — 1977
Rockwell Commander 114 — 1977, 1989
Rockwell Commander 114A — 1979
Rockwell Commander 114B — 1993
Rockwell Astafan Commander — 1977
Rockwell B-1B — 1987
Rockwell X-31 — 1995
Rogerson-Hiller RH.1100M
Roitelet — 1949
Rombac One-Eleven — 1983
Rotorway Executive — 1995
Rutan Long-Eze — 1985–87
Rutan Vari-Eze — 1977–81

R.W.F. R.W.3 Multoplane — 1958
Ryan NYP (reproduction) — 1987

SAAB MFI-15 Safari — 1971, 1977–79
SAAB MFI-17 Supporter — 1975
SAAB J-22 — 1995
SAAB J-32B Lansen — 1959
SAAB J-35 Draken — 1959, 1965, 1969
SAAB J-35D Draken — 1963
SAAB J-35XD Draken —1971
SAAB J-37 Viggen — 1969–1973
SAAB AJ-37 Viggen — 1977
SAAB JA37 Viggen — 1979
SAAB SF.37 Viggen — 1981
SAAB SH-37 Viggen — 1973–75
SAAB JAS 39 Gripen — 1995, 1999
SAAB 91 Safir — 1953, 1959
SAAB 105 — 1965, 1977
SAAB 105G — 1973–75
SAAB 105XT — 1969
SAAB MFI-17 — 1973
SAAB-Fairchild SF340 — 1983–87
SAAB-Fairchild SF340A — 1989
SAAB-Fairchild SF340B — 1991
SAAB 2000 — 1995–97
SAFCA Lignel 46 — 1949
Santos-Dumont 14bis (reproduction) — 1991
Santos-Dumont Demoiselle — 1973
SATIC Beluga — 1995
Saunders Roe Skeeter — 1955–57
Savoi S.66 — 1932
Scheibe SF-34B — 1995
Schweizer 269C — 1991
Scottish Aviation Twin Pioneer — 1957–59
Scottish Aviation Bulldog — 1971–75
SECAN S.U.C.10 Courlis — 1946
Sepecat Jaguar — 1969–73
Sepecat Jaguar A — 1977–79, 1991
Sepecat Jaguar International — 1977, 1983
Sepecat Jaguar GR.1 — 1977–77
Sepecat Jaguar GR.1A — 1991
SFERMA Beech PD.146.01 Marquis — 1961
Shenyang F-8 II — 1989
Short Sealand — 1953
Short SC-5 Belfast — 1965, 1983
Short SC-5 Belfast 2 — 1985–87
Short SC-7 Skyvan — 1965
Short Skyvan 3 — 1969, 1971
Short Skyvan Srs. 3M — 1971–75, 1979
Short Skyvan QSTOL Skyliner — 1971
Short Skyliner Executive — 1973
Short SC.1 — 1961
Short SD330 — 1979–81, 1989
Short SD330 Sherpa — 1983, 1987
Short SD360 — 1981–89
Shorts Tucano — 1987, 1991
Shorts Tucano T.52 — 1991
SIAI Marchetti S.205 — 1965, 1969, 1971
SIAI Marchetti S.208 — 1969–1973, 1977
SIAI Marchetti S.208R — 1975

SIAI Marchetti S.208M — 1969, 1971
SIAI Marchetti S.210M — 1971–73
SIAI Marchetti S.210T — 1971–73
SIAI Marchetti S.211 — 1981–87
SIAI Marchetti SF.250 — 1965
SIAI Marchetti SF.260 — 1969–75, 1979, 1983
SIAI Marchetti SF.260AM — 1975
SIAI Marchetti SF.260C — 1983–85
SIAI Marchetti SF.260MC — 1971–73
SIAI Marchetti SF.260SW — 1977
SIAI Marchetti SF.260TP — 1981–87
SIAI Marchetti SF.260W — 1977, 1981
SIAI Marchetti SF.260WX Warrior — 1975
SIAI Marchetti FN.333 Riviera — 1961, 1965
SIAI Marchetti SF.600 Canguru — 1979
SIAI Marchetti SF.600TP Canguru — 1981, 1985–87
SIAI Marchetti SM.1019 — 1971–83
SIAI Marchetti SM.1019A — 1971
SIAI Marchetti Y 4 — 1965
SIAI (MBB) S.223K.1 Flamingo — 1969, 1971
Boeing Sikorsky RAH-66 Comanche — 1999
Sikorsky CH.3B — 1963
Sikorsky HHS-2 — 1961
Sikorsky HH-52A Seaguard — 1969
Sikorsky H-53 — 1975
Sikorsky MH-53 — 1995
Sikorsky NH-53E — 1997
Sikorsky HH-60G — 1995
Sikorsky MH-60G — 1995
Sikorsky UH-60 Blackhawk — 1983, 1999
Sikorsky SH-60B Seahawk — 1991, 1997
Sikorsky UH-60A Blackhawk — 1991–93
Sikorsky UH-60A/L — 1997
Sikorsky/Weser WF-S64 Skycrane — 1963
Sikorsky H-76 Eagle — 1985
Sikorsky H-76B Eagle — 1991
Sikorsky S-58T — 1971
Sikorsky S-61 — 1965
Sikorsky S-62 — 1959
Sikorsky S-76 — 1975, 1981–87
Sikorsky S-92A Helibus — 1999
Sikorsky AUH-76 — 1983
Silver Arrow Hermes 4505 — 1999
Silvercraft SH-4 — 1969, 1971
Silvercraft SH-200 — 1977
Simmering-Graz-Pauker SGP222 Flamingo — 1963
SIPA S-12 — 1949, 1953
SIPA S-20 — 1946
SIPA S-50 — 1946
SIPA S-70 — 1946
SIPA S.200 Minijet — 1951–53
SIPA S-251 Antilope — 1963–65
SIPA 300 — 1955
SIPA 901 — 1949, 1953
Siren C15-38 — 1979

Siren CE.75 Silene — 1977
Siren CE.78 — 1981
Siren D.77 Iris — 1977–79
Siren E78 — 1979
Siren/Wassmer Cerva CE.43 — 1971
Slingsby T.67A Firefly — 1981
Slingsby T.67M Firefly — 1997
SM-92 Finist — 1995
Sman Petrel Amphibian — 1993–97
Smith DSA-1 Miniplane — 1973
Smith Aerostar 601P — 1977
SNCAN N.1402 Gerfaut — 1955
SNCAN N.2100 — 1949
SNCASE-Sikorsky S.E.55 Elephant Joyeux — 1953–55
SNCASE S.E.210 Caravelle — 1955–57
SNCASE S.E.212 Durandal — 1957
SNCASE S.E.2010 Armagnac — 1953
SNCASE S.E.2410 Grognard — 1953
SNCASE S.E.3120 Alouette I — 1953, 1957
SNCASE S.E.3130 Alouette II — 1955–57
SNCASE S.E. Alouette Gouvernour — 1957
SNCASE S.E.5000 Baroudeur — 1955
SNCASE S.E. Mistral (Vampire) — 1953
SNCASE S.E. Aquilon (Sea Venom) — 1953–55
SNCASO S.0.30P Bretagne — 1953
SNCASO S.0.30R — 1946
SNCASO S.0.90 — 1946
SNCASO S.0.95 Corse II — 1949
SNCASO S.0.1100 — 1946
SNCASO S.O. 1120 Ariel III — 1951
SNCASO S.O. 1220 Djinn — 1953
SNCASO S.O. 1221 Djinn — 1955–57
SNCASO S.O. 4050 Vatour — 1955–57
SNCASO S.O. 6000 — 1946
SNCASO S.O. 6020 Espadon — 1949, 1955
SNCASO S.0.7010 Pegase — 1946
SNCASO S.0.7060 Deauville — 1949
SNCASO S.0.9000 Trident — 1955
SNCASO S.O.M.1 — 1946
SNCASO S.O.M.2 — 9149
SNECMA Atar Volant C-400 — 1957
Socata Rallye 180T — 1979
Socata Galopin — 1979
Socete Gabier — 1979
Socata Gaucho — 1979
Socata Guerrier — 1979, 1985
Socata MS.250 Banc Volant — 1997
Socata ST.10 Diplomate — 1959
Socata TB.9 Tampico — 1979, 1983, 1991–95
Socata TB.9 Tampico Club — 1997
Socata TB.9 Sprint — 1999
Socata TB.10 Tobago — 1979, 1983, 1991–95
Socata TB.10 Tobago XL — 1993
Socata TB.20 Trinidad — 1983, 1991–93, 1997–99
Socata TB.21 Trinidad — 1991–93, 1997

Socata TB.30 Epsilon — 1983, 1991–99
Socata TB.31 Omega — 1991–93
Socata TB.319 — 1995
Socata TB.200 Tobago XL — 1991–99
Socata TB.320 — 1995
Socata TB.360 Tangara — 1997
Socata TBM 700 — 1991–99
Sofca Paramoteur Agrion — 1993
Soko Galeb — 1963, 1969, 1971
Soko Super Galeb G4 — 1991
Soko Jastreb — 1969, 1971
Soko Orao — 1985
Sokol 3-seater — 1946
Sopwith 1-A2 — 1973
Specialized Aircraft TriTurbo 3 — 1979
Sportavia RF.10 — 1981
Sportavia RS.180 — 179
Sportavia-Putzer RF.4D — 1959
Sportavia-Putzer RF.5 — 1969
Sportavia-Putzer RF.5B
Stampe & Renard SV-4 — 1953, 1997
Stampe & Renard S.R.7B — 1955
Starck AS.57 — 1949
Start + Flug H-101 Salto — 1975
Start + Flug Hippie — 1975
Stemme S-10 — 1989, 1995–97
Stemme S-10VC — 1991, 1997
Stemme S-10VT — 1999
Stemme S-15 — 1999
Streak Shadow — 1991
SUC-10 Courlis — 1991
Sud Caravelle III — 1975
Sud /BAC Concorde — 1969
Sud Djinn — 1963
Sud Alouette II — 1963–65
Sud SA.330 — 1963
Sud SE.3120 Super Frelon — 1963
Sud SE.3160 Alouette III — 1961–65
Sud Marquis — 1965
Sud Moynet 360 Jupiter — 1965
Sud (Gardan) GY 80 Horizon — 1965
Sud (North American) T-28 — 1961
Sud Vatour — 1961, 1965
Sukhoi Su-25 — 1989
Sukhoi Su-26 — 1991
Sukhoi Su-26M — 1987–89, 1995, 1999
Sukhoi Su-26MX — 1991
Sukhoi Su-27 — 1993–95
Sukhoi Su-27UB — 1993
Sukhoi Su-29 — 1991–93
Sukhoi Su-29KS — 1995
Sukhoi Su-29M — 1991–93
Sukhoi Su-30MK — 1999
Sukhoi Su-31 — 1993–95
Sukhoi Su-31M — 1995–97
Sukhoi Su-31T — 1995
Sukhoi Su-32FM — 1995
Sukhoi Su-32FN — 1997
Sukhoi Su-35 — 1995
Sukhoi Su-37 — 1997

Sunray 100 — 1987
Sup Aero Petit Canard — 1985
Supermarine Scimitar — 1961
Swearingen SA.32T — 1991
Swearingen Merlin II — 1979
Swearingen Merlin III — 1971, 1977, 1983
Swearingen Merlin IIIB — 1979–81
Swearingen Merlin IV — 1971
Swearingen SA.227AC Merlin IV — 1991, 1999
Swearingen SA.226AT Merlin IVA — 1977, 1989
Swearingen Merlin IVC — 1983
Swearingen SA.227AC Metro — 1979, 1987–89
Sewaringen Metro II — 1981
Swearingen Super Metro III — 1981–83, 1993
Swearingen Metro MMSA — 1993
Synairgie Skyranger — 1995
Synairgie float plane — 1995
Taylor Titch — 1971
Techaero TR.260 — 1987
Techaero/Robin TR.200 — 1991
Techaero/Robin TR.300 — 1991
Terzi T-30C Katana — 1991
Tetras — 1995
Texas Helicopters Hornet — 1985
Texas Helicopters Wasp — 1985
Thruster TST — 1987
Tipsy Nipper — 1965
Titan Tornado II — 1997
Transall C.160 — 1963, 1977–85, 1999
Transavia Skyfarmer T300A — 1981
Tri CX Firebird — 1983
Tri CX Firebird MI — 1983
Tupolev Tu-114 — 1961
Tupolev Tu-124 — 1965
Tupolev Tu-134 — 1965, 1969
Tupolev Tu-134A — 1971–73
Tupolev Tu-144 — 1971–75
Tupolev Tu-154 — 1969–73, 1979
Tupolev Tu-154A — 1975
Tupolev Tu-154B-2 — 1981
Tupolev Tu-154M — 1985
Tupolev Tu-160CK — 1995
Tupolev Tu-204 — 1989–91, 1995
Tupolev Tu-204 Cargo — 1993

Ultralair Campana — 1993
Ultralair Weedhopper AX.3 — 1993
Ultralair Weedhopper Europa I — 1993
Ultralair Weedhopper Europa II — 1993
Ultralair Microlight Chaser — 1993

Valmet L-70 Miltrainer — 1979–83, 1987
Valmet L-90 Redigo — 1993
Valmet L-90TP Redigo — 1987, 1991
Valmet PIK 20EF — 1981
Valmet PIK-23 Towmaster — 1981–83

Vertol H-21 Hawnee — 1957
Vertol 44 — 1957
Vertol 107 — 1959
VFW FK.3 — 1969
VFW H.3 — 1969
VFW/Nord Transall C.160 — 1969
VFW CH-53G — 1973
Vickers FB.27A Vimy (reproduction) — 1969
Vickers Supermarine Spitfire — 1999
Vickers Supermarine Spitfire PR.19 — 1973
Vickers Supermarine Spitfire (P7350, UO-T) — 1975
Vickers Viscount — 1953
Vickers Valiant — 1959, 1963
Vickers Vanguard — 1959
Vintel WA.116 — 1983
Vintras JPV 30 Joker — 1977
Virgin Lightship airship — 1997
Vought F4U Corsair — 1999
Vulcanair (Partenavia) AP 68TP — 1999
Vulcanair (Partenavia) PC 68 C — 1999
Vulcanair (Partenavia) PC 68 Observer — 1999
Vulcanair (Partenavia) SF 600A Canguru — 1999

Waco YMF — 1997
Wassmer WA.28 Espadon — 1975
Wassmer WA.43, then CE-43 Guepard — 1975–77
Wassmer WA.51 — 1969
Wassmer WA.52 Europa — 1971
Wassmer WA.54 Atlantic — 1973–77
Wassmer CE.75 — 1975
Wassmer WA.81 Piranha — 1977
WDL 1 airship — 1987
Weedhopper Europa 1 — 1987
Weedhopper Europa II — 1987
Westland Belvedere — 1961
Westland Whirlwind — 1957–59, 1963
Westland Whirlwind 10 — 1965
Westland Widgeon — 1957–59
Westland Scout AH.1 — 1965, 1969
Westland Sea King — 1969
Westland Sea King HAS.5 — 1981
Westland Sea King AEW — 1983
Westland Wasp HAS.1 — 1965, 1969
Westland Wessex 1 — 1959, 1963
Westland Wessex 2 — 1965
Westland Wessex 3 — 1965
Westland Wessex 5 — 1965
Westland Westminster — 1959
Westland WG.30 — 1979–83
Westland/Aerospatiale Lynx — 1971–83, 1987
Westland Lynx HAS.2 — 1981
Westland Super Lynx — 1987
Westland WS.70 — 1987–89
Westland S.70C — 1987
Windecker Eagle — 1979

Windex 100 — 1989
Windex 1100 — 1985
Wing Derringer D.1 — 1971
Wright 1903 Flyer (reproduction) — 1973
WSK An-28 — 1991
Wyman Gordon (Rutan) Proteus — 1999

Yakovlev Yak-3 — 1985, 1993
Yakovlev Yak-18T — 1975
Yakovlev Yak-40 — 1969–75
Yakovlev Yak-42 — 1979–81, 1985
Yakovlev Yak-42A — 1993
Yakovlev Yak-42D — 1993
Yakovlev Yak-42E — 1991
Yakovlev Yak-42F - 1991
Yakovlev Yak-50 — 1979
Yakovlev Yak-52 — 1981
Yakovlev Yak-52W — 1999
Yakovlev Yak-54 — 1993–95
Yakovlev Yak-55M — 1991
Yakovlev Yak-58 — 1997
Yakovlev Yak-112 — 1993
Yakovlev Yak-130ATS — 1995
Yakovlev Yak-AEM-130 — 1997–99
Yakovlev Yak-142 — 1995

Zenair CH-601 — 1997
Zenith — 1977
Zenith 90 — 1977
Zenith 100 — 1977
Zlin M.2 Skaut — 1949
Zlin N.3 Bonzo — 1949
Zlin 37T — 1985
Zlin 42 — 1969, 1973
Zlin 42MU — 1973
Zlin 43 — 1969, 1973
Zlin 50L — 1977, 1989
Zlin 50LS — 1985–87
Zlin 142 — 1987–89
Zlin Z.126 — 1959
Zlin Z.143L — 1993, 1999
Zlin Z.226 — 1959
Zlin Z.242L — 1993, 1997–99
Zlin Z.326 Trener Master — 1959
Zlin Z.526A — 1969
Zlin Z.526L — 1971
Zlin Z.526AS — 1971
Zlin 726 Universal — 1975

INDEX